My Family

ISBN: 9798368358727

Published by:
The Jenkins Institute
thejenkinsinstitute.com

Professional Editing:
Becky Blackmon

Logo & Cover Design:
Andrew Jenkins

Interior Layout:
Joey Sparks

Order additional copies of this resource at:

thejenkinsinstitute.com/shop

or

tji@thejenkinsinstitute.com

Dedication

With great appreciation to wives of church leaders and preachers who support, encourage, partner with, and strengthen their husbands in the work they do for the Lord. We owe a great debt of gratitude to these godly women who often are the glue that holds our families together.

Contents

Week 1	Why Did God Create Families?	Jeff Jenkins	1
Week 2	The Christian Family Confronts Culture	Chuck Monan	7
Week 3	The Family and Bible Study	Larry Acuff	13
Week 4	Train Up a Child	Kerry Williams	19
Week 5	Husband Love Your Wives	Kirk Brothers	25
Week 6	Blended Families	Mark Ray	31
Week 7	Teaching Our Children Not to Be Prejudiced	Doug Burleson	37
Week 8	Teaching Teenage Children	Logan Cates	43
Week 9	Relationships with Adult Children	Andy Connelly	49
Week 10	Godly Grandparents	Bill Watkins	55
Week 11	Discipline and Children	Mike Johnson (FL)	61
Week 12	Teaching Our Children to Pray	Gantt Carter	67
Week 13	Teaching Our Children to Teach	Bo Shero	73
Week 14	Teaching Our Children to Work	Don Delukie	79
Week 15	Teaching Our Children to Worship	Barry Grider	85
Week 16	Teaching Our Children Faithfulness	Dale Jenkins	91
Week 17	Teaching Our Children Compassion	Robert Dodson	97

Week 18	Teaching Our Children About Our Heritage	Scott Harp	103
Week 19	Teaching Young Children to Serve	Anthony Warnes	109
Week 20	Teaching Your Children About Finding a Spouse	Russell Smith	115
Week 21	Helping Our Children Become Christians	Steve Higginbotham	121
Week 22	Helping Our Children Learn How to Choose Good Friends	Wayne Jones	127
Week 23	Glorifying God in the Family	Steve Lusk	133
Week 24	Encouraging Young Men to Become Leaders	Jerry Elder	139
Week 25	The Family and Service to the Church	J.J. Hendrix	145
Week 26	The Family and Service to the Community	Paul Cartwright	151
Week 27	Making Your Home a Safe Harbor	John McMath	157
Week 28	Beyond Children	John Moore	163
Week 29	Single and a Church Family	John Podein	169
Week 30	Staying Together in Difficult Times	Marcus McKee	175
Week 31	Patience in the Family	David Morris	181
Week 32	Loving What You Have	Keith Parker	187
Week 33	Teaching Our Children to Be Kind to Others	Dan Hammitt	193
Week 34	Teaching Our Children About Dating	Steve Bailey	199
Week 35	Dealing with the Loss of a Child	Jeff Jenkins	205
Week 36	Helping Children To Be an Influence Rather Than Being Influenced	Chris McCurley	211
Week 37	Making Your Home a Haven of Happiness	Paul Shero	217
Week 38	The Family and Evangelism	Graham McDonald	223
Week 39	Balancing Our Time	Billy Smith	229

Week 40	Putting God First	David Shannon	**235**
Week 41	When a Family Member Fails	Ralph Gilmore	**241**
Week 42	Letting Our Children Go	Myron Bruce	**247**
Week 43	When I've Lost My Spouse	Dean Miller	**253**
Week 44	Sports and Spirituality	Chris Pressnell	**259**
Week 45	Helping Our Children When There Is a Divorce	Bryan McAlister	**265**
Week 46	Encouraging Your Sons to Be Preachers	Jon Warnes	**271**
Week 47	Teaching Our Children to Be Spiritual Leaders	Mike Johnson (KY)	**277**
Week 48	Helping Our Children to Think Positively About the Church	Anthony Warnes	**283**
Week 49	Dealing with Conflict within the Family	Dale Jenkins	**289**
Week 50	Having Fun in the Family	David Salisbury	**295**
Week 51	Encouraging Your Daughters to Marry Faithful Men	Kirk Sams	**301**
Week 52	Teaching Our Children to Respect Authority	Brock Johnson	**307**
Week 53	Encouraging Your Minister's Families	Craig Evans	**313**
	More from TJI		**319**

With Thanks

A project on this size takes a lot of humble servants. Over 100 ministers helped in making this material come to life. We are thankful for them all. We hope you'll write some of them as the material blesses your life.

We are thankful for our overworked but multitalented friend, Joey Sparks. He sees our projects through to the end and puts up with our (Dale's) constant irritation about when it will all be done. He handles our formatting, helps with editing and does it all with great skill.

Our thanks to Becky Blackmon who has joyfully preformed the task of editing over 50 different writers material for this book.

We are thankful to congregations who purchase copies of this book for their members to aid in their growth and for those people who gift this book to others.

We're thankful for you and pray this book blesses your life.

But most of all, thanks to the Lord who designed the family as a place for us to grow and flourish in. All glory and praise for this work goes to Him.

How to Use This Book

There are a number of ways to use this devotional guide. You might just read it a section a day each weekday for a year. It might be that each member of the church will have a copy and you will all be reading and growing together. It might be a book you'll use for a class, a small group, or some other Bible study group. There is a Digital version you can have if you would rather read online. In some churches the preacher will use the sermon companion that goes with this devotional guide and preach his lessons around the theme for this year.

All materials can be ordered at *TheJenkinsInstitute.com*.

WEEK 1

Why Did God Create Families?

JEFF JENKINS

God's Idea

Today's Scripture: Ephesians 3:9-11

Our beloved brother Paul could very well have been including marriage and raising children in his statement about God's Eternal plan (Ephesians 3:9-11; Ephesians 5-6). As well, he compares marriage to the Divine relationship between Jesus and His Bride. (Ephesians 5:22-33)

Our homes as well as our lives will be better, richer, fuller, when we understand fully that the family was not our idea. No government entity, no higher education committee, or no corporate board came up with the idea of marriage and the family. Prior to His creating the world, our loving Father decided that every person He made would need family.

After God created mankind in His Image (Genesis 1:26, 27), He declared that it was not good for any man to be alone. (Genesis 2:18) In all of God's creation there was nothing He had made that was "suitable" to man. (Genesis 2:20) God knew that man needed someone who was a part of man, someone who was like man, and someone who was close to man's heart. God put man to sleep and took from his side a rib. He then fashioned a woman who would stand with the man for life (Genesis 2:23-25).

God also instituted the concept of a family unit when He said, "Be fruitful and multiply, and fill the earth..." (Genesis 1:29). Our Father was so committed to the family that He gave us a manual, His Word, to guide us in every decision and every choice we would make in regard to our family (Exodus 20, Matthew 5-7; Ephesians 6:1-4). In the following lessons we'll look at some areas that can help us build strong, faithful families!

Today, I will...*thank God for creating the family, and I will recommit my life to relying on His plan for our family.*

Learning Life

Today's Scripture: Ephesians 6:4

Because God gave us a mind and a heart, we have within us the ability to learn. When it comes to life lessons, the question isn't, "Will we learn?" The question is, "Who will teach us?" Surely, our loving Father allows children to be born into a family so that they can learn how to "do" life.

The Word of God commands parents (particularly, fathers) to bring their children up in the "discipline and instruction of the Lord." We seem to be highly interested in teaching our children daily skills that will get them through life. We want our children to learn to walk, talk, eat, take care of themselves, and we want to teach them other basic life skills.

Then there are some big lessons we should teach them. Perhaps the most important lesson we should teach our children is about relationships. First is their relationship with the Lord. We want to teach them God's Word and what it means to live a life that Glorifies Him. We want to teach them about marriage and family. We should speak often to them about the kind of people they will date and how to choose a mate. We want to teach them about how to humbly submit themselves to authorities. This would include parents, teachers, officers of the law, employers, and the elders in the family of God.

And, we should teach them about prayer. They should hear us pray and they will learn how to approach the Father's throne. Our children will learn what is important to us about life. They will learn how we feel about God, His Church, and our involvement in the family of God. We would challenge fathers to pray with and for their children daily.

Today, I will... *do my best to create a learning environment in my family that will build a greater faith in the lives of each family member.*

Abundant Joy

Today's Scripture: John 10:10

Jesus came to bring us an abundant life (John 10:10). The Word of God commands us that we should always be rejoicing in the Lord (Philippians 4:4). As we all know, this life can be tough and challenging. Relationships can be difficult. It has often been said, that life isn't fair, and as we grow older, we come to realize the truthfulness of this statement.

Children today are exposed to more violence, crime, and injustice than those of us who are older were when we were young. Television, internet, and social media have created an atmosphere of insecurity, depression, and ugliness. On the surface, there doesn't seem to be a lot of reason for joy. We should do everything within our ability to let them see the joy that come come into their lives through Jesus. We should talk about the ways that we have joy in Jesus. We should allow our children to spend time with other Christians who understand the joy we have in Jesus. We should show them through the ways we handle the difficulties of life that Jesus still gives us reasons to be filled with joy.

There are specific reasons that we can share with our family to let them know that for children of God, there is always reason for joy. We can have joy, knowing that we have been redeemed by the blood of Jesus. There is joy in the family of God when we worship and fellowship with one another. We can experience joy as we make decisions based upon the Word of God. Great joy can be found when we live according to His Word and when live in such a way that we bring glory to God. Joy is present when we see others who are living life to the glory of God. Why not talk to your children today about reasons that you have as a family to be joyful?

Today, I will... *allow the joy of Jesus to be seen in my attitudes and my actions.*

THURSDAY

Serving Others

Today's Scripture: Acts 16:15

Most translations inform us that Stephanas and his family had "devoted themselves to the ministry of the saints." (Acts 16:15) However, the KJV (or as brother McCord would be known to say, "my Mother's Bible") says that this family had, "ADDICTED themselves to the ministry of the the saints." Typically, being addicted to something is not considered healthy or wise. We often see families addicted to sports, hobbies, getting ahead, or things. Too much of some things can be bad for our families. But in this case, addiction would be a tremendous blessing to our families as well as to many others! What if every Christian man and his family became addicted to ministering to others. Let's consider some ways we can lead our families into this beautiful addiction!

(1) Make everyone in the family aware of concerns of fellow church members by praying specifically and by name for those who are hurting.

(2) As a family, visit those who are shut-in. Pray for them. Take them some homemade bread or a dessert.

(3) Take an elder or minister, and their family for ice cream so that your children can see them in a setting other than church.

(4) Put together a gift box and send it to a missionary who is serving God in a foreign country.

(5) Plan a family project to serve people in your neighborhood because you want them to know the love of Jesus.

(6) Prepare a meal for someone in the church who is sick or has some other special need.

(7) Spend an evening signing cards to be sent to encourage someone who has done something good or who needs some kind of special encouragement.

One other thought is that we can discuss with our family how Jesus has served those around Him—whether it's washing the feet of His disciples or dying on the cross for our sins. For even the Son of Man did not come to be served, but to serve, and to give His life as a ransom for many" (Mark 10:45).

Today, I will... *search for ways I can help my family serve others!*

5

FRIDAY
Telling Everyone About Jesus

Today's Scripture: Matthew 28:18-20

Most large corporations today have a mission statement. The idea is that every decision made by each employee in the company will be tied back to the mission. In short, everything revolves around the mission. Many churches have picked up on this idea and developed mission statements to help the church family stay focused.

What if every family had a mission statement? What if that statement included the goal to tell as many people as possible who are not Christians about Jesus? We know that we are commanded to share the message of salvation with those around us (Matthew 28:18-20; Acts 1:8-9). What if everything we do as a family brings us back to our family mission?

This wasn't my idea, I've tried to incorporate it into my life on a daily basis. A family eating in a restaurant could say to the waiter, "We are about to pray and thank God for our meal. Is there anything we can pray for you about today?" They may say no, but it might open a door of opportunity to begin building a relationship. You might be able to invite them to worship and ask them to sit with your family.

If we engage people around us on a regular basis, it can become second nature to us. If our children see and hear us engaging others with the mission of talking to them about Jesus, it might become a part of their life. One way to do this is make a list of people in our lives that we want to reach with the message of Jesus. We then can take these names before our Father's throne on a regular basis. We can also talk about tangible ways we can reach these people we love for Jesus.

Today, as a family, we will... *pray for people we love who need to know Jesus and we will do what we can to help them learn God's plan for saving us.*

WEEK 2

The Christian Family Influences Culture

CHUCK MONAN

Model a Healthy Family

Today's Scripture: 1 Peter 2:12

Raymond Kelcy used to use an illustration of the power of the real vs. the fake. Kelcy had a friend who worked for the government as an expert in recognizing and exposing counterfeit currency. Wondering how agents prepared to decipher the difference between the genuine and the fraudulent, Kelcy was surprised when the expert told him the only thing they studied was the genuine article.

After years of studying legal tender, it was easy to spot a counterfeit.

Our world would similarly benefit by studying God's original design for the family.

Even as human frailty and sinful choices keep any family from being perfect, our culture has brazenly imagined that traditional family roles are unnecessary and even oppressive. The idea of a husband and wife raising children together has given way to same-sex marriage, polygamy, polyamory, cohabitation, open marriage, transgenderism, and a host of other sinful practices.

As the inevitable backlash of pain and heartache is sure to come from all this, can you imagine what influence Christians can have simply by modeling the family as God would have it? Families where love, respect, and character abound. "Victory has a hundred fathers, but defeat is an orphan," as John F. Kennedy said of the Bay of Pigs fiasco. Show the world happy, successful families, and they will pay attention.

Today, I will... *work to love my family and encourage them in the way of Christ, asking the Lord's blessing in being a good influence on those who truly desire a peaceful, godly home.*

Give Generously

Today's Scripture: Matthew 6:19-21

"We make a living by what we get. We make a life by what we give," writes Winston Churchill. This is quite different from the attitude of the Rich Fool who said, "I will tear down my barns and build bigger ones...And I'll say to myself, "Eat, drink, and be merry" (Luke 12: 16-21).

Few things say as much about us as the way we spend our money.

When he was growing up in rural Arkansas, Bill E. Smith attended a tiny church attempting to have "regular preaching." They needed $15.00 a week. His father told them he would give five dollars a week on it if they could rake up the other ten.

He was making $20.00 a week.

Decades later, Smith writes "Little did I realize what my father bought that day. From that day forward, the church meant something to me. I wasn't quite sure, at first, what it meant, but I knew there must be something pretty important about it for my dad to give $5.00 a week for it."

As our culture models and encourages selfishness, we can live counter-culturally by being unselfish and generous. Rather than piling up riches, we can use the money God gives us to build up His kingdom and help others. When we do this, people will notice - starting with our children, grandchildren, and our neighbors. And when they ask, "Why?" The answer will point to Jesus.

Today, I will... *use money to make a difference in the lives of others, to live out the giving nature of Christ, and to store up treasures in heaven that will last eternally.*

Refuse to Worship Sports

Today's Scripture: 1 Corinthians 10:14

Our youngest son was an accomplished athlete, making All-state in two sports in high school. He was nearly as good at several other sports as well, from a very early age. Like his parents, he loved to compete.

As is all the rage these days, eager coaches and parents recruited him to join AAU teams, travel leagues, and the like. They came to my wife and I, describing in great detail the future glories that awaited him if he really devoted himself to these athletic pursuits.

Our answer was always the same. No.

Sunday is the Lord's Day. It is not for tournaments, travel, or anything that causes us to miss the assembly of the saints (Heb. 10:25). As a family we enjoy sports of all kinds, but we worship the God of all creation. "For while bodily training is of some value, godliness is of value in every way, as it holds promise for the present life and also for the life to come" (1 Tim. 4:8).

What effect could our families have on our culture if we said, "Enough!" to this ridiculous obsession with enrolling our children in an endless schedule of games? What effect would it have on our kids if we set the rule that Jesus, not sports, rules our lives? John Wimber says, "Show me where you spend your time, money, and energy, and I'll tell you what you worship." By this metric it would be difficult to disprove the assertion that too many parents and children these days are worshiping the wrong thing.

Today, I will... *refuse to give in to our culture's priorities, choosing instead to pursue spiritual blessings over a wreath that will fade over time.*

Treat People Equally

Today's Scripture: Acts 10:34-35

As a 21-year-old baseball coach at Ohio Wesleyan University, Branch Rickey recruited a black player named Charles Thomas. In 1903 when the team traveled to South Bend, Indiana to play Notre Dame, the hotel refused to allow Thomas to stay because of a whites-only policy. Rickey persuaded the clerk into allowing Thomas to stay in his room.

Later that evening Rickey found Thomas crying, rubbing his hands and arms convulsively, lamenting, "It's my skin. If only I could wipe off the color they could see I am a man like everybody else!" Rickey told him, "Buck up! We will beat this one day!"

Forty-four years later as the President and General Manager of the Brooklyn Dodgers, Rickey made good on his promise. With a remarkable man named Jackie Robinson, the color line in Major League Baseball was broken.

How different would this country be if Christians long ago had lived up to their faith in a God who shows no partiality? It is never too late to do the right thing. Even as our culture struggles with racism, prejudice, and hatred, we can influence it for the good by showing love, respect and acceptance of all people, not just those who look like us. The Gospel is for all because Jesus is for all. It is time for the church to take the lead in modeling the beautiful picture of Ephesians 2:14-18. When our families are devoted to living out this ethic, our influence will spread like wildfire to a divided world.

Today, I will... *imitate our Heavenly Father in not showing favoritism, but treating everyone with love and acceptance as we show the world that Christ has torn down the walls that separate people.*

Think of Yourself Less

Today's Scripture: Philippians 2:1-11

It's doubtful that Hirashi Ueda truly understood what his invention would do for the cause of narcissism.

Ueda designed the prototype for the first selfie stick in the 1980s. An avid photographer, he was motivated to invent the selfie stick after he asked a child to take a photo of him and his wife outside of the Louvre…and the kid ran off with his camera.

The phenomenon of selfies has exploded across the world, leading stadiums, concerts, museums, and even the next Apple conference to ban selfie sticks.

Banning people from thinking about themselves too much will prove far more daunting.

We do our families a disservice when we put ourselves before others. We do our children a disservice when we make them the center of the universe. And we do our Creator a disservice when we worship and serve created things instead of Him (Rom. 1:25).

C.S. Lewis offers some brilliant insight in saying, "True humility is not thinking less of yourself, it's thinking of yourself less." When our families follow this wisdom, it will have a transformative effect on others. Few lessons are more needed in today's culture of narcissism.

Today, I will... *follow the Bible's advice by considering others before myself, and to practice humility by thinking of myself less.*

WEEK 3

The Family &
Bible Study

LARRY ACUFF

Study the Bible Together

Today's Scripture: Deuteronomy 6:6-8

Moses, in his final days and writing his last book emphasized the instruction that is to be family driven. Among his thoughts are three words he used to convey his message.

The first word is "words" (vs. 6). What words? Moses wrote, "And these words…" The words he commanded, the words that came to him from God. Listen to God. Read God's word. The Bible later records, "Your word is a lamp to my feet and a light to my path" (Psalms 119:105).

The second word is teach (vs. 7). Instruction is valuable. Solomon wrote, "Hear, my son, your father's instruction, and forsake not your mother's teaching" (Proverbs 1:8). Instruction is a family matter. We learn from one another. In this passage of scripture, we see father, mother, and child. There is a difference in reading and teaching. I can read an instrument panel on an airplane but knowing what they mean and how to use them is very different. That is why he wrote, "Teach them diligently to your children." The word of God must not only be read but taught.

The third word is "bind" (vs. 8). That word "bind" carries with it togetherness. Do you think of a rope? Bind cords together to make a rope. When you do that, the rope becomes stronger than the cords. When the word of God is bound in the heart and life, it makes a real difference.

When a family studies the word of God together, they teach the family and then strengthen the family. As a result many a child has had his or her faith energized.

Today, I will... *pray for my family that we always have togetherness in Christ, and I will work to that end.*

14

Study the Bible with Enthusiasm

Today's Scripture: Ecclesiastes 9:10

Families studying the Bible together is a joy. There are several words in the New Testament that encourage this enthusiasm. Before looking at those words, think about how young children will get their Bible story books or Bibles and are eager to sit in your lap or sit beside you while you read to them. God wants us as a family to have that same attitude. Focus for a few minutes on the following words that express the joy and enthusiasm of studying the word of God.

Zeal! "Do not be slothful in zeal, be fervent in spirit, serve the Lord" (Romans 12:11). When it comes to zeal the scriptures teach us not to be slothful and then tells us to be fervent. Two wonderful words – zeal and fervent! Study the Bible with zeal and fervency.

Eager! "So Christ, having been offered once to bear the sins of many, will appear a second time, not to deal with sin but to save those who are eagerly waiting for him" (Hebrews 9:28). Eagerly waiting! This great passage helps, "Now these Jews were more noble than those in Thessalonica; they received the word with all eagerness, examining the Scriptures daily to see if these things were so" (Acts 17:11). Study the Bible with eagerness.

Earnestly! "O God, you are my God; earnestly I seek you; my soul thirsts for you; my flesh faints for you, as in a dry and weary land where there is no water" (Psalm 63:1). Study the Bible earnestly.

Today, I will... *pray that as our family studies the Bible together that it will be done with a joy and enthusiasm because we have a love for God.*

Study with Obedience in Mind

Today's Scripture: Ephesians 6:1-2

Remember that great Judge of the Bible, Samuel (1 Samuel 3)? The Lord would call him, and he thought it was Eli, so he would get up and go to Eli. Eli said, "I did not call; lie down again" (1 Samuel 3:5). After the third time, Eli said to Samuel, "Therefore Eli said to Samuel, "Go, lie down, and if he calls you, you shall say, 'Speak, LORD, for your servant hears.'" So, Samuel went and lay down in his place" (1 Samuels 3:9). As our family studies the Bible together should that not be our goal? "Speak, Lord, for your servant hears."

There are several passages that encourage us to be obedient. As a family, we study for the joy of knowing God's word, we study so that our children may see the beauty of studying the Bible, and we study to know what God's will is for us.

The Psalmist has taught us:
> "Blessed is the man who walks not in the counsel of the wicked, nor stands in the way of sinners, nor sits in the seat of scoffers; but his delight is in the law of the LORD, and on His law he meditates day and night" (Psalms 1:1-2).

We walk in His counsel. We do not obey the ungodly or walk their walk. We obey God and walk His walk. Not only do we "walk the walk," but we also meditate upon it. Meditate means more than simply reading it or looking it over.

Our study encourages us to do as Samuel was told by Eli, "Speak, Lord, thy servant hears."

Today, I will... *pray that as our family studies the Bible that we will do so with the determination to be obedient to the will of God.*

Study the Bible Together to Be Approved of God

Today's Scripture: 2 Timothy 2:15

Most all Bible students know 2 Timothy 2:15. It is great verse, one that many know, but do not realize the significance of it. Notice the statement, "Do your best to present yourself to God as one approved." Children want the parent's approval. Employees want approval from the boss. All want approval. When we study as a family together, God approves. Do you want to be approved of God? Sure! Here are three ways.

One: "Do your best!" Do not try to serve God in a half-hearted manner. Years ago, in the 1950's, there was a commercial for a hair product for men called, "Brylcreem." In the commercial the following statement was made, "A little dab'll do ya." That is the way some folks look at the Bible, "A little dab'll do ya." God wants our best.

Two: "Be a worker!" Nothing makes a person feel better than to be a worker for the Lord. Do I want to be approved of God? Be a worker. Jesus said, "We must work the works of him who sent me while it is day; night is coming, when no one can work" (John 9:4). When you visit the sick, teach a class, door knock with the congregation, attend a gospel meeting, have a Bible study with a non-Christian, guess what? You know that you have God's approval.

Three: "Rightly handling the word of truth!" Approval of God means that we have some understanding of how to handle the word of truth. When the Bible says that Judas went out and hanged himself (Matthew 27:5), it does not mean that I must go out and hang myself. To be approved of God, we must rightly handle the word of truth.

Today, I will... *pray that as we study the Bible together as a family that we will do so with the idea in mind that we want to be approved of God.*

Study the Bible Because Of the Love of God

Today's Scripture: Galatians 2:20

God is love (1 John 4:16). God loves man (John 3:16). We are taught to love God (Matthew 22:37). What a great reason to study the Bible as a family, and that is, the love of God. Paul expresses it like this, "I have been crucified with Christ. It is no longer I who live, but Christ who lives in me. And the life I now live in the flesh I live by faith in the Son of God, who loved me and gave himself for me" (Galatians 2:20). This passage does three things.

First, it identifies the Love of God. "…The life I now live in the flesh I live by the faith in the Son of God, who loved me…" His love is a divine love (John 3:16). His love is an ancient love (Jeremiah 31:3). His love isn't something that just started a day of two ago. His love is immeasurable (Psalms 103:11-13), and it is unchanging (Numbers 23:19).

Second, it individualizes the love of God. "I have…I who live…Christ who lives in me…I now live…I live by faith…who loved me…gave himself for me." In that verse alone there are seven personal pronouns. Yes, Christ died for the world, but the Holy scriptures individualize it. Christ died for me.

Third, it involves me in the love of God. "The life I now live in the flesh…" This means that I do not love the world (1 John 2:15-17), but rather it means that I seek first the kingdom of God (Matthew 6:33). This means that I love the brethren (John 13:35), and it also means that I work in the kingdom (Ephesians 2:10).

The Bible says, "We love because he first loved us" (1 John 4:19).

Today, I will... *pray that as we study the Bible together as a family that our love will grow stronger and stronger because He first loved us.*

WEEK 4

Train Up A Child

KERRY WILLIAMS

To Love the Lord

Today's Scripture: Deuteronomy 6:5-8

The responsibility of raising children in the "discipline and instruction of the Lord" (Ephesians 6:4) can be overwhelming. What greater obligation could God place upon Christian fathers and mothers than to mold children into adults who live their lives to His glory?

Developing real love for God in the hearts of our children begins with our daily example. Our Father chose to reveal Himself through the metaphor of Father and child. From God's first reference to Himself as the Father of Israel in Exodus 4:22-23, He adopts the imagery of parent and child over and over throughout the scriptures. Why did God choose to reveal himself in this way? Hebrews 12:5-11 shows us His purpose as the author describes the discipline we receive from our earthly fathers and compares it to the training provided to us by God. Therefore, God intends that children relate to Him as a divine Father through their experiences with their earthly fathers. In this way, parents literally demonstrate the love of God to their children every day. As parents, we are a living, breathing example of parental love that our children can use to understand God – how He loves them, how He takes care of them, and how He has sacrificed for them. When your child thinks of you as a parent, their impressions will be transferred to God. In this way, we serve as God's surrogates with our children.

Deuteronomy 6:5-8 describes the process of teaching our children to love the Lord, as Israel was instructed to love the Lord with "all your heart and with all your soul and with all your might." Then, they were further commanded to teach their children to love Him with the same intensity through daily training. Do we fulfill this divine charge? Do we talk to our children about our love for God every day?

Today, I will... *demonstrate my love for God in ways my children can observe and commit to discussing the goodness of God every day with them.*

TUESDAY

To Resist Temptation

Today's Scripture: 1 Corinthians 10:13

As Christians, we struggle every day against the world and its evils. Paul tells us that we are engaged in a spiritual war "against the spiritual forces of evil in the heavenly places" (Ephesians 6:12). To aid us in this fight, God has equipped us with powerful defenses (the Armor of God) and the Sword of the Spirit (the Word of God). Our daily lives are a perpetual struggle against evil as "we destroy arguments and every lofty opinion raised against the knowledge of God and take every thought captive to obey Christ" (2 Corinthians 10:5). Yet, we often don't see our lives as a warzone. We go through our daily routines without much thought to the struggle that rages around us in the spiritual world. When we are oblivious to the fact that we face an ever-present enemy who seeks our destruction, we place ourselves, and our children, in great danger.

As we face off against Satan, most of our battles will involve temptation. The Devil seeks to deceive, causing us to abandon our morals and yield to sin. Yet, the Lord has provided us with everything we need to defeat the enemy by resisting temptation. If we resist the temptation, God promises Satan will flee from us (James 4:7). Additionally, we will never face a temptation that is too powerful for us to resist, as God promises a way of escape (1 Corinthians 10:13). The Devil is not the only source of temptation. Paul instructs us to resist our "flesh" (Galatians 3:16-17). Paul himself struggled in his inner man as he strove to transform his carnal desires and conform to the will of God (Romans 7).

Do we prepare our children for the spiritual war that rages all around them or do we focus solely on earthly concerns? As believers, they too are soldiers of the cross and must wage war against the Devil and their flesh. We must never neglect their training as we prepare them for the fight!

Today, I will... *discuss the spiritual war with my children and teach them to resist temptations.*

To Navigate the Wilderness of Life

Today's Scripture: Deuteronomy 8:1-4

Life is not easy. Although there are certainly moments of great joy, our physical lives are filled with disappointments, sufferings, and death. Although children are often insulated from the pain through the wonder of childhood, parents must prepare them for the inevitable hurts they will one-day experience in life.

In Deuteronomy 8:1-4 Moses tells the Israelites that God allowed them to suffer in the wilderness so that He might know their hearts. For the Israelites, the wilderness represented the hardship and pain they endured to ultimately reach the promised land. Many Old Testament events have great relevance to us as well, as they serve as shadows of the realities we experience in Christ. As the Passover lamb represented a shadow of the true Lamb of God (Christ), the wilderness also serves as a shadow of the challenges we must all pass through to reach our ultimate "promised land" (heaven). What an accurate image. This life is a "wilderness" filled with struggle as we march to glory, and our children must also pass through and survive it to finally make it home. This is a sobering truth when we realize that it is our responsibility to lead them along the way.

Praise God we do not walk through this world alone! As He journeyed with the Israelites, providing for and protecting them, our God has promised to "never leave you or forsake you" (Hebrews 13:5). We see God's companionship through our struggles in the shortest verse of the Bible (John 11:35). Although Jesus was about to raise Lazarus and turn all of their sadness to joy, still He wept. He wept because we, His people, must walk through a land of death. He wept because He feels our pain. He wept because He cares, and He walks this road with us. We must prepare children for the wilderness while reassuring them that they will never have to walk it alone.

Today, I will... *talk to my children about the difficulties of life while assuring them that God will never leave or forsake them.*

To Be a Friend of God

Today's Scripture: Luke 10:27

Is it better to be your children's friend or to be their parent? The problem with this question is that it presupposes that the two roles are exclusive of one another. It assumes that it isn't possible to be both a parent and a friend to our children.

Godly parents must exercise authority. They must command respect, discipline, train, and guide their kids in His way. But, can an authority figure still enjoy a meaningful friendship with a subordinate without compromising their authority? When we assume that such a relationship is impossible, what do we inadvertently communicate to our children about their relationship with God?

Our God had always desired a deep, intimate relationship with mankind. He desires that we love Him with all of our heart, soul, and mind (Luke 10:27). Abraham certainly held God in the highest respect, yet his relationship with the Lord was so meaningful that God says, "You, Israel, my servant, Jacob, whom I have chosen, the offspring of Abraham, my friend" (Isaiah 41:8). Paul also sought after a deeper relationship with the Lord, as he said, "that I may know Him and the power of His resurrection, and may share His sufferings, becoming like Him in His death" (Philippians 3:10). Paul desired intimacy with Christ to the degree that he was willing to even suffer and die to achieve it.

The Lord also pursues intimacy with us. Sin separated mankind from Him, as was demonstrated by man being separated from His presence in the temple by the veil. When Christ died on the cross, the veil was torn in two, giving us access to God's presence (Hebrews 10:19-22). Part of God's purpose in establishing the New Covenant was to accomplish greater intimacy with us by writing His law on our hearts and making us His people (Jeremiah 31:31-34). Let us, therefore, encourage our children to respect and honor God, but know that if they "draw near to God and He will draw near to you" (James 4:8).

Today, I will... *encourage my children to seek out an intimate friendship with God.*

To Strive for Excellence

Today's Scripture: Colossians 3:23

Christianity is a pursuit of excellence in all things. Complacency is never acceptable regarding holiness, service, spiritual maturity, or prayer. The transformative nature of our faith demands that we ever strive for change as we give ourselves daily over to God as "living sacrifices" (Romans 12:1), having been "crucified with Christ" (Galatians 2:12), and no longer living for ourselves.

We live in a world of mediocrity, where mankind often defaults to the "path of least resistance" by choosing the easiest course. As children of God, we have been called to rise above the meager efforts of "behaving only in a human way" and strive to be better (1 Corinthians 3:3). Paul prayed for his beloved brethren in Philippi that they would abound in love so that they might, "Approve what is excellent" (Philippians 1:9-10). If we are to instruct our children in the way of the Lord, we must therefore instill a desire and demand for excellence within them, so that all of their endeavors glorify Him (Colossians 3:23).

The pursuit of excellence is a precious gift for our children. It will yield spiritual growth, strengthened relationships, and even earthly success. However, it also bears a cost. Excellence exposes mediocrity, and, as a result, those who seek to put forth less effort can become jealous and aggressive. Daniel's story demonstrates this well, as He had an "excellent spirit" that distinguished him above the other officials of Babylon (Daniel 6:3). His contemporaries became envious of Daniel and sought to destroy him, resulting in him being thrown to the lions. Everyone who strives for excellence will, at some point in life, face the scorn of others. As we train our children, we need to prepare them for when it comes and reassure them that, just as God rescued and rewarded Daniel, they too will be victorious if they stay the course by always putting forth their best.

Today, I will... *start teaching my children to be the best they can be in all things, not for glory or praise, but to glorify God.*

WEEK 5

Husbands, Love Your Wives

KIRK BROTHERS

Lead Like the Lord

Today's Scripture: Ephesians 5:23-24

Building codes provide standards for builders and rubrics provide standards for students writing research papers. What is our leadership standard? When we study or teach on Ephesians 5:21ff, we may tend to focus on issues of authority and submission. I would like, instead, to focus on the Lord factor. Paul says that the husband is the head "as Christ." That is a critical phrase. We may focus on the "head" part of the verse and not on the "as Christ" part of the verse. Paul is saying that Christ is the standard for what it means to be a leader! What kind of "head" is Christ? Paul says that He is the kind of leader that saves (verse 23) and sacrifices (verse 25). He is the kind of leader that would allow himself to be crucified in place of those who follow Him.

Jesus shared His philosophy of leadership with his disciples in Matthew 20. He is nearing the end of His earthly ministry and wants to make sure his disciples understand what true leadership looks like. The text says, "But Jesus called them to him and said, 'You know that the rulers of the Gentiles lord it over them, and their great ones exercise authority over them. It shall not be so among you. But whoever would be great among you must be your servant, and whoever would be first among you must be your slave, even as the Son of Man came not to be served but to serve, and to give his life as a ransom for many'" (Matthew 20:25-28). Jesus did not only teach servant leadership, He modeled servant leadership. The take away is this: leaders who lead like the Lord serve for the benefit of others, not themselves.

Today, I will... *put my wife first and lead for her benefit.*

TUESDAY

Love Like the Lord

Today's Scripture: Ephesians 5:25-30

I remember when I studied and participated in debate in college. A key element in any formal debate is the two sides coming to an agreement on the definitions of the key terms in the debate. There is a saying in the debate world, "The one who determines the definitions, wins the debate." In other words, if I get to define the key terms in a way that best supports my position, it is harder for the other side to defeat me. How we define things is important. In light of this reality, one of my favorite sayings is this: "Definition determines doing."

How do you define love? How we define love will influence how we do love. Paul calls on husbands to love their wives "as Christ loved the church." Just as Jesus is the leadership standard (previous devo), He is also the love standard. The night before His death, our Lord told the apostles, "A new commandment I give to you, that you love one another: just as I have loved you, you also are to love one another" (John 13:35). Now, to "love one another" was not a new commandment (cf. Leviticus 19:18). What was new then about this commandment? The answer is found in the "just as I have loved you" part of the command. Jesus was giving them a higher standard for love. He was raising the bar. Jesus' love focused on doing what was best for others. Is that how I love my wife? Are my actions driven by what she needs, what is best for her, and what make her happy? That is what Jesus would do.

Today, I will... *focus on what my wife needs and what makes her happy instead of myself.*

27

The Scariest Words in the Bible

Today's Scripture: 1 Peter 3:7

I wrote this devotional on October 31, Halloween. It is appropriate because I want to talk about something scary. We will return to that thought in a moment. How do you live out your faith when you are being persecuted? Are persecution and mistreatment an excuse to rebel and act in ungodly ways? Those were some of the questions that the persecuted Christians who read the letter of 1 Peter were struggling with. The letter addresses the "proper perspectives and practices of the persecuted" (I use 1 Peter 1:6-7 as the theme verse). In spite of persecution, Peter challenges them, "Keep your conduct among the Gentiles honorable, so that when they speak against you as evildoers, they may see your good deeds and glorify God on the day of visitation" (1 Peter 2:11). In the following verses he calls them to submit to the government, masters, and in the home in spite of persecution. He also gives Jesus as an example of submission (2:21-25).

Yet, in his discussion of submission in the home, he gives a word of warning. In chapter 3 he calls wives to submit to their husbands. Likely, many women were being converted to Christ and they were married to men who were not Christians. He still wants them to be submissive and godly in spite of this. He then speaks to husbands and states some words that should send a chill up every husband's spine. He in essence says that God will not accept our prayers if we do not respect and understand our wives. We find similar language in Malachi 2:13-16 where God says he rejected Israel sacrifices because the men were faithless to their wives. God is watching how we treat our wives and treats us accordingly.

Today, I will... *treat my wife with understanding and respect as a fellow heir of God.*

THURSDAY

The Vow

Today's Scripture: Deuteronomy 23:21-23

The Hebrew term nādar means "vow" or "solemn promise"(HALOT). There were certain things that Jews were required to do, such as giving 10% of all their blessings to God (tithing). Sometimes Jews would make promises in God's name or they would make a promise to do certain things if God would bless them. In Deuteronomy 23:21-23, God is saying that it is their choice to make such vows or promises but if they make them, they better keep them. In other words, do not make a promise to God or in the name of the Lord if you do not plan to keep it. You find a similar statement in Ecclesiastes 5:4.

What does that have to do with our devotional theme of "Husbands love your wives?" Well, everything. I have performed and witnessed many a ceremony with wording similar to these: "I _____, take you _____, to be my wedded _____. To have and to hold, from this day forward, for better, for worse, for richer, for poorer, in sickness or in health, to love and to cherish 'till death do us part." We call these types of statements wedding vows. . . i.e., wedding promises. Every wedding sermon I have presided over began with the words, "We are gathered here in the presence of God . . ." When we marry, we make a promise to God and in the presence of God. Those passages from the Old Testament tells us how God feels when we break a promise to Him and in His name. Jesus spoke of the important of keeping our marriage promises when He said, "What therefore God has joined together, let no man separate" (Matthew 19:6). Paul stressed the importance of being people of our word when he said, "Therefore, having put away falsehood, let each one of you speak the truth with his neighbor, for we are members one of another" (Ephesians 4:25). When you said, "I do," did you tell the truth?!

Today, I will... *remind myself that I made a promise and I will always be faithful to that promise and my wife.*

HALOT – Hebrew and Aramaic Lexicon of the Old Testament.

FRIDAY

Partners

Today's Scripture: Acts 18:1-3

"Strength in numbers" has been the moto of the world champion Golden State Warriors for several years. They have won four championships in the last eight years, in part, because they understood that it takes a team, not individuals, to win championships. The same is true in ministry and in marriage. When God made Eve, He said, "It is not good that the man should be alone; I will make him a helper fit for him" (Genesis 2:18). The word "fit" translates a word meaning "that which is opposite, that corresponds to" (HALOT). The New American Standard translates it as "suitable for him." The New Revised Standard Version says, "I will make him a helper as his partner." When God made Eve, he was not making a servant for Adam. He was making someone who corresponds to him, a perfect match, a partner that he could face life with. From that moment forward, he would not face any struggles alone. He had a partner.

I cannot help but think of Aquila and Priscilla in the New Testament. They are mentioned six times in the biblical record (Acts 18:2, 18, 26; Romans 16:3; 1 Corinthians 16:19; and 2 Timothy 4:19). They worked with Paul in ministry and in tentmaking. They guided Apollos in a proper understanding of baptism. A congregation met in their home. They did ministry together. They were partners. The two most important decisions in life are God and your best friend. If you put God first and chose the right best friend, everything will be alright even when everything is not alright. When choosing who you will marry, you are choosing a partner to share life and ministry with. Do ministry together. Do life together. Be a team. Ecclesiastes 4:9-12 was read when Cindy and I married: "Two are better than one, because they have a good reward for their toil. For if they fall, one will lift up his fellow. But woe to him who is alone when he falls and has not another to lift him up! Again, if two lie together, they keep warm, but how can one keep warm alone? And though a man might prevail against one who is alone, two will withstand him—a threefold cord is not quickly broken." That day we became better. We became partners. We became a team. Strength in numbers.

Today, I will... *I will thank my wife for partnering with me in life and ministry.*

HALOT – Hebrew and Aramaic Lexicon of the Old Testament.

WEEK 6

Blended Families

MARK RAY

My Heroes

Today's Scripture: 2 Timothy 2:1

It is good to have heroes, people that you can look up to and imitate in life. For some people heroes come from the sports world or the political world. For others, a mentor is someone who is closer to us in life. Some of the people I admire are step parents. These people step up in times when needed and fulfill a very important role.

Timothy, the young man we read of in the Bible, had an active mother and grandmother who taught him the Scriptures from childhood, 2 Timothy 1:5. Yet his father seemed absent in his life at least in a spiritual way. Acts 16:1 tells us that Timothy's mother was a Jew, but his father was a Gentile. After this short introduction, we don't read anything more of Timothy's father in the text. Paul filled the role of spiritual mentor in Timothy's life and helped him as a preacher and leader in the Lord's church (1 Timothy 1:2). Under Paul's encouragement, Timothy grew from a religiously mixed home into someone who was faithful to God and who encouraged others.

We need these kind of heroes today. We are in need of heroes in foster care, adoption, step parenting, and spiritual mentoring. One of the glaring deficiencies in today's homes is the lack of people to whom kids can look up to and imitate. Seemingly our society encourages adults to not be involved in lives of children. Our churches need to encourage and support those who will rise up and fill the need to be a hero to these kids today. This can be done in the home through adoption, fostering, or being in a blended family. This can be done in the church by teaching Bible classes, helping with youth group activities, and caring for children.

Today, I will... *pray for kids and be an example to them.*

God Loves Families

Today's Scripture: 3 John 1:4

We know artists by their most significant creations. Michelangelo is known for the ceiling of the Sistine Chapel, Beethoven by his "Fifth Symphony," and George Lucas by the "Star Wars" movies. Each masterpiece reveals something of the creator. The same is true of God, especially in his design and purpose of the family.

In the first two chapters of Genesis we see God create the universe and all that is in it. When He saw it, He called it good. When He saw man alone, He said that was not good. God's masterpiece is the family (Genesis 1:27-28). The two essential elements of family—marriage and parenthood—reveal God's character like nothing else in creation. The love between a husband and a wife shows Christ's passionate devotion toward us as His bride, and the ups and downs of parenthood show us a compelling picture of God's tenderness and patience toward us as His children.

But what about single parent homes? What about blended families? Families sometimes look different because of circumstances and decisions. Yet these families also hold a special place in the mind of God. As a matter of fact there are times when an extra measure of God's grace is seen in the dedication of a single parent to his or her children. As she takes her kids to church and makes sure they are provided for spiritually and physically, we are reminded of the great lengths God goes to in order for us to have our daily needs met. As we see a blended family, we see the selfless nature of the Lord in the actions of step-parents who raise kids the same as their biological children. As we see growth and love grow through the hard times, it reminds us that the Lord Himself has promised to never leave us nor forsake us in our troubles.

The family is one of God's greatest masterpieces. We need to shape our families to reflects God's priority.

Today, I will... *shape my family into a place God is welcome and pray for my family.*

What You May Not Know About Blended Families

Today's Scripture: Ephesians 6:1-4

While most of our focus in sermons and Bible classes has been on the traditional family structure, it is important that the church recognizes and ministers to blended families as well. Here are some things that many people do not know about blended families. Let's use the word "family" to help us to see them.

Looking at the letter "F" we see that non-traditional families are dealing with new familiarities. There are new links created between step-parents and new siblings that take a while to get used to in life. Secondly, the letter "A" reminds us that blended families are constantly making adjustments. What do you call your step-parents? What expectations are there from children and others in this new arrangement? Thirdly the letter "M" shows us that blended families are dealing with memories of the past. There are times that traumas such as death or divorce have to be dwelt with. Grief and changes are real things that have be be gone through. The letter "I" can remind us of insecurities. When great changes happen, we don't always know what to expect in the future. Many people in insecure families have difficulty in understanding the true definition of love. The letter "L" shows us that links are often broken in a blended family. When a new family combines, traditions that occur at Thanksgiving, Christmas, and other holidays will change. There is often not a shared history with some family members and new ways and traditions must be made. Lastly the letter "Y" stands for years. Hallmark-style families are not created in an instant. A good, supportive family will take time to be created well. We must be patient while that occurs.

Today, I will... *take note of blended families and keep them in prayer.*

Ministering to Blended Families

Today's Scripture: Hebrews 10:24-25

What should churches know about blended families? What things can we as members of a congregation offer to families with single parents or those who have gone through death or divorce? As a quick reminder I remember the word "family" when thinking about a church's responsibility to families.

The letter "**F**" stands for Fellowship. Fractured families need a place to belong. They need a stable group of friends and mentors to help. We need to be encouragers to all families as they continue their walk with God (Hebrews 10:24-25). Secondly, the letter "**A**" stands for assumptions. Some are tempted to judge a person by his past or his difficulties. We should recognize that God is working with each person—adults and children—though their lives to call them to Himself. We must see people as God sees them (Romans 5:8), and know that all of us are in need of grace. Thirdly, the letter "**M**" stands for marriage. Great care needs to be taken by the congregation to support good relationships. We must teach the importance of Ephesians 5:23-6:4 as it relates to marriage, parenting, and family structure. The letter "**I**" stands for instill. That is, instill spiritual traits such as those found in Galatians 5:23-33. The fruit of the Spirit is love, joy, peace, patience, kindness, goodness, faithfulness, gentleness, and self control will help us live more like Jesus every day. The letter "**L**" of course stands for love. The Bible type of love is one that unselfishly wants what is best for others in every situation, John 13:34-35. It is the sort of lifestyle that seeks to serve and to help in every circumstance. Finally the letter "**Y**" stands for years. It takes time to create spiritual maturity, Philippians 4:6. Spiritual maturity is the sum of knowledge and experience. We must continue to be faithful and to grow spiritually over time to be what God expects of us. Don't expect maturity in a day when God is working over a lifetime.

Today, I will... *send a card of encouragement to a family with young children.*

FRIDAY

A Great Mission Field

Today's Scripture: John 4:35

Among the final words of our master was the command to go and preach the gospel to every creature. Many congregations have had great success in the far reaches of the globe in telling the lost about Jesus. Every soul needs to hear the gospel and be encouraged to obey. But let me tell you about a great mission field right next to your church building. While many of our church programs are designed for families with a mother and father and 2 kids, a large percentage of our nation's population consist of single people, single parents, and members of blended families. These souls, who are in untraditional family arraignments, need Jesus also. As a matter of fact, due to their life experiences they may be more open to the gospel than those who are in traditional family types. When Jesus shared the gospel to the Samaritan woman in John 4, she eventually brought her entire town out to listen to Him. His willingness to reach out to her helped His ministry to grow.

There are some members of the church who feel uncomfortable reaching out to people who have had different circumstances and experiences than they do. But the church is a place where all disciples can feel accepted and loved (Galatians 3:28). It is so important for us to remember that the church is a hospital for those who are hurting, not a museum of people who have every thing figured out (Luke 5:31). When we see the need we have to grow in Christ, we will see that there is room for others to grow among us as well. Today let's reach out to people who are open to the gospel so that they can have this opportunity as well to follow Jesus.

Today, I will... *reach out to those who may not look just like me.*

WEEK 7

Teaching Our Children Not to Be Prejudiced

DOUG BURLESON

God Does Not Play Favorites

Today's Scripture: Deuteronomy 10:17-19; Acts 10:34-35; Romans 2:11

Racial prejudice is not a mere political hot topic.

The Bible has much to say about how we think about and treat other people.

The story of Scripture begins with God's desire not only to create a world in which a people dwelt, but that He could bless all people through His presence and instruction. God created a man with whom all humanity shares a connection and who also affected all humanity by his sin (Genesis 5:1; Romans 5:12-21). He created from man a woman, Eve, who was called the mother of all humanity (Genesis 3:20). With Scripture beginning in this fashion, one wonders how any reader could conclude that God loves some people more than others?

Prejudice is what results when a person makes a judgment about a person or people group as being either inferior or superior, which demonstrates partiality and sinful bias. God has never thought in this way. Even in His instructions through Moses for the chosen people of Israel under the old covenant, God is "the great, the mighty, and the awesome God, who is not partial and takes no bride" (Deuteronomy 10:17). This is the same reality that allowed the apostle Paul, who spent his ministry striving to reach Gentiles to write, "God shows no partiality" (Romans 2:11). Peter, the apostle to the circumcised, concluded after seeing what God did for Cornelius, "Truly I understand that God shows no partiality, but in every nation anyone who fears Him and does what is right is acceptable to Him" (Acts 10:34-35).

God's word consistently shows that God does not play favorites but instead desires a relationship with all people. If God refuses to favor some people more than others, why should we think or behave with prejudice?

Today, I will... *be impartial towards people in a way that honors God. I will help my children not to make snap judgments about people based on their race, age, or gender but instead see others as God sees them.*

TUESDAY

No Group Can Claim Cultural Superiority

Today's Scripture: Genesis 1:26-27; Acts 17:26

There is no doubt that some people groups have been oppressed more than others.

The Gospel of Jesus can give light to all. On the sixth day of creation God said, "Let us make man in our image" (Genesis 1:26). God concluded that both Adam and Eve were made in His image, even after they sinned (Genesis 9:6). Paul recalled in his sermon in Athens that God "made from one man every nation of mankind to live on all the face of the earth" (Acts 17:26). Scripture demonstrates that all human beings come from a common source of origin, namely God.

Over time as people scattered in a post-Babel reality (Genesis 11:1-9), people groups gained much diversity in culture, language, and race. Even though Pentecost offered a glimpse of global unity in language (Acts 2:6-12), diversity among people groups became more apparent over time and sadly more divisive as people wrongly assumed some cultures were superior to others. When Paul dealt with this in Corinth and Rome, his message was always Christ-centered. Any strategy that attempts to confront these behaviors and practices that is not rooted in the Gospel of Christ is misguided.

Dr. Martin Luther King, Jr. wrote in his 1963 Letter from a Birmingham Jail, "The contemporary church is so often a weak, ineffectual voice with an uncertain sound. It is so often the arch supporter of the status quo." Sixty years later Dr. King's words still ring true because some even among God's people maintain that their cultures are superior to others. This is not what the Word of God teaches. The kingdom of Christ is superior to any worldly culture. The church should be a place where all races are welcome and where cultural standards ought not to divide us (Romans 14:1-21).

Today, I will... *speak and live out a message that is different than that of the world. I will help my family to see the healthy aspects of our cultural perspectives, while learning more about the perspectives of others, particularly that are different than our own perspectives.*

39

Our Assemblies Should Not Be Segregated

Today's Scripture: Ephesians 2:14-19; James 2:1-9

Due to the separation Israel was called to have from the world, the temple in Jerusalem did not give equal access to all. Women and Gentiles were not granted the same levels of access. Even the suspicion that Paul brought a Gentile into the temple led to a riot (Acts 21:27-30).

Long before this tense moment, Isaiah spoke of how the temple would "be called a house of prayer for all the peoples" (56:7). Jesus cited this passage when He cleared the temple (Mark 11:17). The temple had partitions that kept Jews and Gentiles separated, but Christ "has broken down in his flesh the dividing wall of hostility" (Ephesians 2:14). The people who were once outside of Israel were now the beneficiaries of Christ's work (Ephesians 2:11-12).

While understanding that God's people no longer worship on the mountain in Jerusalem (John 4:23-24), why would God's people choose to segregate themselves by race on Sundays given that Christ has torn down the dividing wall between us? If a congregation is segregated because its members hate people of different race or background, that is sinful. In James 2 we are warned about showing partiality in our assemblies based on social status or wealth. The message is clear, "if you show partiality, you are committing sin and are convicted by the law as transgressors" (James 2:9). But what about when God's people just settle for keeping things "the way they've always been"? What effort has been made to come together as God intended. Christians surely can set an example for the rest of the world in the way we love one another. God tore down the walls of division and has brought us together. The Gospel of reconciliation will always be superior to the tradition of segregation, especially among God's people.

Today, I will... *be intentional about not upholding old divisions that have been torn down in Christ. I will seek out opportunities for my family to worship with a congregation of God's people made up of Christians who are different than ourselves.*

THURSDAY
Paul Did the Right Thing

Today's Scripture: Matthew 7:12; Galatians 2:11-14

Paul rebuked Peter to face. Was it just because Peter was being inconsistent in his behavior (Galatians 2:12)? Peter was guilty of conduct that did not accurately represent what it means to be Jesus' disciple. Peter "drew back and separated himself, fearing the circumcision party. And the rest of the Jews acted hypocritically along with him, so that even Barnabas was led astray by their hypocrisy" (Galatians 2:12-13). Though when Paul took Titus and Barnabas with him to Jerusalem and was extended the right hand of fellowship (Galatians 2:1-10), Peter was rebuked to the face by Paul in Antioch.

Are there moments when our children would learn helpful lessons based on our response to the prejudice of others? How would our families be blessed if we never allowed prejudiced speech to be used in our presence, including jokes? Our children and grandchildren would be blessed to hear us talk to them about how people have been mistreated in the past and how these same prejudices sometimes prevent justice in the present. How could our families benefit if we were intentional about inviting those of different cultural or racial backgrounds into our homes for opportunities to fellowship, while also seeking out opportunities to be in their homes?

Jesus has invited His people to treat one another with fairness. He said, "So whatever you wish that others would do to you, do also to them, for this is the Law and the Prophets" (Matthew 7:12). The Golden Rule should be lived out among the people of God. May we be consistent in our love towards others, even when we feel pressure to do something different. May we have the courage to speak the truth I love, even when it requires that we rebuke those who speak and act in ways that are ungodly.

Today, I will... *cut off any speech or activity from my home that promotes prejudice, striving to have the courage to speak to my family about the value of others and to protect them from worldly influences.*

41

Heaven Will Be Filled with Various Tribes and Tongues

Today's Scripture: 1 Timothy 2:4-5; Revelation 7:9

Though Jesus' mission was primarily for the lost sheep of the household of Israel, we also know that Jesus spoke highly of non-Jews, anticipating a mission that would go to the ends of the earth. Paul's mission was "to bring about the obedience of faith for the sake of his name among all the nations" (Romans 1:5). The Old Testament anticipates the response of the nations to God's work, and Jesus' ministry causes readers to anticipate even more God's promised work that would be realized throughout the world.

The God who made all people in His image "desires all people be saved and come to a knowledge of the truth" (1 Timothy 2:4). Notice that there are no qualifying statements about the people that God desires to be saved. As the missionary to Japan, J.M. McCaleb wrote in his hymn, "The Gospel Is for All." Furthermore, we can rejoice that God's plan for the world will bring about good results. John's visionary description of the new Jerusalem includes his seeing "a great multitude that no one could number, from every nation, from all tribes and peoples and languages, standing before the throne and before the Lamb" (Revelation 7:9).

May we as the people of God take the Gospel to all races without prejudice. May we "do good to everyone, and especially to those who are of the household of faith" (Galatians 6:10). I long to be in a glorious heaven where there will be no segregation or partiality. Let us commit to working in the kingdom as those who desire to show the world how God really intended for things to be.

Today, I will... *show my family what it is that God has always desired for His people. I will talk about Jesus' commission, Paul's mission, and John's vision. I will prepare my children and grandchildren for a heavenly reality that will be greater than our divided context on earth.*

WEEK 8

Teaching Teenage Children

LOGAN CATES

MONDAY

Teenagers Absorb More Than We Know

Today's Scripture: John 17:14-19

Several years ago, my wife and I had a number of people in our home, and as we all sat down to eat, someone nudged me. They discreetly pointed at their glass of tea as if something wasn't right. I quickly tasted the tea, and it tasted so much like soap I spit it out. I politely asked my wife to make us more tea, but the new pitcher tasted exactly the same. We were all so perplexed about this predicament until we all figured it out. We had been storing the tea bags in the same area as the washer and dryer, and all the tea bags in the box soaked up the soap in the air. Every tea bag smelled like fabric softener.

Just like the tea bags, we are all in the environment of the world, but we must overcome the world. Are we to conform? (Romans 12:1-3) Or be transformed? Jesus said, "They are not of the world" (John 17:16), yet in verse 15 Jesus says, "I do not ask that you take them out of the world" (John 17:15).

We absorb our environment far too easily. We may not see it, but whatever environment we place ourselves in, we are inwardly absorbing the good and the bad. Just because a teenager "doesn't drink", do they even belong at the party? When we justify every movie, every app, every immodest clothing, we begin to appear more like we are conformers. Is that what Holy means? We begin to smell so much like the world it is hard to see Christ living in us.

Every parent has a difficult task of leading his or her teenager to live "in this world" but not "of it." Our Savior prayed diligently to the Father, "But that you keep them from the evil one" (John 17:15). Sin has a way of absorbing itself into our families and many times without our notice. Let us remain diligent and study to learn of Satan's trickery.

Today, I will... *pray for my teenagers and their battle to be in this world, but not of this world.*

44

"It Is Not My Way (or The Highway)"

Today's Scripture: Isaiah 55:8-9

The author Art Murphy once wrote, "Parents must remember God wants your child in His kingdom more than you do." Teenagers are printed copies of their parents, their surroundings, and their own wishes or desires. With this realization, we immediately become better parents. Quite often parents focus more on the Proverbs of discipline than on what Paul says, "Do not provoke your children to wrath" (Ephesians 6:4). I have raised three teenagers and could write many books about all my failures.

It is not my way or the highway. I am lovingly leading them to love God's way. "For My thoughts are not your thoughts, and neither are your ways My ways, declares the Lord" (Isaiah 55:8,9). Too many times parents make every argument and every demand about following "our ways." I don't want them to follow my way. I want to teach them God's way. If this is not the foundation of our parenting, then what is?

There will be times when arguments arise and words are exchanged. There are times I stop the momentum of an argument and consider something extremely important: Am I simply trying to get them to submit to "my way" or am I explaining to them the depth of what God wants in our relationship? Have I communicated why this means so much to me? What does God want for their life and mine? Can we turn arguments into a calm biblical conversation? Winning the battle should not be my first priority. My first priority ought to be helping them align their life to God's will.

Young people need communication more than any other age. If we could create a peaceful atmosphere where everyone knew, "We will follow God's Word first and foremost," it would help everyone be on the same page. Again, I do not want them to follow my ways. I want them to love His ways and be reverent to Him.

Today, I will... *stop and pray; I will seek His guidance. Then I will do my very best to show my children the same.*

They Have to See It, Not Just Read It

Today's Scripture: Matthew 23:1-12

Words won't do it and louder isn't better. If we aren't living what we are teaching, retention will not happen. Have you ever demanded your teenager to do something you don't do? Brethren, if we want desirable outcomes in our young people, it will only occur when they actually see us living it, not just preaching it. Lynn Anderson wrote that great leaders are not sherriff flashing a badge or CEOs contained in an office, enforcing policy from a conference room. If we, as parents, hold on to the value of Christ's example, we must understand He showed us all how to live by His life not just His words. A quiet father and mother living out Christ's example will do exceedingly more for the next generation than a loud voice and little action. We, as parents, must bear this in mind. As a parent of three teenagers, I have learned this the hard way.

This may surprise you, but one of the strongest studies for me is Matthew 23, where Jesus cites the hypocrisy of the Pharisees. It may not be the most uplifting chapter, yet it carries me to be a better father and husband. Do I preach but not practice (Matthew 23:3)? Have I laid burdens on my teenagers I am not willing to carry myself (23:4)? Have I been doing deeds just to be seen by others (23:5)? These individuals were to be the religious elite helping others learn about God, but were falling down on their job.

I am supposed to be the spiritual Mufasa of my home, but there are times when I am more like the Pharisees and Scribes, and I forget. Jesus uses what some call harsh words, but Jesus' goal was to win soul. May our leadership be revived to see the most important part of teaching is when our actions match our words!

Today, I will... *examine my heart to see if it matches my words!*

THURSDAY

Where Is Your Teenager's Weapon?

Today's Scripture: Ephesians 6

Imagine your teenager is being pressed to the front lines of an intense battle, and the enemy is striking repeatedly using harmful, deceitful methods. We send our teenagers into battle with something in their hand, but it's not a weapon; it's a phone. In fact, they have somehow become addicted to holding on to the enemy's greatest tool rather than the Word of God. Woops! Wait, How did that happen? Can we fix it? Peeling it from their grasp is becoming virtually impossible. As a church camp director for seventeen years, I'm amazed how parents don't understand our reason for asking for restraint with phones. Parents, we are left watching our teenagers attempt to fight deep, dark, terrible, intense battles without the very weapon God begged us all to take.

"Put on the whole armor of God, that you may be able to stand against the schemes of the devil" (Ephesians 6:11). Do our children have it? The devil helps us all relinquish the Word of God and replace it with the world. From the beginning, Adam and Eve relinquished God's word and chose to sin. By putting on the full of armor of God, we will be able take our stand against the devil's schemes. This text isn't designed to make a great youth class, it is to provide victory for us and our family through Christ.

My first task as a parent of teenagers is to empower my teenagers to soak deeply and completely in the illumination of God's word. There is not a greater and more honorable task on this earth. The secular trophies, medals and certificates on the wall are not our first priority. We must defy the world's attempt to glue them to technology and lead them to see and love the inspired Word. It certainly true that, "without the armor of God, they cannot stand against the schemes of the devil."

Today, I will... *lead my teenagers to a deeper love of God's Word.*

Motivate Teens to Serve

Today's Scripture: Mark 10:33-45

The vapor of selfishness naturally lingers over every teenager, and the more they are permitted to inhale it, the harder it will be to turn them into servants later. Today, if you find a teenager even remotely interested in doing anything for anyone else in the church, you might want to go thank their parents or grandparents and take the youth to lunch. I'm afraid it has become very easy to raise a generation into feeling entitled to receive much more than they give. So what do we do?

As followers of Christ we are called to be implementers of His life and teaching. I remember my own mother dropping me off at an older widow's home to mow her grass when I was only twelve. Now every time I drive by that house, I am reminded of the good my mother was trying to accomplish (even though at age twelve I rolled my eyes).

Mark 10:33-45 is a fantastic nightly bible discussion for your teenagers. James and John are like teenagers fighting to see, "who gets to sit shotgun first" next to Jesus. They were caught breathing the vapor of selfishness. His response would leave them all in shock because He tells them greatness is paired with a servant-heart. Is that what we find in our teenagers today? As parents, are we showing them how to serve others every day? This will not happen just by sitting them in worship week after week. Jesus consistently shows us that we must be disciple-makers not just parents. We must show our teenagers what service to others looks like.

How? Attend church activities, sharing with them the plan to help before or afterward. Help them make cookies to take to someone struggling. Make one day a week "card day" where you have cards for them to sign to encourage others. Are your teenagers involved when there is a service project? Show them how to call someone struggling and encourage them. It is easy to get busy and forget we are training disciplines not just having kids.

Today, I will... *show my teenagers the servant heart of Christ and lead my home after Him.*

WEEK 9

Relationships with Adult Children

ANDY CONNELLY

MONDAY

Start Early

Today's Scripture: Proverbs 22:6

While Proverbs 22:6 is a well-known scripture regarding God's view of parenting, the back half of the verse has always brought a few different considerations. However, to begin a week in consideration of relationships with adult children I want to begin by focusing on the words at the beginning of the verse, "train up a child." My wife is a career schoolteacher, having now taught in both a public-school setting and a private Christian school setting for a combined 24 years. Also, in addition to being a long-time preaching minister, my father was a Christian college professor for 33 years. One constant theme heard from each of them has been the evident difference in young people whose parents started cultivating positive relationships early and those that waited too long.

Many parents are heartbroken today over difficult relationships with their children. I vividly remember a conversation with a good friend who was in severed anguish over choices made by a child that were vastly different than those things taught and exemplified in the home. Lashing out in a very human nature, he screamed the phrase, "What did we do wrong?" I stopped him at that point and took him to the parable of the prodigal in Luke 15:17-18, where that son came to his senses and made the choice to return home. The logic is that he knew he could go there. The most pitied among us is the one who feels he has nothing to which he can return. If it's just Monday in your time of raising children, I beg of you to start early. Good relationships with adult children are more likely when they start early. Give them something to which they want to return. Help them feel confident you will always be there.

Today, I will... *not assume I can build the relationship later, and prioritize teaching those things to which they can always return.*

Knowing What Time It Is

Today's Scripture: John 21:15-23

When our first son was born, I was handed the tool to cut the cord. When they handed him back to me, I couldn't help thinking this was the God who had knit him in his mother's womb saying to me, "Now build me a man." It was both exciting and humbling. After 26 years I find myself wondering where that time has gone.

In John 7 Jesus references His time had not yet come. Later, John 13 says Jesus knew the time was upon Him, and in John 17 He prays knowing that time was now upon Him. Our Lord always knew what time it was in His ministry, and in His purpose. For parents, it is vital that we know what time it is. Having older children calls for different things that it did when they were younger. Christian parenting is a God-given ministry. Scripture reminds us that children are "a heritage from the Lord" (Psalm 127:3). While specifics may change with age, there is still a vital Christian stewardship to consider.

Jesus experienced many conversations with Peter—some that were necessitated by Peter's "infancy" as a disciple of the Lord. However, Jesus always knew what time it was in His work, and He changed those conversations, challenging Peter differently than ever before in John 21. Asking Peter three times if he loved Him, Jesus made sure Peter knew why He was asking, telling him the truth about what was to come. As children reach adulthood, life throws new things their way, and our conversations should change and challenge. By illustration, as the Lord knew what was coming to Peter, we probably know much of what is coming to them. Jesus could not leave Peter and the disciples in their infancy, as there was much for them to do. Like our Lord, I must not leave my children in their infancy.

Today, I will...￼*pray that God leads me to know what time it is for my children, and how to change the conversations where necessary.*

Good Counsel

Today's Scripture: Proverbs 24:6

It is said that there is a time when parents are the smartest people in the world, then the time when they seem to know nothing or don't understand, and finally you find they became smart again. Have you ever felt like this from either end of the spectrum, or now from both? The Bible is not silent on seeking wise counsel, and parents hope that chosen counsel will be an aid in various forms of protection. As parents, where do we tell our adult children to go?

Well, here are three important reminders. First, every Christian should remember that as we grow, we should strive to grow with the Word of God. So we must teach our children to go to the Scriptures. Paul reminds fathers and parents that children should be raised, "in the discipline and instruction of the Lord" (Ephesians 6:4). There is no substitute for that which is inspired of God and not from culture, education, or friends.

Secondly, wise counsel doesn't just send them to the scripture, it sends them to counselors that are indeed wise. My parents taught me to have a team of brothers and sisters in Christ that were like- minded, proven, and trustworthy, seeking God's counsel themselves. Adult children must maintain close voices that are listening to God themselves. In other words, to achieve and maintain moral integrity, one should seek morally excellent people for counsel. As Paul stated, as children begin to select their own advisors, remind them that "bad company ruins good morals" (I Corinthians 15:33).

Finally, as they marry, remind them to go to their spouse. Scripture says it was the plan of God that after marriage, a man should "hold fast to his wife, and they shall become one flesh" (Genesis 2:24). One flesh means sharing, listening, and valuing the other in their thoughts. A marriage that devalues this is not built to last, nor does it honor the God who created the home. Advise them to make one another their closest confidant.

Today, I will... *begin praying my children find wise counsel beyond just their parents.*

THURSDAY

Why Am I Coming in Second?

Today's Scripture: Luke 2:41-52

Adult children who begin to move forward through life are doing just that, moving forward, meaning they are entering and accepting new challenges and opportunities just like parents. As time moves swiftly, often the parents are not quite ready for this. When my children went away to college, I did not handle it well the first few weeks. We were buddies, and I had specific things we did every week that could no longer be done as often. I missed it terribly.

In Luke 2:52, we read that Jesus "increased in wisdom and in stature and in favor with God and man." This was part of God's necessary plan not just to save man from sin, but to be the perfect High Priest, able to understand both our needs and pain, and learning obedience "through what He suffered" (Hebrews 5:8). The same writer reminds us that we have a high priest "who has been tempted as are we" (Hebrews 4:15), which allows for His identification with man. God had a job for His son to do, and those things being allowed were necessary to be the most effective High Priest. Friends, our sons and daughters coming into adulthood will have jobs to do, and opportunities for great influence. When we see them begin to take on other things, people, and opportunities, this was in God's design, as it was for Jesus. Remember, we want growth in those same areas cited in Luke 2:52.

I still review photos, videos, and simply recall and discuss those things we have done together. They will also come back to those things soon. As they have moved into adulthood, we have chosen to celebrate things where they are, and because they see us doing that, they love being together. Fostering good relationships with adult children requires flexibility of what we as parents begin to champion. We cannot merely hold to great past memories, but learn to celebrate them for the new journeys they are now taking.

Today, I will... *select a current part of my adult child's journey, and send a message that supports that.*

Once a Man ... Twice a ...

Today's Scripture: Ecclesiastes 3:1-8

There is a time for everything. That's not just conventional wisdom, that's scripture. You may know it well, and it comes from Ecclesiastes chapter 3, which begins by saying, "For everything there is a season, and a time for every matter under heaven" (Ecclesiastes 3:1). From that point forward, the writer covers the seasons of life. No, not winter, spring, summer, and fall. These are the seasons that life throws our way, and at times more than one of those seasons is in full bloom. In chapter 12 of the same book, the writer gives a vivid description and urges one to remember his creator early, before some of those seasons occur. It's a most accurate depiction of the aging process and life's ultimate futility if lived without that remembrance.

That time is coming for adults with adult children themselves. When that time comes, the man in that life may in some way become the child again. Life has changed, along with abilities, comfort with some things, and opportunities. It's in this moment those with adult children can help themselves by admitting and allowing into practice the idea that some things are best trusted to the child, now the adult. It's hard when you want to still view them as being in diapers, or yourself much younger. God has put mankind in families for a reason, and it was one of the bigger pieces of evidence to His wisdom. I urge you, regardless of which side of this equation you find yourself, to pray to find this necessary give and take. To adult children, be willing to take on things you are now best suited to handle that they are willing to give you. Don't forget however to "honor your father and mother"(Ephesians 6:2) in another way, by being careful to allow their dignity to remain intact. To parents with adult children, let them love you this way, and remember, you trained them well. Please have this conversation, and pray about it often.

Today, I will... *begin to pray for this time down the road, and begin the conversation.*

WEEK 10

Godly Grandparents

BILL WATKINS

Grandchildren Are the Crown Of the Aged

Today's Scripture: Proverbs 17:6

We were getting ready to leave for preschool when I noticed my grandson, Knox, had his boots reversed. I stopped him and said, "Knox, you have your boots on the wrong feet." He looked at me with all the sympathy that his four-year-old heart could muster and said, "PAH-op! These are the only feet I have!"

I love being Pop to my grandchildren—all 24 of them! A few years ago, we took them all for a few days to Disney World along with their parents. On Thursday, Beverly (my wife) told all the parents, "You guys go to the park today and enjoy it. Bill and I will keep the kids with us." I thought she had lost her mind! "What are we going to do with all these kids?!?" The day was raucous, challenging, sometimes unorganized, and exhausting, but at the end of the day, I realized it was my favorite time in the park. I loved it when people said, "Who do all these kids belong to?" and I could say, "Me!"

Time with grandchildren is precious. They are so full of energy and potential. It is often true that their parents—because of work or other concerns—do not have the time or energy to devote to all the needs of their children. As grandparents, we have been granted the wonderful opportunity to help shape and point them toward the future, and to enjoy them when their days are so full that 24 hours doesn't seem to be nearly enough time.

Today, I will... *thank God for the blessing of children in my life. I will take some time out of my busy schedule to pray for them, and I will call or visit with them. I will take their concerns seriously and seek to help them on their way to heaven.*

Blessing Your Grandchildren

Today's Scripture: Genesis 48:8-9

Grandchildren are such a blessing! When I can, I take two of my grandsons to breakfast before school. It's one of the favorite parts of my day. Once while we were eating Kash asked, "Pop can I have five dollars?" I thought he might want it for a toy or a game, so I asked, "What do you need it for?" He said, "There's a man sitting at the table behind you. I think he's homeless and I want to help him." I gave him the five dollars and he said, "Can you buy him a sausage biscuit and some orange juice? I think he's hungry." So I gave Kash enough to get breakfast for the man. He ordered and paid for the food, took it to the man, gave him the five dollars, and said "God bless you." I think I'll keep taking my grandsons to breakfast.

As a grandfather, I want to give my grandchildren a blessing. I'm certainly not Jacob. I have no supernatural power or prophetic insight to share with them. But I know that I can bless them by reflecting their potential in Christ and in the world back to them. I can help them discover their unique talents. I can listen to their dreams and help guide them toward a better future and the best eternity. I can pray with them and for them every day. I can show them confidence, honesty, sincerity, and courage and bless them with words from God. As grandparents, we can make a difference.

Today, I will...thank God for the privilege of knowing the best of His creation. I will pray for my grandchildren to grow in wisdom and stature and in favor with God and man. I will remember what a privilege it is to be in their lives.

The Value of Experience

Today's Scripture: Psalm 37:25

When I'm with my grandchildren, they always want me to tell them stories about when I was younger. I love a good story, and I happen to think that everyone's life is an amazing story. Sometimes the stories are comedies, sometimes tragedies, sometimes drama, sometimes success stories, sometimes failures, but they are always incredible adventures.

Stories—especially true stories—give perspective to life. What we often accept as obvious and a matter of course have become that way to us because of the stories that we have lived out. Our grandchildren have not had those experiences, and therefore some things are not obvious to them.

The perspective of a grandparent helps our grandchildren to see that obstacles are not the end of the road, that setbacks are simply a part of life, that trials make us stronger, and that adversity leads us to hope. We can share the longer view that sees beyond today's traumas, and trials, and temptations, and tensions to possible outcomes. We can share with them that there is always hope and always Someone we can trust.

We can say, "I've been where you are. I know how you feel. Trust me, there is a lot more life to be lived than you can see right now." Because we are getting closer to our eternal home, we can truthfully say, "The best of my life and the best of yours is still in front of us. I'm not giving up and you don't need to either."

We've seen life, and it's bigger, and more confusing, and more frightening, and more beautiful, and better than many have ever imagined. Life is worth living, and with God, it's good!

Today, I will... *encourage the depressed, weep with the weeping, rejoice with the rejoicing, and point them to my Father. In all my years He has never failed me, and He won't fail now!*

THURSDAY

Passing on a Heritage

Today's Scripture: Psalm 103:17-18

What will you leave behind for your grandchildren when you have left this planet? I've seen many leave behind generous gifts of money and property. I've also seen many families torn apart by conflict over whether or not everyone has gotten their fair share.

What will you leave that is guaranteed to bless them with hope and joy? I think there is only one thing. Leave them the godly heritage of obedience and righteousness. It will keep blessing them long after you have gone.

For better or for worse, we will leave an indelible imprint on our children and grandchildren. When God was giving the ten commandments to Moses He said, "I the LORD your God am a jealous God, visiting the iniquity of the fathers on the children to the third and the fourth generation of those who hate me, but showing steadfast love to thousands of those who love me and keep my commandments" (Exodus 20:5-6).

If you live your life in disobedience, you will affect even your great grandchildren in a negative way. But if you live in love and obedience to God, you will affects thousands of generations to come. Long after they have forgotten your name—long after your tombstone has been lost to the world—the generations will continue to be blessed with mercy and love because of the life that you lived while on earth.

We are not here to live for ourselves. In fact, our lives aren't really about us at all. We were created for the glory of God, and He made us to reflect that glory for our time and for the generations to come.

Today, I will... *remember that I am a part of a much larger picture than myself alone. I will live and make decisions today in such a way as to bless those who have never yet taken their first breath. I will live for eternity today.*

FRIDAY

Staying Young

Today's Scripture: 2 Corinthians 4:16; Isaiah 40:28-31

One of the things that keeps many older people from having an influence on the young is that they have begun to think "old." Their emphasis is now centered on preserving what they have. They don't want to lose their health, or their wealth, or their mind.

But all of that is self-defeating. No football team ever won a game by trying not to lose! You must play to win! You must have something to live FOR!

George Burns lived to be 100 years old. When he was asked the secret to such a long and successful life he said, "You can't help getting older, but you don't have to get old."

The moment you quit dreaming, the moment you stop striving for something more, the moment you stop hoping, is the moment you start dying. People, especially grandchildren, will be attracted to you if you still stay involved, interested, and invested in life.

What have you always wanted to try or do? Where have you always wanted to go? What have you always wanted to know? What piques your interest? What fascinates you? You still have time! Pursue what you can! Dream big dreams! Pursue your loves!

Your grandchildren will want to be like you, and they'll want to be around you. So think young! Don't regret what you can't do – pursue what you can! Life is still worth living!

Today, I will... *dust off the cobwebs from my dreams. I will try something I've never tried, but have always wanted to. I will invite my grandchildren to experience it with me. I will relearn to love my life!*

WEEK 11

Discipline & Children

MIKE JOHNSON
(FLORIDA)

Begin with the End in Mind

Today's Scripture: Psalm 78:1-7

There's a baby in my house! I'll never forget that feeling 23 years ago when Joshua came home for the first time. We had prepared for months, but now he was here. And the question that we and every new parent must ask in that moment is, "now what?"

What do we want for our children physically, mentally, emotionally, and socially? More importantly, what do we want for them spiritually? If we try to make these decisions in the moment, our tossing back and forth will disorient our children, leading to confusion and rebellion.

What are you aiming for when it comes to raising your children? Have you written it down? Have you talked about it with your children? If we you aim at nothing, you'll hit it every time.

For followers of Jesus, the goal of parenting is the same as Jesus' commission to the apostles. "Go therefore and make disciples of all nations" (Matthew 28:19). Our ultimate goal is to raise a disciple of Jesus. And making a disciple requires discipline, the discipline to stay on course (children and parents) when multiple detours entice us. God hasn't called us to help our children get into Harvard. God has called us to help them get into Heaven.

Our prayer is that our children's grandchildren will be disciples of Jesus. We've made the commitment of the Psalmist:
> We will not hide them from their children but tell to the coming generation
> the glorious deeds of the Lord, and his might, and the wonders that he has done.
> He established a testimony in Jacob and appointed a law in Israel,
> which he commanded our fathers to teach to their children,
> that the next generation might know them, the children yet unborn,
> and arise and tell them to their children, so that they should set their hope in God
> and not forget the works of God, but keep his commandments.
> (Psalm 78:4-7)

Today, I will... *raise my children to pursue the only prize that really matters.*

TUESDAY

Guardrails

Today's Scripture: Proverbs 1:1-7

Kids need safe spaces. The idea of safe spaces has become politically charged in our culture. But no one can argue that for children to thrive, they need to be able to exist in a physically, emotionally, and socially safe environment.

When driving down a highway, guardrails are extremely valuable. Guardrails warn us that we're swerving off the path. Guardrails can keep us from going too far and keep us moving in the direction we need to go. For children, the safest spaces are between the guardrails.

What guardrails do you have in place for your children? Are your guardrails clearly marked? Are your guardrails consistent? Are your guardrails in alignment with your child's stage in life and personality traits? When your children push the guardrail boundaries, do you correct and redirect with conviction and consistency, but without anger? Some children will push the edges of the guardrails, while others will joyfully thrive at a safe distance from them. But clear, consistent, appropriate guardrails can be a matter of life and death.

If you're looking for guardrails, may I suggest a reading of the book of Proverbs? After all, a Proverb a day keeps Satan away. Here are the first words of Proverbs.

1 The proverbs of Solomon, son of David, king of Israel:
2 To know wisdom and instruction, to understand words of insight,
3 to receive instruction in wise dealing, in righteousness, justice, and equity;
4 to give prudence to the simple, knowledge and discretion to the youth—
5 Let the wise hear and increase in learning, and the one who understands obtain guidance,
6 to understand a proverb and a saying, the words of the wise and their riddles.
7 The fear of the LORD is the beginning of knowledge; fools despise wisdom and instruction.
(Proverbs 1:1-7)

Today, I will... *make certain there are clear, consistent, appropriate guardrails in place so that my children can thrive in a safe space.*

WEDNESDAY

More than Rules

Today's Scripture: Deuteronomy 6:4-9

Kids need rules! Don't miss that. They need to know the rules. They need to experience consequences for not following those rules. But we are not running a business. We are raising a family, and for a child to grow to be a disciple, discipline must be about more than rules.

In Exodus chapter 5, Moses reminds the people of the Ten Commandments, and then in the first three verses of chapter 6, Moses emphasizes the importance of following those commands. Then in verse 4, Moses says there's something even more important than rules. "Hear, O Israel: The Lord our God, the Lord is one. You shall love the Lord your God with all your heart and with all your soul and with all your might" (Exodus 6:4-5).

While emphasizing the commandments, Moses establishes a new commandment that supersedes all commandments. That new command is love! These words of Moses indicate that the primary motive for obedience is relational.

Moses is warning the people about the danger of passing down rules without the context of a loving relationship. Parents tend to buy into the myth that what is most important is passing down the rules and the reasons for the rules. If we simply explain why we have the rules, it will result in an appropriate response from our children. But I can't recall a time when I gave such a wonderful explanation of the rules that my children agreed and said in unison, "O wise father, we now fully understand and we will fully obey." The problem with reasons and rules is that you can debate them. But you cannot debate a trusted relationship. It's not that parents shouldn't have rules. They must. It's just that rules never carry more weight than a healthy relationship.

What are you doing to grow your relationship with your child? How eager will they be to come home once they're grown and gone?

Today, I will...*intentionally pursue a more intimate relationship with my child.*

THURSDAY

Influence

Today's Scripture: Ephesians 6:4

The quality of your relationship determines the weight of your influence.

When our children first come into our lives, our influence does not hinge upon the strength of the relationship. We have a size and position advantage. We can pick them up and put them somewhere. We can make them eat what we put on their plates. They are dependent on us.

But eventually, all that goes away. If we do not shift to parenting from strength and depth of the relationship instead of from size and position, we will be tempted to parent from size and position even when we no longer possess those advantages; and parenting that way erodes the relationship.

In Ephesians 6:4, Paul says, "Fathers, do not provoke your children to anger, but bring them up in the discipline and instruction of the Lord." The word, 'provoke,' means to make one hostile. It means you have abused your size and position to get what you want, but in the process, you've harmed the relationship. Paul is saying, "Don't put your kids in a position where they cannot win with you."

Instead, "bring them up." Those three words are one Greek word that means, "to nourish and replenish." We should be a nurturer, a partner, a guide and coach. Our best bet for preparing our children for the future will come through relational channels, not from size and position.

That does not mean you no longer discipline. It just means that if you want to make that transition on your terms, now is the time to prepare. We always want to be sitting in the seat of influence with our children, especially when they start making their most important decisions. And the key to that future influence is the richness and health of the relationship that we are cultivating right now.

Today, I will... *do something specific to make my child feel valued and accepted.*

Train & Trust

Today's Scripture: Proverbs 22:6

Do your best, and trust in God.

Doing our best as a parent means training. Proverbs 22:6 says, "Train up a child in the way he should go; even when he is old, he will not depart from it." Some see this as a reference to training in the path of right-eousness. Others claim the Hebrew phrase is better interpreted as refer-ring to training that aligns with a child's unique personality and gifted-ness. It can mean dedicate the child to God or prepare the child for fu-ture responsibilities.

I'm not sure it matters which idea you cling to; all of them are expound-ed upon elsewhere in Scripture. But what we as parents must be careful of is clinging to this verse like a rabbit's foot. This passage doesn't say wayward children will come back. It says they will never leave! That's why we must remember that Proverbs are general principles, not iron-clad guarantees.

Children are not mindless lumps of wet clay. The accomplishments or sins of our children don't always reflect our parenting skills or godliness. If you don't believe that, ask God about Adam and Eve. Could they have had a better Father than God himself? Could there be a better home than the Garden of Eden? It doesn't get any better than the perfect envi-ronment and a perfect parent. If child rebellion happened in the Garden of Eden, it can happen anywhere.

Our job is to train our children to the best of our ability to love and obey God. If we do, they're likely to follow, but they might not. Our children aren't a possession that we own and that we can manipulate to do what we want. They are a trust that we manage for a little while before turning them back over to their original owner.

Today, I will... *train as if it all depends on me and pray as if it all depends on God.*

WEEK 12

Teaching Our Children to Pray

GANTT CARTER

MONDAY

Do They See You?

Today's Scripture: Luke 11:1

Your children are watching you, watching you all the time. They watch you at the supper table; they watch you as you visit with friends, and they watch how you interact with your spouse. The question is not whether they are watching you, the real question is, "What do they see when they watch you?"

As we pick up Luke's gospel account, we read: "Now Jesus was praying in a certain place, and when he finished, one of his disciples said to him, 'Lord, teach us to pray, as John taught his disciples'" (Luke 11:1).

Why did the disciples ask Jesus to teach them to pray? What did they see? He is their teacher, and they do mention that they want Him to teach them "as" John taught His followers. The fact that Luke tells us that Jesus is praying when His disciples arrive with their request does not appear to be a mere coincidence. The disciples wait until He is done praying, and then they express their desire to learn from Jesus about prayer.

How might that work with our children? This is not to suggest that we must wait until our children come to us and ask us about prayer before we teach them, but there is a lesson here about the subtle power of example. Do your children ever see you praying? Is mealtime the only time they see you pray? Granted, prayer is not something we want to brag about or turn into a show (Matthew 6:1, 5-6). However, we can pray before our children and with our children, finding ways for them to know that we pray fervently and frequently.

Have you ever had to tell your child to not interrupt you when you were speaking to God, perhaps just in your head (Nehemiah 2:4-5)? It is a wonderful opportunity to then teach about praying to God on a consistent basis, and to share how prayer can occur only in our thoughts.

Today, I will... *seek to set a clear example of a healthy prayer-life for my children.*

TUESDAY
Simplicity & Dependence
Today's Scripture: Luke 11:2-4

As we keep reading in Luke, we discover the way Jesus taught His disciples to pray: "When you pray, say: 'Father, hallowed be your name. Your kingdom come. Give us each day our daily bread, and forgive us our sins, for we ourselves forgive everyone who is indebted to us. And lead us not into temptation'" (Luke 11:2-4; see also Matthew 6:7-15).

This model prayer is sometimes called "The Lord's Prayer" or "The Disciples' Prayer." Regardless of how we label it, it is an example of how to pray from the King Himself. His words provide us with a pattern for our own prayers, and they are one way for us to share prayer with our children.

Jesus' prayer here is quite simple; it is short and to the point, as it might be said. The simplicity involved makes His prayer especially helpful in teaching children. Jesus begins by addressing God as "our Father," a distinct reminder of the intimate relationship we can have with Him. He also stresses God's holiness and authority, pointing us to the reverence appropriate as we worship our Father. He is our Father, but He is still the Sovereign God of the universe. We are honored by His grace to get close to Him and to come boldly before His throne through Jesus (Hebrews 4:14-16; Ephesians 2:17-18). May our intimacy never turn into a frivolous attitude toward Him, and yet may our reverence never cause us to feel distant from Him.

Jesus includes a request about daily bread in this prayer. It is totally appropriate for our prayers to contain references to physical needs. Children can easily appreciate these types of prayers. Then He turns His attention to the need called forgiveness of sins, and to the danger of temptation. Praying for spiritual aid as we interact with others is so vital. As we face the battles against Satan, we cannot do so effectively without prayerful dependence on our Lord. Do your children know this?

Today, I will... *share these beautiful realities about prayer with my children.*

Bringing Them Up

Today's Scripture: Ephesians 6:4

As parents, especially Fathers, God expects us to fulfill our role in specific ways. He blesses us with children, and we are to direct their hearts toward Him. Based on the imagery of Psalm 127:3-5, we may perhaps describe parenting as forming arrows to eventually launch into society, all in a manner that makes for a godly impact in the world.

Inspired by the Holy Spirit, the apostle Paul writes: "Fathers, do not provoke your children to anger, but bring them up in the discipline and instruction of the Lord" (Ephesians 6:4). In a parallel text, he cautions: "Fathers, do not provoke your children, lest they become discouraged" (Colossians 3:21).

How do we bring our children up in Jesus' discipline and instruction? In short: We live the way we want them to live (be who you want them to be); we teach them verbally about God and life, and we provide needed discipline and structure. Teaching our children to pray is a wonderful part of training up our children in the Lord!

We cannot expect anyone else to teach them about prayer. What the world will teach them about praying to God will not be healthy. Communicating with our Creator is far too important for us to leave to chance, to the world, or to anything of the sort. Our example alone is invaluable in raising kids, but may we also intentionally train them to pray to God.

Let us teach our children about the simple, yet profound truth of prayer. Prayer is both crucial and costly for us, connecting our will to God's will. God speaks to us in His written Word. We speak to God when we pray. Prayer is not some mystical experience or some magical wand. Prayer is talking to the greatest being in the entire universe. God is not our personal genie; God is our heavenly Father.

Today, I will...*intentionally bring up my children in a way that teaches them to communicate with our God.*

THURSDAY
How Early Is Too Early?

Today's Scripture: 2 Timothy 3:14-15

Think on Paul's inspired words to young Timothy: "But as for you, continue in what you have learned and have firmly believed, knowing from whom you learned it and how from childhood you have been acquainted with the sacred writings, which are able to make you wise for salvation through faith in Christ Jesus" (2 Timothy 3:14-15).

Please take note of the phrase, "from childhood," in the beginning of verse 15. From a very early age, Timothy's mother and grandmother were working to share their sincere faith with this young man (see 2 Timothy 1:5-7). They helped to instill a rugged faith in him by teaching the Scriptures to him. Surely, praying was an essential part of that parental effort. Their work paved the way for Timothy's faith in Jesus!

Can we teach an infant to fold their hands and talk to God? What about a toddler or a preschooler? Am older kid? A teenager? We may easily underestimate the comprehension of a child; it is amazing just how much they can retain, and a joy to see just how well they can learn spiritual truths. Teens tend to get a bad rap, unfortunately, but they can be some of the most sincere and strong servants of Jesus. It is, however, often more difficult to teach older children who have not been taught during the earlier stages of their life. Are we helping our children to know God and to love God and love people? What better way to do that than to teach and encourage them to pray to God and to pray for others?

It is so vital for our children to learn to acknowledge God in their formative years – childhood is such a great time to teach our children to pray. Consider cautions like Ecclesiastes 12:1. Let us help our children to remember their Creator in the time of their youth!

Today, I will... *recognize the value of taking the time to teach children to pray during this time called childhood.*

71

Daily Opportunities

Today's Scripture: Deuteronomy 11:19

As God calls His people to love and serve Him, He tells them to store His words in their heart, and to carefully teach their children. Look at part of the instruction: "You shall teach them to your children, talking of them when you are sitting in your house, and when you are walking by the way, and when you lie down, and when you rise" (Deuteronomy 11:19; compare Deuteronomy 6:7).

God intends for parents to consistently train their children in His ways. This brings us back to the concept of teaching prayer both by words and by example. If we are praying throughout our days (1 Thessalonians 5:17; Romans 12:12), then we are well on our way to leading our children to a life of prayer themselves.

Jesus sets the example for us all: His earthly life was devoted to prayer. Consider the intensity of His prayers: He prayed all night prior to a major decision (Luke 6:12), and He prayed at times with "loud cries and tears" (Hebrews 5:7). May we first align our own hearts to His heart, and then share His heart with our children. Are we pointing our little ones to Jesus?

Our 6-year-old son usually leads the prayer at our family meals. He is never forced to do it but is encouraged to do so and rarely does he not want to pray. There are times when gentle feedback is provided to guide him in the future. He recently asked if praying prior to a meal is something "we have to do", or just something "we do because it's what we do." His inquiry provided a great occasion to talk about the Biblical teaching and example for offering thanks for our food (1 Timothy 4:1-5; Matthew 14:18). We also discussed the third option outside his initial question, praying at mealtimes and at other times, as something we desire to do in our relationship with God.

Today, I will... *enjoy and appreciate the daily opportunities to help my children grow in their clarity about God and in their closeness to God.*

WEEK 13

Teaching Our Children to Teach

BO SHERO

My Treasure

Today's Scripture: Matthew 13:44-46

In these parables (Matthew 13:44-46) Jesus tells of a farmer and a merchant who sell all that they have in order to own a treasure and a great pearl. Jesus was teaching of the value of the kingdom of God to those who know what they have found. It is to them of such great worth, they would be willing to give up everything in order to have it.

If you want your children to become Bible teachers, it would be good for them to see you treasuring God's word. My dad was a preacher who raised three sons who are preachers. A big part of the reason I preach and teach the Bible is because it was treasured by my dad. Sundays and Wednesdays were not enough for him. He was so much in love with the Bible that he set up private studies in our home or the homes of those he taught. Most of those studies resulted in his students being baptized into Christ Jesus. Natural family conversations were often centered around a passage of scripture and its application in our lives. I remember my dad sitting in a quiet room with his worn Bible with all the underlined passages studying the treasure that meant so much to him.

I love the Bible as my dad who loved it before me. My son has reminded me of the excitement with which I would tell him of some new treasure that I had uncovered in my own Bible study. My son tells me the greatest motivator for him being the Bible teacher and preacher that he is today was watching me treasure the word of God.

You have no secrets from your children. Your children know what you treasure. If you want them to become Bible teachers, treasure the Bible before them and teach the Bible when they can see you.

Today, I will... *read the Bible and treasure it and seek an opportunity to share this great treasure with someone else.*

TUESDAY

My Example

Today's Scripture: John 5:19

Abraham lied that Sarah was his sister not his wife in Egypt and to Abimelech (Genesis 12:10-13, 20:1-2). Then Isaac told the same lie about his wife to Abimelech (Genesis 26:7). Jacob deceived his way through his early life, and his sons learned to deceive him (Genesis 37:31-33). Amnon must have learned to take any woman he wanted (2 Samuel 13) from his father David (2 Samuel 11). Apparently we teach our children a lot by our own behavior. They see, and often follow, the bad and the good that they see lived out by us.

If you want your children to be Bible teachers, it would be very good for them to see you teaching the Bible. If they see you preparing your lessons and materials, or better yet, if they help you prepare your materials they may be drawn to that service. Many of our Bible teachers came from parents who taught Bible themselves. Likewise many of the mere consumers, who sit in class and worship but never teach, learned this from their parents. If your children see the sacrifice you make and the fear you overcome, they will understand the treasure that you consider the Bible to be.

Along with your example, you should also consider your conversation. If you speak of Bible teaching as a drudgery to be endured, they will likely see Bible teaching is best avoided. If you talk of Bible teaching as a gift from God in His great kingdom, they will likely see it as a gift as well.

Your children are watching you. You have no secrets because they live with you. If you want them to only sit in a pew, then do that yourself. But if you want them to share and serve, to teach and participate, then you should show them how we do it.

Today, I will... *sign up to teach Bible or to learn to teach the Bible so that my children might see the passion for the treasure that is God's word and one day share that passion.*

WEDNESDAY

My Blessing

Today's Scripture: Genesis 49

It was 46 years ago, but I still remember everything about the scene when a friend of my parents told me of his expectation of my athletic performance. It would take years to attain the goal he set for me. But his words echoed in my head so often as I strove to reach it. Do you know the power of voiced expectations in the lives of your children?

Jacob nearing the end of his life called his sons to him and blessed them with his vision of what they and their families would become. I know he was speaking at this time as a prophet of God and that we are not in that role today. But we should not cast this example aside merely because we are not prophets. There is great power in telling a child of the service to God's kingdom that you see them doing in the future.

Someone will set goals for your children. The world will set goals of popularity, wealth, fame, power, athleticism, pleasure, beauty, humor and the like. If they hear no other goals, sadly these may dominate their lives. But it doesn't have to be that way. We can speak a blessing to them that says how we hope God will use them to His glory in the service of His kingdom.

When you speak of future service for a child, set the goal high. No mere pew sitting. Serving, leading, teaching, preaching, evangelism, and sacrifice should be declared. This kind of blessing can be spoken or written in a card or note. We also should not limit our "blessing talk" to our own children. Seek out opportunities to tell a child in your congregation how you hope God will use them in His kingdom. I've seen Christians have a "blessing dinner" after a young person's baptism just to tell them what they hope God will do through them.

Today, I will... *encourage a child by writing or telling of my hope that they will serve God by teaching His word.*

Heroes for Your Children

Today's Scripture: 2 Samuel 23:8-39

Today's scripture tells the names and some of the exploits of David's mighty men. This is not just a record of history. In part, it was record- ed because Israel needed warriors, and telling of these mighty men would cause children to aspire to be mighty men themselves. The ac- count of Benaiah going down into that pit on a snowy day and killing a lion must have motivated many young Israelites to become brave warriors. In much the same way, if you want your children to become Bible teachers, it would be good for your children to have some he- roes who were Bible teachers.

When searching for heroes for your children, the Bible is a great place to start. Little ones need to hear of the faith of so many heroes from the Bible. But they also need to know, and know of people, who are serving God and teaching His word today. If you can, introduce your children to your childhood Bible teachers. If you are unable to intro- duce them, tell of the important change they made in you and brag on the blessing they gave you. When you introduce your children to a visiting preacher, use language that stresses the importance of that role of sharing God's word. And your children should see you treating missionaries the way the world treats celebrities.

Our children are listening more often than we might think. Chatting with your spouse about the boring Bible class teacher or dull sermon, won't help your children want to teach the Bible. But, relating stories of missionaries swimming jungle rivers or crossing the Iron Curtain to share the gospel, or a Bible teacher who confronted racism at his own peril, or even the member of your own congregation who over- came their own fear in order to teach a Bible class, will give your child the opportunity to see Bible teachers in a heroic light.

Today, I will... *search out a heroic teacher of the Bible and introduce my child to him or her or to their story.*

The Opportunity

Today's Scripture: Mark 6:6-13

When Jesus sent out the twelve to preach repentance, they really did not understand the nature of Jesus ministry. But they were going to be the ones to preach the message of Jesus after the resurrection. Jesus thought it good for them to go out and practice a bit of the job that they would one day have.

My dad was a preacher, and I wanted to preach since I was two years old because I saw how he treasured the Bible. Our heroes were Bible teachers, preachers, and missionaries. I often heard the blessing of adults telling me that they believed I would one day be a preacher of God's word. Before the School of Biblical Studies, before university, before the internships, my parents intentionally sought out opportunities for me to practice or learn by doing. I participated in my parent's home Bible studies by entertaining the children while they taught the gospel. There were training classes where we led songs, learned to present lessons, and practiced on each other and later on the congregation. Later my mom drove me to preaching appointments before I received my driver's license.

If you want your children to be Bible teachers, it would be good for you to seek out opportunities for them to practice early in life. There are many organized programs that teach children the skills needed to serve in the church. These programs also provide opportunities for our children to practice. If such a program is not currently on going in your congregation, maybe you could ask the leaders if one of the organized programs is right for your congregation or if you should start something of your own.

We would never expect an athletic team to succeed without instruction and practice. Why would we expect our children to become Bible teachers if there is no "little league" for future Bible teachers?

Today, I will... *seek an opportunity for my child and the children of my congregation to practice the roles that are needed in the body of Christ.*

WEEK 14

Teaching Our Children to Work

DON DELUKIE

Work Is a Biblical Principle

Today's Scripture: Proverbs 22:6

When I was a youngster in my teens, I would occasionally ask my Dad for money. He would then ask why I needed it. I might say I wanted to take my girlfriend to the movies. He would say something like, "Well, we'll see what we can do" then "How much do you need?" As I anxiously awaited his answer, I would notice he was writing. Usually the next day he would say something like, "Well ten dollars should cover this and give you a little extra for popcorn." (I guess that shows how long ago that was). Then he'd hand me his writing and say, "Here's what you can do to earn the ten dollars." Amazingly I felt much better about receiving the money because I had earned it. I had a better understanding of the value of ten dollars. I was also rewarded by taking my girl (now my wife) on a date. This gave me an excited view of how positive it was to earn things. I was free from guilt and from being what we used to call a "moocher".

He also encouraged me to take mundane jobs and praised me for it. I delivered newspapers on my bicycle. One judge bought one every day. I found out years later he had a paper but was buying from me to encourage me to be productive. I washed cars at a service station on Saturdays. It was hard work washing them by hand and pleasing the customers. One guy would run his hand under the fender to see if I washed there. From such experiences I learned labor and duress but stayed with it. Several other guys worked one or two Saturdays and quit because it required a lot of effort. I got raises, all because of a dad who instilled not just the knowledge of God, Christ, and the Holy Spirit in me, but biblical principles as well.

"Train up a child in the way he should go; even when he is old he will not depart from it" (Proverbs 22:6).

Today, I will..._teach my children to work hard for everything they want to accomplish._

Don't Enable Sloth

Today's Scripture: Proverbs 12:11, 24

Satan has succeeded in ruining many youth's initiative by utilizing the following: modern media (especially from television and handheld devices) and culture changes like rewarding indolence, peer pressure conclusions, and hectically busy parents.

Why work if you can evade it? Why seek to be productive when the "deck is stacked against you"? Or, why exert so much energy when you can play a video game in total safety, with an exciting format, when you can succeed so much greater in the metaverse? Parents and guardians must learn what the "metaverse" is about and what a dangerous thing it is to our youth. Proverbs 12:11 says "Whoever works his land will have plenty of bread, but he who follows worthless pursuits lacks sense." Some young people are not developing people skills, work skills, or being productive as they spend hours sequestered in a room totally enveloped with mechanical and technical manipulation. Howling protests may ensue, but to allow this to continue is counter-productive to their future. Do our children have any responsibility? Some use the care of animals as a good way to teach productivity, staying with something, and realizing this creature won't live if they don't do their job. Simple tasks like taking out the trash, making up beds, and helping to do chores help build a framework of responsibility. Have we ever heard someone characterized as "handsome, likable, courteous, neat and well- dressed but he won't get a job?" When he occasionally does get one, he doesn't stay with it. He's living with his parents again. "But let each one test his own work, and then his reason to boast will be in himself alone and not in his neighbor. For each will have to bear his own load" (Galatians 6:4-5). Unwittingly some parents and guardians have become enablers to their youngsters who are getting addicted to laziness and sloth. "The hand of the diligent will rule, while the slothful will be put to forced labor" (Proverbs 12:24).

Today, I will... *slow down and consider things in proper perspective, especially when it comes to the future of my youthful loved ones.*

The "Ethic" In "Work Ethic"

Today's Scripture: Proverbs 13:4

Those wishing to instill a work ethic in their children may need to consider enlightening them on some things in our culture that are confusing to them. They may see their parents or grandparents retired and no longer working a regular job. Children may be wondering why they can't do that. Or they wonder, "How come the grandparents don't work, but are pressing me to work?" Imagine how confused some of our youth must be right now. Especially after Covid when so many paradigms have changed. People are no longer going to work, but are working from home, etc. or receiving a check from the government to "help" them. There's the idea of some who get grants from the government to start a business and soon close the business because the grant money was their goal, not the business. Or there are chronic abusers of welfare who boast about the many checks they receive for various situations so that they would never make that much in the work force. What do they think when they see someone asking a friend to punch their log in card at a company to get a day's pay when they weren't even there?

Obviously in our quest to instill a work ethic we must put some time and meaning to that second word—ethic. In addition to emphasizing labor and effort, we must also emphasize ethical behavior and accountability. The wrong-doers won't get away with it. While they may get rich, they must answer to God someday. Playing the system can be fun, and some savvy youngsters can win big and get rich—but if it was not done ethically there will be a reckoning. "The soul of the sluggard craves and gets nothing, while the soul of the diligent is richly supplied" (Proverbs 13:4).

Today, I will... *give an honest day's work for an honest day's pay, and model truth to my children, while warning them of those seemingly being rewarded for dishonesty, that they will be accountable to God someday.*

THURSDAY

God-Given Talents

Today's Scripture: Deuteronomy 4:9

Recently I watched with awe as a six year old was playing drums. Nothing about it was cumbersome. He could do moves that would take some drummers years to master. It appeared to be second nature to the lad. Intrigued I watched some other youngsters playing difficult instruments with absolute finesse. Obviously there is something God-given here. They have a talent that others could never approach after years of trying. Also there are some involved parents and guardians who have given opportunity to, and support and provision to allow the young prodigy to excel. In addition the young boy was all smiles —he was loving it! What might happen if they insisted he paint, or learn atomic scales, or aspire to be an attorney or something like his dad? Fortunately they saw where the propensity was.

There's an old saying, "If you love what you do, you'll never have to work a day in your life." The meaning is that loving certain pursuits are so rewarding, performing them doesn't seem like labor. Then work is fun. Are we observing what God has given our children and encouraging them in it? Again we say "Train up a child in the way he should go; even when he is old he will not depart from it" (Proverbs 22:6). There's more to that principle than just God awareness. Forcing children to seek a life journey that we want rather than what God enabled them to do can be disastrous to all involved. "Only take care, and keep your soul diligently, lest you forget the things that your eyes have seen, and lest they depart from your heart all the days of your life. Make them known to your children and your children's children"(Deuteronomy 4:9).

Today, I will...*see my children the way God made them, knowing what He has given them. May their life's work follow God's gifts to them so that they may be happy all the days of their lives and be a blessing to others.*

FRIDAY

Let Us Labor Every Day

Today's Scripture: Matthew 21:28-32

Aesop, the ancient Greek fable writer, told of a thirsty crow who found some water in a bucket. His beak was too short to reach the water. So he went to work and dropped pebbles in the bucket until the water level was raised to his usefulness.

Work can be tedious, monotonous, and boring but the end result can be very rewarding. Children need to be taught to finish a task, stay with it until it's finished, and be prepared to be tired from the labor. But, great reward will result. "One who is faithful in a very little is also faithful in much, and one who is dishonest in a very little is also dishonest in much" (Luke 16:10). We remember Jesus saying not to put our hand to a task and look back in Luke 9:62. It grieved me on one occasion to see a mother send her child to bed without supper because he had not performed a task. However, the child made sure to finish the task next time!

Matthew 21:28-32a says, "What do you think? A man had two sons. And he went to the first and said, 'Son, go and work in the vineyard today.' And he answered, 'I will not,' but afterward he changed his mind and went. And he went to the other son and said the same. And he answered, 'I go, sir,' but did not go. Which of the two did the will of his father?" They said, "The first."......

Let us work, let us pray, let us labor every day

Today, I will...*teach my children that work can be hard but rewarding. I will do my best to raise productive people who will be a light to this world and a great help in God's kingdom.*

WEEK 15

Teaching Our Children to Worship

BARRY GRIDER

Sing

Today's Scripture: Psalm 100:2

I love singing. I especially love singing "psalms, hymns, and spiritual songs" (Ephesians 5:19) to the praise of my heavenly Father. Singing is an authorized act of worship (Colossians 3:16). Christians, through singing, worship God and edify one another. On many occasions I have met with a Christian family to plan the funeral service of a loved one. Sometimes when asked about favorite hymn selections to be sung during the service a family will respond, "We don't really have any favorites that come to mind." This is always a strange response to my ears. Is it possible that a Christian can go through life and never be touched with the sentiments expressed in certain hymns? Is it possible that individual Christians can live a lifetime on earth and never sing a hymn outside the assembly? Is it possible that one could sit in the assembly for many years and never take to heart the words of the hymns being sung? Sadly, it is possible.

A love for singing should be instilled in the hearts of children early in life. When these children witness parents who love singing hymns at home, these children will eagerly learn to join in with them. Neither will they have to be persuaded to offer praise in song during the assembly. I well remember my maternal grandmother (who could not carry a tune) washing dishes as she sang "Heavenly Sunlight," and my paternal grandmother, sitting in her rocking chair, and cutting loose with "I'll Fly Away." A wonderful memory for me is harmonizing with my parents as together we sang "Mansion Over The Hilltop." Going to an "all night" singing was quite common during my childhood. Through these examples, singing hymns became part of my everyday life. Why is this important?

When we sing hymns we express our adoration and praise for God. This gift called singing lifts our souls above the mundane things of earth. The lyrics contained in these hymns teach us about God's love and His gift of salvation, encourage us to be faithful, and remind us of our heavenly home. So it is helpful to study carefully the words written in these songs. Through the singing of hymns our hearts become filled with joy (James 5:13). Some sing because they are happy; most are happy because they sing. Keep a song in your heart and mind all day long and, "Come before his presence with singing" (Psalm 100:2).

Today, I will... *take time to sing a hymn of praise with my children.*

TUESDAY

Pray

Today's Scripture: Acts 2:42; 1 Thessalonians 5:17

Praying is an authorized act of worship (Acts 2:42). Likewise, prayer should be a regular daily exercise for a Christian (1 Thessalonians 5:17). While we are commanded to pray, what a privilege it is to carry everything to God in prayer. Yet we often struggle for various reasons. Allowing sin to remain in our hearts could hinder our prayers. Failing to trust God can keep us from praying. It may be we refuse to pray simply because we have become lazy. I remember hearing James Watkins say, "If you are having trouble praying—talk to God about it." I loved that answer because talking to God is the very definition of prayer.

How do we teach our children to pray? First, Christian parents must pray in front of their children. Let them hear their parents praise and petition God in prayer. As these children witness their parents pray, they will learn about the priority of this relationship between God and man. These prayers that are offered should be frequent and not offered just at the dinner table. Sit down with your children in a special place at a special time to pray.

Second, we Christian parents must love their children. By loving our children, which includes appropriate discipline, we help them develop a healthy understanding of the nature and character of God and why it is a blessing to call Him our Father whenever we pray. Third, let our children pray. God loves our children even more than we love our children. Jesus loved nothing more than holding little children in His arms. He said, "Let the little children come to me" (Matthew 19:14). He loves their prayers. A child may pray a simple and sweet prayer that has been memorized, such as, "God is great and God is good, let us thank Him for our food." Likewise, that is a sublime prayer, for there is no greater truth that could ever be expressed than God is great and God is good. Fourth, always praise a child's prayers and never mock them. By so doing we will develop the child's confidence and the child will keep developing a strong prayer life that will continue long after that child has left home. Some things we will regret as parents. Teaching our children to pray we will never regret.

Today, I will... *take time to pray with my children.*

WEDNESDAY

Study

Today's Scripture: Acts 20:7; 2 Peter 3:18

What is the connection between preaching and worship? When a group of Christians assembled together on the first day of the week in the city of Ephesus, Paul preached to them (Acts 20:7). Preachers have an obligation to study so that God's will may be made known and to therefore, help Christians grow spiritually (2 Peter 3:18). After all, Christianity is a taught religion. Sadly, many mock the idea of preaching today. Occasionally I will hear a public speaker talk about an important issue and say, "I'm not here to preach to you," as if preaching is somehow a bad thing. Preaching is God's method to bring the message of salvation to the lost (1 Corinthians 1:21), to help Christian's mature in their faith (2 Timothy 2:15), and to provide comfort during times of struggle (Acts 20:27).

How do we help our children appreciate the time in worship that is spent studying God's word? It is encouraging to live in a house where the décor speaks of a love for God and His word. I love looking around my house at art portraying such scriptures such as Joshua 24:15 or Psalm 23. We must let our children grow up in atmosphere where they can see the word of God reverenced. The psalmist said, "For you have exalted above all things your name and your word" (Psalm 138:2). Children will learn to respect and appreciate the place of preaching in worship when at home we regularly open our Bibles and study. Sometimes I told my children that I could not talk to them at the moment because God was talking to me through His word—I needed to concentrate and meditate on what He was saying. I wanted them to realize just how special such a time was for me and how they could experience the same as they grow in His word. Regular devotional periods with children will help them to increase their appreciation for the Bible. On Saturday evenings we must challenge them to listen to the sermons and take notes as to what they hear the next day. On Sunday evenings we must discuss the sermons presented and ask questions regarding Bible classes. Finally, we must pray that what has been learned will be lived out in each family member's everyday life.

Today, I will... *take time to study the Bible with my children.*

THURSDAY
Take, Eat. Take, Drink.

Today's Scripture: Matthew 26:28

According to New Testament teaching, first century Christians came together upon the first day of the week to particularly remember Jesus sacrificial death on the cross (Acts 20:7). They did this by partaking of what is commonly called the Lord's Supper. Jesus instituted this memorial shortly before His crucifixion. Regarding the bread, He stated, "Take, eat; this is my body." Concerning the cup, He said, "for this is my blood of the covenant, which is poured out for many for the forgiveness of sins" (Matthew 26:28). Through the blood of Jesus we have been saved. While we partake of the Lord's Supper upon the first day of the week, as Christians we cannot help but remember His sacrifice every day.

The apostle Paul said we ought to keep Christ's crucifixion always before us (Galatians 3:1). When we learn to do this, we help our children to appreciate our remembrance of His death when we assemble on the Lord's Day. Since the various acts of worship are all interrelated, let us regularly sing with our children about the cross. When we pray, let us never forget to offer thanksgiving for the cross. In a devotional setting, frequently explain what the bread and juice represent. As it is fitting according to age, explain how agonizingly painful the cross was to Jesus and that what He did was done for each one of us personally (Galatians 2:20). Ask your child what the cross means to him. The answers will be interesting and give insight into his thinking.

At some point your child will no doubt want to be baptized. As a Christian parent you will rejoice at such a moment. But perhaps you will also ask yourself some questions. Is he old enough? Does she understand what she is doing? Among other questions you might ask your child, "What will you think about when you partake of the Lord's Supper." One little bright-eyed girl who wanted to be baptized responded to this question by saying to her mother, "I will be sad that Jesus had to die on the cross to forgive me of all my sins, but I am so glad He did." What a great answer. She is well on her way to having the proper understanding of why one should become a Christian.

Today, I will... *reflect on the cross with my children.*

89

FRIDAY

Give

Today's Scripture: 2 Corinthians 8:5; 9:7

"Now concerning the collection for the saints: as I directed the churches of Galatia, so you also are to do. On the first day of every week, each of you is to put something aside and store it up, as he may prosper, so that there will be no collecting when I come" (1 Corinthians 16:1,2). Christians are to be givers not takers. This must be taught because it is so easy to be selfish. Our Lord Jesus said, "It is more blessed to give than to receive" (Acts 20:35). I have witnessed a few children who had a hard time letting go of a quarter to drop in the collection plate. Likewise, older folks can struggle with giving of their means to the Lord, as well.

If we are to help our children understand the importance of giving to the Lord, they must first see a spirit of sacrificial giving in every area of their parents' lives, including that which is monetary. Do we aid the poor? Do we feed the hungry? Do we sacrifice time that we may teach? Do we mow the yard of that Christian who is unable and has no family to help? Do we assist our living parents? How we answer these questions determines to some degree our willingness to give of ourselves (2 Corinthians 8:5).

When teaching your children to worship God through making a monetary offering, let them know how serious you take this command. Explain that you have an income paid to you through your employer and from that income you return a portion to the Lord so that His work might go forward through the local church. When your children are young, provide them with some money to place in the collection plate to help develop this good habit. Teach them that when they begin working, regardless of how minimal their pay may be, to give to the Lord in proportion to their income.

Furthermore, share with them the joy that comes through giving. God loves to see a cheerful giver (2 Corinthians 9:7). Finally, help them understand that everything that's "yours" is really God's and that you cannot outgive Him (Luke 6:38; 2 Corinthians 9:6).

Today, I will... *engage in an act of sacrificial service with my children.*

90

WEEK 16

Teaching Our Children Faithfulness

DALE JENKINS

Faith

Today's Scripture: Luke 7:1-9

"Faith" is such a neat word. It is both a noun and a verb. It is a noun in Acts 6 where a great many of the priests "were obedient to the faith" (Acts 6:7) or in Jude 3 where we are to "earnestly contend for the faith." It is a verb in Hebrews 11, as by faith Abel offered, Noah constructed an ark, Abraham obeyed, Sara conceived, Jacob blessed, etc. James will use the word both ways: "My brethren, have not the faith of our Lord Jesus Christ, the Lord of glory, with respect of persons" (James 2:1) and "But someone will say, "You have faith and I have works." Show me your faith apart from your works, and I will show you my faith by my works" (2:18). I like to say for the Christian faith is a noun (a set of beliefs in truths) that becomes a verb when you add water (baptism).

God is interested in faith. Abraham believed God (faith) and it was counted to him for righteousness (Romans 4:3). Jesus will come looking for faith (Luke 18:8). Faith impresses the Lord (see Luke 7:1-9).

For people of faith, from the moment we learn a child is coming into our families, most everything is centered around ensuring that this child will have a shared faith in the Lord. For the Christian we want our children to be good students, to excel in extra-curricular activities, to be socially well adjusted, for them to be good citizens, but none of these come close to the ultimate desire. At times parents can end up maladjusted and focus too much on sports, or getting into the right college, or finding their child's perfect mate. While those things have a place in life, what if your child does not know Jesus? When we are old and gray, nothing else will matter, and we'll live with the regret that we led them wrong. So, how do we keep our focus where it should be?

This week we will think about helping our children to faith.

Today, I will... *pray for my children and all children that the next generation will have greater faith than ours has and that we can lead them in the right direction.*

TUESDAY

Faithful

Today's Scripture: Joshua 24:15

We really know nothing much about Joshua's family, but we do have one of the great family statements in all the Bible from his words: "...as for me and my house, we will serve the Lord" (Joshua 24:15). Every Christian parent "Amens" Joshua. We have the words stenciled on our walls, painted on a sign, embroidered on a hanging, and tattooed on our hearts. But, how do we do this?

When it comes to helping our children become faithful, there are two elements. Talk and action. Teaching and doing. Teaching faith without living faith will produce the next great hypocrite. Living faith without teaching faith will make for great Boy/Girl Scouts but not great Christians. I am a statistician and need to state that those who are putting out numbers of how many children we are losing in churches of Christ are way off. They are inflated for various agenda driven reasons. But the fact is if that number is 1%, it is higher than any of us as Christians should be satisfied with. Yet here is a stat that will hold up. When both mom and dad are both active, faithful Christians, the children in every study that has been conducted have the greatest chance to grow up to be faithful Christians. Therefore, the single most important thing you can do to help your children be faithful, is to strive to be faithful yourself.

Children who grow up in a family where faith is promoted on Sunday and taught other times but not lived out in front of them learn to spot hypocrisy very quickly. The text says "a double minded man is unstable in all his ways" (James 1:8). James says they are doubters. They embrace faith as a concept but are not willing to risk living it out in the day to day.

Children who grow up in a house where faith is beautifully lived out have a great advantage. BUT, if it is lived out without being taught, then they have a house with no foundation. And it might produce people who are tremendous servants, and caring people but who are unstable and are tossed about easily by every new and exciting doctrine that blows through. They know what to do, but not why. We seek to give our children the best opportunity to succeed spiritually. They need a faith that is taught and demonstrated in the lives of those teaching it.

Today, I will... *examine my own life and my beliefs and strive to have them both come in line with Jesus.*

WEDNESDAY

Faithfulness

Today's Scripture: 1 John 1-2

"God is faithful" (1 Corinthians 10:13). Along with such things as kindness, love, grace, mercy and longsuffering, His faithfulness is known as what are called the moral attributes of God. These are things God is by His nature. Paul will tell Timothy that even "if we are not faithful, he will still be faithful, for He cannot deny Himself" (2 Timothy 2:13).

This among many other things is one that lets us know how wholly (and Holy) different God is from us. Yet 1 Corinthians 4 instructs us "Moreover, it is required of stewards that they be found faithful" (vs. 2).

But while God is perfect in His faithfulness, faithfulness does not mean perfection. Moses is called faithful (Numbers 12:7), Samuel is called a faithful priest (1 Samuel 2:35), as is/are Hezekiah, David, Isaiah, Daniel, Timothy, the city of Jerusalem, two of the stewards in Matthew 25, Tychicus, the church at Ephesus, Epaphras, Onesimus, etc. Were these people clad in clay perfect? Of course not. We know of the sin of several of them. But they were faithful. And while we are called to perfection (Matthew 5:47), we won't by our own merit attain that earthly goal, but we can be faithful.

You've probably heard it best illustrated like I have. If you ask Melanie (my wife), if I am a perfect husband she'd laugh and ask if you have a fever. But if you ask her if I'm a faithful husband, she would say that I am. I suppose one of the most challenging aspects of being a parent is knowing that your children, whom you are trying to teach to not sin...sin. And in that disappointment it becomes easy for our children to feel like utter failures when they...fail.

I love John's writing in 1 John 2:1, "My little children these things I write to you that you sin not." Ahhh, John is calling for perfection. But the very next words are, "Yet if any does sin we have an advocate with the Father, Jesus Christ, the righteous" (vs. 2). The Spirit moving John's pen knew we would (excuse me), not, not sin. He knew we would fall short of the desire, so He assures us of our advocate. Perhaps that's the balance we teach our kids. A child who thinks he must always be perfect will either have his spirit crushed, carry a ton of guilt, or become a hypocrite or heretic. Train them in faith and faithfulness. And assure them that you too are striving, imperfectly, but that you too are striving for faithfulness.

Today, I will... *have a talk with my children about faithfulness.*

THURSDAY

Faithfully

Today's Scripture: Deuteronomy 6:1-9

"Cleanse me from secret faults" (Psalm 19:12, NKJV) does not mean the sins I am committing in secret, as if we can somehow bargain with God to let us hold onto some sin we enjoy in private and be right with Him. It means the sins I commit that even I do not know about. David, post sin with Bathsheba, so desired to be right with God that he didn't even want to commit sins unconsciously or subconsciously.

Faithfully is an adverb. It modifies or describes the verb, faith.

Faithfully: We faithfully train our children in the faith. This is not a one-time visit to the mountain to see some guru to impart faith upon them. It is Sunday, Monday, and every other "day that ends in 'y.'" Moses talked about this for the Israelite parents in what is called the Shema: "These are the commands, decrees and laws the Lord your God directed me to teach you to observe...so that you, your children and their children after them may fear the Lord your God as long as you live by keeping all his decrees and commands that I give you, and so that you may enjoy long life...Hear, O Israel: The Lord our God, the Lord is one. Love the Lord your God with all your heart and with all your soul and with all your strength. These commandments that I give you today are to be on your hearts. Impress them on your children. Talk about them when you sit at home and when you walk along the road, when you lie down and when you get up. Tie them as symbols on your hands and bind them on your foreheads. Write them on the doorframes of your houses and on your gates" (Deuteronomy 6:1-9).

This is not just a weekly trip to the church building, or even a daily devotional time. Read it carefully, it is in the day to day. It is when you are driving down the road and see beauty and you attribute it to God. It is when you witness injustice and you teach them to love justice. It is when you are kind when someone cuts you off in traffic or is rude to you at the ballgame. It is in the every day of life. That is where faith is taught. And how it is taught is faithfully.

Today, I will... *actively look for opportunities to see God at work and attribute His work to Him in teaching children.*

FRIDAY

Faith Finished

Today's Scripture: 2 Corinthians 57

We train our children in faith because the day is coming when faith will no longer be needed. There is no doubt that today "we live by faith, not by sight" (2 Corinthians 5:7). And while our faith is not a blind leap, Luke talks about Jesus being proved to be the Son of God by many "signs, wonders, and *infallible truths*" Acts 1:3, emp DJ). Paul brings a multitude of living witnesses to the stand in 1 Corinthians 15 who saw Jesus after His resurrection. Yet faith is belief without sight but with incredible evidence.

Jim Hill wrote it this way around 1950:
What a day that will be
When my Jesus I shall see
When I look upon His face
The one who saved me by His grace
When he takes me by his hand
And leads me to the promise land
What a day, glorious day that will be (There is Coming A Day, Jim Hill, 1950).

And on that day, faith is lost when proof is given. Faith in the unseen will be proven in the seen. Today EVERYONE has faith. The day will come when NO ONE will have faith. "Every knee will bow, every tongue will confess" (Philippians 2:10) what we have confessed by faith already. And our faith will be done. Faith will give way to sight, to substance that is intangible. That which is temporary to that which is eternal, that which is unseen to that which is seen (2 Corinthians 4:18).

Until then you are, as a believer, at war with invisible forces who do not fight fair (Ephesians 6:11). So, live, teach, model, love, indoctrinate, train, your children against the schemes of the devil (2 Corinthians 2:11). There are excellent materials out there from sources like Apologetics Press, The Daily Apologist and others in the larger religious world by such scholars as Josh McDowell, L.O. Richards - "It Couldn't Just Happen: Knowing the Truth About God's Awesome Creation." Some day, when all the scoffers will be put to silence (2 Peter 3), it will be worth it. Forever.

Today, I will...*search for excellent materials that deal with Christian Evidences and strive to equip my children and grandchildren against the evil ones tricks.*

WEEK 17

Teaching Our Children Compassion

ROBERT DODSON

Let Them Hear It in Your Prayers

Today's Scripture: Matthew 19:13-15

Every child deserves to hear his parents pray. And, to have parents that believe God hears and answers prayer. When children hear their parents earnestly pray for others, they can see how much they really care. It teaches them to have compassion on others, and to pray for them, too. Parents may express their concern for those suffering around the world, as well as those they know and that are involved in the lives of their children. They should certainly express God's heart of compassion for lost souls in prayer.

Praying with your children about their own struggles is especially important, too. It reminds them that they are not alone, but that God cares for them and so do you. It will help give them the encouragement and confidence they need to overcome whatever it is that troubles them. All of this reminds me of how Jesus blessed the little children. "Then children were brought to him that he might lay his hands on them and pray" (Matthew 19:13).

Here are some examples from the Bible that may help you to pray with your children, so that they may see your compassion for them and for others:

• Genesis 17:18 And Abraham said to God, "Oh that Ishmael might live before you!"
• 2 Samuel 12:16 David therefore sought God on behalf of the child. And David fasted and went in and lay all night on the ground.
• 1 Chronicles 22:12 Only, may the Lord grant you discretion and understanding, that when he gives you charge over Israel you may keep the law of the Lord your God.
• 1 Chronicles 29:19 Grant to Solomon my son a whole heart that he may keep your commandments, your testimonies, and your statutes, performing all, and that he may build the palace for which I have made provision.

Today, I will... *pray with and for my children, remembering to express the compassion of God for them and for all others, too.*

Teach Them from the Bible

Today's Scripture: Luke 10:25-37

Children love to hear stories—and the best stories are found in the Bible. One of my favorite stories of the Bible is found in Jesus' parable of the Good Samaritan. It's a story about compassion. You may know the story but why not read it again with your children? They will learn, and you will be reminded that two men in the parable who appear righteous fail in compassion. It could be that they are more concerned about themselves than others, especially if the others are different from them. But the good Samaritan teaches us that it doesn't matter who the person is, only that he is in need, and that we can help him.

Be sure and carefully notice with your children the lengths to which the Samaritan was moved to do what he could for the half-dead stranger on the side of the road. Point out the action verbs that are italicized here demonstrating the compassion of the Samaritan. "He went to him and bound up his wounds, pouring on oil and wine. Then he set him on his own animal and brought him to an inn and took care of him. And the next day he took out two denarii and gave them to the innkeeper, saying, 'Take care of him, and whatever more you spend, I will repay you when I come back'" (Luke 10:34-35).

Then, your child will be thrilled to answer Jesus' question, "Which of these three, do you think, proved to be a neighbor to the man who fell among the robbers?" (Luke 10:36). The lesson is unforgettable: If we are truly compassionate, we will do what we can to help others, too. "But if anyone has the world's goods and sees his brother in need, yet closes his heart against him, how does God's love abide in him? Little children, let us not love in word or talk but in deed and in truth" (1 John 3:17-18).

Today, I will... *read and learn about compassion with my children from the Bible.*

Give Them an Example

Today's Scripture: 1 Corinthians 11:1

Carlos recently departed this life to be with Christ. What his two daughters remember most about him was his compassion for other people. They spoke of how he would do anything for anybody to help them. Carlos worked all around town. At times he would take his girls with him to the job site and pay them to do some things for him. On other days he would donate his time and money to help a charity or someone in need. His girls would go with him to donate their time and money, too. It was not uncommon for Carlos to mentor friends or coworkers to help them with their problems or encourage them in their work. He would adopt them like they were his own family. Carlos always talked to his girls and others about the Lord. He cared for their souls.

I wonder, what will our children remember most about us? Will they have learned from our example to be compassionate towards others? Will they be able to tell others about what we did to help and serve others? Let's check and see what kind of example we are to our children. Be honest in your answers. Do you talk about what's wrong with people or about what you can do to help and save people? Are you mean and ugly to others or are you kind and respectful to them? Are you trying to get even with others or are you willing to love and forgive them? Are you totally wrapped up in selfish pursuits or are you sharing your time and money to do something for someone else? What do your children see in you?

Remember, children are great imitators (Eph. 5:1-2). If we want them to learn compassion, we must set the example, so we can say to them, as Paul, "Be imitators of me, as I am of Christ" (1 Corinthians 11:1).

Today, I will... *be careful how I walk before my children, letting compassion lead me in my steps.*

THURSDAY

Provide Them an Opportunity

Today's Scripture: John 6:1-14

There were thousands of people following Jesus that day as He went about healing the sick. When it came time to eat, Jesus' disciples didn't know what they were going to do to feed them. But Jesus did. He would let a boy share his loaves and fish. Miraculously, this became enough to feed the people all they wanted, and there were twelve baskets of left-overs.

Have you ever wondered why Jesus used the boy's food? Surely, He could just as easily have turned stones to bread or just make it appear out of thin air. But the way Jesus did it gave the boy an opportunity to help feed the people. And I'm sure he never forgot what happened that day. I am also convinced that he learned to never be selfish with what he had but always willing to share with others in need.

Perhaps, the best way we can teach our children compassion is to give them opportunities to show it. When they do, they will experience the joy of giving and helping others. They will see how it can make a difference in the lives of others. It is a good way to show Christ to others and may even lead them to believe in Jesus as it did that day when Jesus fed the crowd with just five loaves and two fish.

When young, our children depend upon us for all they have, and we give them everything. But if we don't give them opportunity to use what they have, to show compassion and to help others, we will deprive them of the greater blessing. Jesus Himself said, "It is more blessed to give than to receive" (Acts 20:35). All our children need is an opportunity.

Today, I will... *give my children the opportunity to show their compassion and to share what they have to help others, so they can experience the greater blessing of being on the other side of the receiving line.*

Remind Them of the Cross

Today's Scripture: Romans 5:8

There has never been nor will there ever be a greater demonstration of compassion than the cross of Christ. At the cross we see God's inexhaustible love, mercy, grace, and forgiveness. It was a sacrifice for all people (John 3:16; Eph. 5:2). It was given unconditionally. "God shows his love for us in that while we were still sinners, Christ died for us" (Romans 5:8).

It was not for anything He had done that Christ suffered on the cross, but it was for our sins. "Surely he has borne our griefs and carried our sorrows; yet we esteemed him stricken, smitten by God, and afflicted. But he was pierced for our transgressions; he was crushed for our iniquities; upon him was the chastisement that brought us peace, and with his wounds we are healed. All we like sheep have gone astray; we have turned—every one—to his own way; and the Lord has laid on him the iniquity of us all" (Isaiah 53:4-6).

Our children need to be reminded of the cross when they find it hard to be compassionate. When another is mistreated by others. When another is hurt. When another is losing. When another is overcome. When another is incapable. When another is without. When another is alone. When another is lost. Ask them, "What would Jesus do?", and remind them of the cross.

Your child cannot become a follower of Jesus without going the way of the cross. Jesus said, "If anyone would come after me, let him deny himself and take up his cross daily and follow me" (Luke 9:23). This is how we all will come to know and show compassion at its best.

Today, I will... *watch for moments when my child needs to learn and show compassion, and I will remind him of what Jesus did for us all at the cross.*

WEEK 18

Teaching Our Children About Our Heritage

SCOTT HARP

MONDAY

Connections

Today's Scripture: Ecclesiastes 12

Would you rather get a new toy or something old that belonged to one of your grandparents? A lot of people would choose to receive something new. Why? Well, we like new things. But there is something special about having a thing that an ancestor owned and used. My granddaddy had an old desk that came out of a railroad depot. He worked many years for Illinois-Central-Gulf Railroad in maintenance. When the station closed, they gave him that desk. He took it home and polished it. For years, when visiting my grandparents, I would arise each morning to see him studying his Bible at that old desk. When Grandaddy died, the desk came to me. Today, it makes for precious memories nearly every time I see it.

One of life's sweetest blessings is to connect with those who have gone before us. Walking where they walked or touching what they touched makes us feel more connected to them. It is especially meaningful when our loved ones are no longer with us. The Hebrews writer encouraged, "Remember your leaders, those who spoke to you the word of God. Consider the outcome of their way of life and imitate their faith" (Hebrews 13:7).

You and I are blessed to have a rich heritage of godly people who have gone before us in the church. Bible Class teachers, preachers, elders, deacons, and so many more have done so much to make it possible for you to have a Bible classroom and a church building in which to worship. Think about it this way, your Bible School teacher once sat where you sit and learned from their teachers. And that person was taught by someone before them. Have you ever wondered who the first teachers in your church family were? Maybe this Sunday, a good question to ask your teacher or preacher is, "Who was your favorite Bible teacher and why?"

Today, I will... *look around my house for things that remind me of my great Christian heritage and share it.*

TUESDAY

Restoration

Today's Scripture: Acts 2

On his fourth birthday, my nephew embarked upon the world of bike riding. He got a brand-new Schwinn Predator BMX bicycle. It had training wheels and all the bells and whistles. That little fellow wore out that bike! Later his sister, and still later, his younger brother, learned to ride on it. When it had run its course, my brother put it in the attic—fast forward about twenty-five years. My nephew was married, and his son was about to turn four. Several months before his birthday, his grandpa got the old bike out of the attic. It was in rough shape, but he took it to a bike enthusiast who completely dismantled it, replaced all the wearable parts, re-chromed the sprockets, and completely restored that little bike to better than new. Imagine my great-nephew's surprise when he saw what he thought was a brand-new bike.

In 586 B.C.E., when Jerusalem lay in ruins, the prophet Jeremiah cried, "Restore us to yourself, O Lord, that we may be restored! Renew our days as of old" (Lamentations 5:21). The temple had been destroyed by Babylon's king Nebuchadnezzar and was rebuilt nearly a hundred years later. But true restoration for Israel then and today is through Christ. Have you ever thought of Jesus as being a restorationist? No, he did not restore bikes. He restored lost souls to God through His great sacrifice on the cross and resurrection. His teachings show us the way to restoration.

We certainly have a rich heritage! In the last 200-plus years, people like David Lipscomb, Barton W. Stone, Alexander Campbell, N. B. Hardeman, and a host of others have led thousands of people to do Bible things in Bible ways. It has been a restoration movement, an effort to leave denominational division to take on the traits of the New Testament church. Do what they were taught to do, and we can be what they were. That restoration spirit can and should be entrenched in us all.

Today, I will... *put on the restorationist spirit by seeing that I follow Christ's teachings completely.*

They Pointed Us to the Word of God

Today's Scripture: 1 Corinthians 2:6-16

The Bible is the Word of God. Since the beginning of time, the final and ultimate authority in all of life has been the Word of God. Moses was the great lawgiver of the Old Testament. To the nation of Israel, he repeatedly pointed to the Word of God as their final authority in all matters of life, e.g., Deuteronomy 27-30. When Israel's faithfulness waned, the prophets, from Samuel to Malachi, pointed the people back to the Word of God as their only hope.

Jesus, His apostles, and the New Testament writers expressed that man's only hope of finding the truth for life is found when one is devoted to the Word of God (Heb. 4:12; 2 Tim. 3:15-17). Fourteen hundred years later, the Word of God gained steam in distribution with the invention of the printing press. Englishmen John Wycliffe and later William Tyndale produced the first translations of the Word of God in the English language. Amidst great religious confusion, these, and other great Reformers of the middle ages, like Luther, Zwingli, Calvin, Huss, Savonarola, and many others, pointed people back to the Word of God. And, when America was settled, still more stood up to break the barriers of religious confusion. "Raccoon" John Smith, B. F. Hall, James A. Harding, and a host of others rose to encourage all to take the Bible and the Bible alone for guidance in matters of life. (Note: You can read about these and others at TheRestorationMovement.com.) Preachers, Bible Class teachers, elders, and deacons make it their mission in life to point us to the Word of God for counsel in all matters of life.

When you think about it, we are standing on the shoulders of giants, great people who sacrificed so much by pointing the people of their day back to the Bible. Our rich heritage spans more than 6000 years. Praise be to God for His precious gift!

Today, I will... *reach out to someone who has pointed me to the Bible and express my thanks.*

Finding the Old Paths

Today's Scripture: Isaiah 35

The Natchez Trace Parkway is one of America's oldest roads. For 440 miles, it stretches from the Cumberland River in Nashville, Tennessee, in the north and heads southwest to the Mississippi River in Natchez, Mississippi. Centuries ago, small animal paths developed into the trail when Native Americans made their way through the dense forest. Pioneers further widened the road in the 18th and 19th centuries as they moved west. Over the years, the paths have been straightened; the road widened and paved. Today it is operated and maintained by the U.S. National Park Service. If you travel the parkway, the speed limit may be lower than on state highways, but the experience of natural flora and fauna is worth the trip.

Riding on the old parkway can feed one's imagination of what it was like in the early days when the Indians hunted, and the pioneers struggled. Often you can see signs that point you off to strips of the old trace that have been abandoned to straighten the road. You can literally see where the old trail veers into a different direction and later where it comes back into the current path. Looking up those abandoned stretches, you can just envision some old wagon stopped, and those pioneers sitting around a late-night campfire. Listen as you hear the owls and the coyotes in the distance.

Recall the words of the old prophet, "Thus says the Lord: 'Stand by the roads, and look, and ask for the ancient paths, where the good way is; and walk in it and find rest for your souls. . .'" (Jeremiah 6:16). And think of the words of the psalm, "He restores my soul. He leads me in the paths of righteousness for his name's sake," (Psalm 23:3). Have you ever considered that God's old paths never had to be straightened? They were and are still as straight as an arrow!

Today, I will...	*walk the ways less traveled. I will follow the paths of God.*

Some Spiritual Genealogy

Today's Scripture: Acts 20:17-38; Hebrews 12:1-2

One of my professors often admonished, "Remember to thank the bridges you have crossed." As odd as that may sound, we owe a debt of gratitude to those who have gone before us and made our lives easier and more successful. For instance, to whom do you owe a debt of gratitude for introducing you to Jesus? If you grew up knowing the Lord, your parents had a part in it, perhaps, others. Here's something to think about—who do you suppose was their most significant influence, and the one before them?

The first in my ancestry to take on New Testament Christianity was my great-grandmother, Hattie Leona Turner (1900-1991). At seventeen, she attended a country tent meeting that an Alabama preacher was conducting by the name of C. A. Wheeler (1851-1937). One night after the assembly, she approached the older minister asking what she should do to become a Christian. He told her to go home and read the Gospels to see what Jesus taught on the subject. Then she should read the book of Acts to see how people became Christians in the first century. He then instructed her to come back and tell him what she should do. Returning home, she read her Bible all night by the light of a coal-oil lamp. The next evening she again attended the meeting. Upon seeing the preacher, she told him she wanted to be baptized for the forgiveness of her sins like they did back in the Bible days. That night she was immersed for the forgiveness of her sins. Her faithfulness led her husband and six generations after the way of Christ.

You, too, have a spiritual genealogy, a bridge of sorts, for which to be most thankful. We will never know all those of our heritage who had a hand in bringing us to this place of faith we enjoy. One thing is for sure; we can see the hand of God's providence in all our lives.

Today, I will..._explore my spiritual ancestry and be thankful._

WEEK 19

Teaching Our Children to Serve

ANTHONY WARNES

Teaching Our Children to Serve

Today's Scripture: Revelation 22

When God gave us children, He gave us a great blessing and a great responsibility. It is within this blessing and responsibility that we are told to teach our children. We teach them many things under the sun: how to brush teeth, hit a ball, make food, clothe oneself, etc. With teaching them comes the greatest item that a parent can teach: "Train up a child in the way he should go..." (Proverbs 22:6).

What way should we teach or train our children? Towards God. Let's teach our children to love the Lord and to follow His ways! One of the many ways that we can do this is by teaching our children to serve Him and serve others. In Matthew 20:26-28, Jesus says "...But whoever would be great among you must be your servant, and whoever would be first among you must be your slave, even as the Son of Man came not to be served but to serve, and to give his life as a ransom for many."

Why did Jesus come to this earth? Was it to be pampered? No, it was for the purpose of serving humanity! In the last chapter of the Bible, we have a glimpse into heaven. And what a beautiful glimpse it is! You have the Lord there. You have the tree of life there. And you have the Lamb's servants there. And what are they doing there? Revelation 22:3-4 says, "And His servants will worship him. They will see His face, and His name will be on their foreheads." Parents, let's teach our children starting at a young age how to serve Him and others.

Today, I will...be prayerful about finding ways that I can teach my children how to serve the Lord and others. Let's teach our children how to serve Him now, so that they will know how to in eternity.

Don't Just Teach Them, Show Them

Today's Scripture: John 13:3-17

Our children may refuse to do good deeds when we ourselves fail to do good deeds. We can tell them all day long that they need to be a certain person. Yet if we are not showing them how to be that person, the words can fall on deaf ears. The best sermon ever preached is the one that is lived. This statement goes for preachers, and it goes for parents.

Parents, how well are we SHOWING our children how to serve? Jesus showed us. Not only did He come and die for us, but He also gave us plenty of examples on how to serve one another. Take John 13 for instance. After Jesus instituted the Lord's Supper, what did He do? He covered Himself up with a towel, got down on the ground, and washed the filthy feet of the apostles. Who should have been doing this deed? The apostles should have been washing Jesus' feet. They didn't, and Jesus wanted to teach them how to serve one another, but He didn't just tell them how; He showed them how.

Parents, it will be hard for our children to learn how to serve others if we do not show them. Start at home. Husbands and Wives: serve your spouse, and make sure your children see you do it. When you decided to settle down and commit yourselves to one another, you were committing to be there for one another "for better or for worse." Do your children see the commitment and service in you? I hope so, because chances are they are going to treat their future spouse in much of the same manner that they see you treat yours.

Parents, serve your children also. Parenthood is often a sacrifice isn't it? All of the time, money, attention given to these precious souls is much. And that is ok. The sacrifice in the long run is easy because we serve from love.

Today, I will..._find a special a new way to show my children about serving others._

Don't Forget to Bring the Children!

Today's Scripture: Mark 19:13-15

You got a phone call from a member of your congregation that needs help moving some furniture. You heard that a sweet new family in your neighborhood had a baby, and you want to bring them a meal. A sweet member of your congregation has passed away to his eternal reward, and you want to go encourage the family at the funeral or visitation. In all of these acts of service and more, don't forget to bring your children along with you!

I understand the struggle. The younger the child is, the harder it is to serve others. It almost seems counterproductive to bring children with us to different service projects because we can get more work down in half of the time without them. I understand that sometimes certain situations call for this. Yet, can I encourage you to rethink this for many of the cases? If the worst possible thing that can happen is that our service for someone else takes longer than we want it to…I promise you that the benefits usually far outweigh that consequence. When our children see us serving our congregation and the community, we are investing in their Service Bank. When we take the extra time to show them how to work hard for others, how to make some banana bread for someone, or how to show someone that we care; then we are enriching our children's lives!

Jesus had to deal with people who didn't appreciate children—and it was His own disciples! We read of people investing in their children by bringing them to Jesus, and the disciples discouraged it. Jesus sets them straight quickly: "Let the little children come to me and do not hinder them, for to such belongs the kingdom of heaven." (Matthew 19:14).

Today, I will…*look for ways outside of the home to serve others. It might be large acts of service, or simple small acts, showing that I care. And I will be sure to have my children come along to watch and help.*

A Service of Initiative

Today's Scripture: James 2:14-17

Sweet Miss Mary was struggling physically. She was older in years, and her health was failing. Out of the kindness of their hearts, many would come by to check on her. And you know what they would say? "If you need anything, you let me know!" Yet the first individual that checked on her failed to see the pile of dishes filling the sink. Oh, she was not going to ask her to do her dishes, so they went unwashed. The second person failed to see the lawn that desperately need tending. Oh, she wasn't going to ask, so the yard went uncut. The third good hearted person failed to notice the door that he walked through wasn't opening and shutting properly and needed mending. Oh she wasn't going to ask him to fix it, so it went unfixed.

How many times do we fall into this trap? We have good intentions, and we offer to help people in any way they may need help. Yet, we fail to just open up our eyes and look for ways to jump in and help on our own initiative.

Let's teach our children to do better with this than we have done. Teach them initiative. Allow them to get creative on how to help people around them. Ask every child to come up with a project. It might be washing windows of a widow's house. Maybe it is mowing someone's lawn. Maybe it is making a meal for someone or dropping off some groceries. Let's foster an attitude of opening up our eyes to service!

Today, I will... *encourage my family as we gather around for family Bible time to come up with a plan to help someone that we know.*

Service in Secret

Today's Scripture: Matthew 6:1-4

As children are raised, rewards can be helpful. From allowance, to trophies, to ice cream cones, there are many ways that children are motivated to do good. I have and will continue to use these in parenting! However, how cool would it be to teach our children to also serve others with the understanding that we will receive nothing in return. One of the ways that we can do this is to encourage them to serve others in a secret way, where the recipients of their service do not even know who served them.

Jesus even preached about this type of service in Matthew 6:2-4 when He said, "Thus, when you give to the needy, sound no trumpet before you, as the hypocrites do in the synagogues and in the streets, that they may be praised by others. Truly, I say to you, they have received their reward. But when you give to the needy, do not let your left hand know what your right hand is doing, so that your giving may be in secret. And your Father who sees in secret will reward you."

Why not try to implement this? You can even make it into a game! Try to see how much you can help people without letting them know. Here are a few ideas: Maybe your neighbor's leaves are in need of raking, so you do it after you have seen them leave for the day. Maybe you help your children sneak over to a friend's house and wash their vehicles windows. Maybe you encourage your children to set aside a little of their money for a small gift card that is just big enough to buy a snack at a favorite fast-food restaurant. Help them bring that card to the church secretary to hand it to the recipient of their choosing. The ideas are endless!

Today, I will...*help my children come up with creative ways to surprise others with service. And we will discuss the reward of doing it in secret for only the Lord to see.*

WEEK 20

Teaching Your Children About Finding a Spouse

RUSSELL SMITH

Be the Spouse You Want Your Child To Be

Today's Scripture: 1 Corinthians 13:4-5

It can be tempting to fall into the trap of putting your children before your spouse - they are often more demanding of our time and love. It can be tempting to fall into the trap of putting your spouse before God— he or she is often demanding of our time and love, too. Keeping God at the top is worth it - and it's hard work!

When we talk about "putting God first", our minds often shift focus to keeping God first in our jobs, our schedules, dreams, personal leisure, priorities, etc. But, it's of extreme importance to show our children that we "put God first" in our marital relationships because it's there that our kids see us most often and in the most intimate setting. They learn how to be a spouse from our example in the home.

They are learning about becoming the spouse you want them to be. They are learning about becoming the spouse their children need to see in them one day. Simultaneously, they are becoming the kind of spouse some other parent is praying for their child to find.

Remember, your children are not watching to see if you're the "perfect" spouse. Is there such a thing (other than my wife)? There will be fusses, frustrations, disagreements. Your spouse will make mistakes; you will make mistakes. The goal is that when those things arise, that your own children see that you handle them with a never-ending agape love for your spouse.

Will you only pick up your shoes IF she washes your clothes? Will you only wash his clothes IF he picks up his shoes? Agape love picks up the shoes regardless of whether the clothes get washed or not, and vice versa. Love leads and is not petty. Love does not insist on its own way.

Your children will become later on what they see modeled in the home today. Be the spouse you want your child to be.

Today, I will..._tell my children that I love them less than my spouse, whom I love less than God._

Answer Their Prayers

Today's Scripture: Matthew 6:24

"Do not be anxious about your life." Aren't those beautiful and awesome words? There are many challenges in life, and I've worried about most of them. I've worried about money, clothes, bills, and I've worried about the bigger things like my kids' futures. I know their future spouse is probably already alive and that that child is growing and learning. And I've prayed and worried about their faith. "Do they love God?" "What was their home life like as a child?" "What will my children be getting themselves into?" Please tell me I'm not the only one, right?

Somewhere today, there is a parent worrying about their child's future. They're praying today by faith that their child's spouse is loving God and learning about His will for them in their life.

They're also praying for you. They're praying that you are sharing with your child everything he or she needs to know about being a Godly spouse. They are praying that the child who will come into their family one day is being taught about God's plans for the home. They are hoping and praying anxiously about the parents (you and your spouse) who are teaching their child's future spouse all about God. They are anxiously praying that their child marries a spouse who has the same set of morals and whose spiritual compass is fixed in the very same truths found in those ancient words that they have passed down to their children from the moment they were born. Will their future spouse love God more than self? Will their future "other" grandparents (you and your spouse) be a teammate in the raising of their grandchildren in a God centered fashion? They are praying faithfully, and yet, they are anxious!

God is answering their prayers today by using you. You can answer their prayers today by living by faith and loving the Lord and by helping your children see all the important things.

Today, I will...*tell my children that their raising, my parenting, and my marriage, if done by faith in God, will be the answer to someone else's prayer for their child.*

Marry Someone Who Will Make You A Stronger Christian

Today's Scripture: 2 Corinthians 6:14

What we are talking about today is using God's wisdom in our lives. To understand this better, study Proverbs 1-9. But doing good doesn't always result in good and life's meaning is sometimes very cloudy. To better understand this, read Ecclesiastes and Job.

A yoke is the beam of wood attached to the oxen pulling a cart or plow. It enabled the oxen to work together. You would never yoke a tall ox with a short ox because then they would pull in a circle.

When a Christian yokes together with a non-Christian in any partnership, business agreement, or union, it's harder to yield maximally great results to the glory of God. Something has to give, and too many times what gives is the conviction of the believer. The closest partnership your children can have is with another in marriage, and so this principle applies to the marriage relationship as well.

Marriages fail to work for many different reasons, but at their core, most fail because either or both spouses fail to love God and keep HIM at the center of their relationship. When a couple's focus is on loving God, it is God that pulls them closer together. But when at least one spouse loves the other spouse more than God or loves himself most of all, the couple will never grow close to God together. Uniting a believer and an unbeliever is like uniting opposites, and mostly makes for a very difficult marriage. Difficult marriages like this seldom result in each spouse making the other a stronger Christian.

This world is difficult. Like you, I pray for my children, and more than anything I want them to grow in their faith, along with their future spouses some day, to accomplish great things in this life for the glory of God. When they are pulling in the same direction, they get stronger, and the stronger they are, the stronger their children will be in the Lord.

Today, I will...*tell my children to marry someone who makes them a stronger Christian.*

118

THURSDAY

Marriage Is for a Man And a Woman

Today's Scripture: Genesis 2:24

Homosexual and polyamorous "marriages" are becoming normal in many societies in the world. Sadly, Christians today are becoming convinced that these kinds of agreements are okay. To understand and define marriage we have to understand that marriage was given to mankind from God. Marriage did not originate in the mind of man. When God created the first man in Genesis 2, He also created for him, out of his rib, someone special as a helper and a companion in life, someone uniquely created for procreation. "Be fruitful and multiply" is a command from God that can only and forever be fulfilled within the confines of a male and female relationship.

Television, movies, music, and streaming services have all created a massive challenge for the Christian family. It seemed Disney could, for the most part, be trusted, but not anymore. Just this year, the website whatsupmoms.com published an article promoting 10 new LGBTQ shows exhorting, "There are so many TV shows for kids with great LGBTQ+ characters, storylines and themes, and that's great news — because representation matters. Here are 10 to check out." The article goes on to promote 10 new shows on Netflix, Disney+, Nickelodeon, and Hulu that Satan has diabolically designed to manipulate and confuse our children.

It's hard to believe that we're at the point where gender misidentification and gender swapping are even words common in our vocabulary. Boys and girls alike are swapping identity pronouns such as "they", "him", "her", "themself", etc.. etc... Social pressures are forcing our children to play along with this delusional game. Society tells us that to ignore someone's selected identity pronoun is to say that that person doesn't exist. To misuse selected pronouns is to increase the adverse effects of social oppression, we are told.

Satan is working overtime to confuse our children. Don't let the world dictate to our children what marriage and their sexual identity should be. Let's make sure we are teaching our children their God-given place in the marriage covenant.

Today, I will...*pray for wisdom and effectiveness in teaching my children/grandchildren/children in my church family that marriage is for a real man and a real woman only. I will filter any shows and characters that Satan is using to confuse the children in my life.*

I Told My Kids to Pray for Their Future Spouse and They Thought I Was Crazy

Today's Scripture: Philippians 4:6

God is all-knowing and all-powerful, so it is completely within His power to know whom your child will marry one day. Yes, we have free will, but even in that, God knows how it will all play out.

When you tell your children to pray for their spouse, the first thing they do is probably look at you like you have a cantaloupe growing on your forehead. But when you explain it, they'll get it. And even when they pray, they may pray about an idea of what type of person their spouse may be. In time, they will come to know the type of person whom God has prepared.

So, while their idea of whom their spouse will be may be vague, God is able to put a name and a face to that prayer. You see, God knows exactly who you are praying for even when you do not. So teach your children to pray very specifically for things for their future spouse.

Pray for their health. Pray for their purity.
Pray for their ability to handle their disappointments.
Pray for their family.
Pray for their safety. Pray for their faith.
Pray for their hurts. Pray for their patience.
Pray for their friends' influence on them; pray for their influence on their friends.
Pray that their spouse will be praying for them.

Today, I will..._sit down with my child and pray for their spouse._

WEEK 21

Helping Our Children Become Christians

STEVE HIGGINBOTHAM

Lessons from the Yellow Brick Road

Today's Scripture: Matthew 6:33

I grew up during a time that was prior to many modern conveniences we take for granted today. For instance, we had no microwave ovens, VCR's, computers, or cell phones.

With that context in mind, CBS would broadcast "The Wizard of Oz" once a year. My memory of that movie was quite different from the memory of my peers. My version of the movie went like this:
Dorothy is a young girl living on a Kansas farm. A tornado lifts Dorothy away to the land of Oz. Her house lands on the Wicked Witch of the East. Dorothy throws water on the Wicked Witch of the West, melting her. Dorothy meets the Wizard of Oz and wakes up safely back in Kansas.

Now, if you know the story of the Wizard of Oz, the above summary is missing a large portion of the movie. In fact, it is missing the entire journey on the Yellow Brick Road. The reason I have no memory of what happened on the Yellow Brick Road is that CBS aired this show at 6:00 p.m. on Sunday night, once a year from 1959 to 1991.

What does that have to do with my sketchy memory of the movie? Well, church services started at 6:30 p.m. on Sunday night, and the residents of my home went to church, movie or no movie. I would see the first 25 minutes of the show, then run home after church just in time to see the Wicked Witch melt.

Although I would have liked to have seen the entire movie as a child, I am so thankful that my memory is not of Dorothy "skipping through Oz" but of our family not "skipping worship services."

If we want our children to be faithful to the Lord, we must model proper priorities before them.

Today, I will... *will examine my priorities to make sure they honor God before my children. "But seek first the kingdom of God and His righteousness, and all these things will be added to you" (Matthew 6:33).*

TUESDAY

The Traffic Light

Today's Scripture: Colossians 3:1-2

When I was a boy and riding in the car with my dad, he stopped at a traffic light. While we were stopped, I noticed several children playing in front of some dilapidated houses. I also noticed that the children were barefoot and barely clothed. It was obvious they were poor, and had little supervision while playing next to a busy road... and I felt sorry for them.

As the light turned green, I told my dad that I felt sorry for those children. In response, my Dad said something to me that I have never forgotten. My dad said, "Yes, it is sad, but unless someone teaches them about Jesus, this is the best it will ever get for them."

I could not shake those words when I was a child, and I have not been able to shake them as an adult. People often ask me when I decided to become a preacher and if my mom and dad ever "pushed" me into my decision. Actually, I don't ever remember having a single conversation with either of my parents in which they "pushed" me to become a preacher. But that is not to say my decision was all my own. My parents influenced me to become a preacher by daily conversations like the one I recounted above.

While those houses have long since been demolished, and the road rerouted, whenever I pass by that area, I relive that brief, but profound conversation with my dad that took place over 50 years ago.

Friends, help your children to understand that for the child of God, one's time on Earth will be the closest he ever comes to Hell, but for the one who rejects Jesus, one's time on Earth will be the closest he ever comes to Heaven.

Today, I will... *search for ways to impress eternity upon the minds of my children. "Set your minds on things that are above, not on things that are on earth (Colossians 3:2).*

Memories from My Mother's Lap

Today's Scripture: Ephesians 6:1-4

I have vivid memories of a time when I was a child and would sit on my Mother's lap while she read to me. She did not read just any books, but she read a book called, "Tiny Tots Bible Reader," written by Jim Bill McInteer.

As the years past, I lost that book and could not remember its name. The best I could do as I searched for a copy was to say it was thin, red, and had simply stick-figure illustrations in it. Finally, someone knew what I was looking for and helped me secure a copy over the Internet. I was so happy and excited to find this book that I called my college-age children and told them that when they came home from break, they were going to be sitting on my lap while I read to them!

Today, although I have thousands of books in my library, this thin, red, book is one of my most prized possessions and is prominently displayed.

While this is a wonderful memory for me, I am aware that it is a memory that is not shared by all. Sitting in my Mom's lap and having her read Bible stories to me was common place in my early years, but those are not everyone's childhood memories. I am certain there are people who have no memories of their mother or father ever reading Bible stories to them, singing, and praying with them at home.

Please carve time out of your busy schedules and make your priorities such that you spend time reading and telling the great stories of the Bible to your children. Let them hear you marvel at these great stories of faith and the power and love of God.

Today, I will...abegin etching deeply into my children's memories my love for God and His word. I will work to make my home, not only a good place, but a "God place," "...but bring them up in the discipline and instruction of the Lord (Ephesians 6:4b).*

Burger King & 11 Cents

Today's Scripture: James 1:22

I once had a discussion with my 10-year-old son at the dinner table. He was explaining how he had benefited on a homework grade because of a mistake his teacher made while grading his paper. I saw this as a teaching opportunity and explained how he would want the teacher to correct the mistake even if it wasn't in his favor. Therefore, it was only fair to inform her of the mistake. I said no more about the matter. However, as he sat silently through the meal, he must have been weighing what I had said to him. Toward the end of dinner, he blurted, "I'll tell my teacher, tomorrow."

To say I was proud of my son is an understatement, but as proud as I was of him, I was equally ashamed of myself. Earlier that same day, I had discovered that after driving away from the drive-thru window at Burger King, I had been given 11 cents too much in change. But I rationalized the error in my favor, remembering all the times they had messed up my order, so I drove off.

However, I was now convicted by my son, and my responsibility to him. I cannot be the father I should be by telling him to do what I, myself was unwilling to do. So, the next morning, I did what I should have done the day earlier. I returned 11 cents to Burger King because it was not mine.

Friends, our children not only need to hear us teach the truth, but they desperately need to see that we embrace and practice the truth we speak.

Today, I will... *remind myself to be a model of integrity for my children. There are many competing voices that call for their attention, therefore I must make sure that my voice rings with clarity by the consistency in what I teach and what I practice. "But be doers of the word, and not hearers only, deceiving yourselves" (James 1:22).*

Mount Moriah Experiences

Today's Scripture: Genesis 22:1-19

Do you remember when Abraham took his son, Isaac up on Mt. Moriah to offer him as a sacrifice to the Lord (Genesis 22)? While we attempt to imagine the internal struggle Abraham must have been going through, do not ignore the thoughts that must have been running through Isaac's mind as well. Yet, in spite of the difficulty of the situation, we simply see faithful compliance on the part of Abraham as well as Isaac.

Scripture tells us what Abraham was thinking at the time. He believed God would raise Isaac from the dead (Hebrews 11:19). However, Scripture does not tell us what Isaac was thinking. But I am certain of this, the memory of being laid on the altar and his father raising the knife in his hand must have burned deeply into his memory. I dare say that for as long as Isaac lived, he vividly remembered the events of this day and just how faithful his father, Abraham, was to the commandments God.

My question to you is, "What kind of life-long memories are you creating for your children in your home?" What events, demonstrating your faithfulness to God, will be burned into the memory of your children? What steps have you taken to impress upon your children that you are completely sold out and committed to the Lord?

Dennis Rainey calls these events, "Mt. Moriah Experiences." Friends, I believe it's time to create some "Mt. Moriah experiences" for our children. When parents, with intention, do something that will be burned into the memory of their children that demonstrates their faithfulness to God, they are walking in the same footsteps of the "Father of the Faithful" (Romans 4:16).

Today, I will... *begin to brainstorm about ways to impress my children with my unwavering faith in God. I will begin creating "Mt. Moriah Experiences" so that long after I am gone from this world, my children will know how deeply I loved the Lord. "And through his faith, though he died, he still speaks (Hebrews 11:4).*

WEEK 22

Helping Our Children Learn to Choose Good Friends

WAYNE JONES

One of Life's Greatest Choices

Today's Scripture: 1 Corinthians 15:33

What we are is often determined by the character and spirituality of the people in our inner circle. Sons become like their fathers. Daughters become like their mothers. And all of us, in one way or another, share in the likes, dislikes, actions, and reactions of our friends. Whether we intend for it to happen or not, our friends are often our role models, We often mimic their behavior, share their viewpoints, and champion their causes. Whose mother hasn't asked him, "If all of your friends were jumping off a bridge, would you do it too?" The reason for the question seems quite obvious – we are influenced (sometimes for good and sometimes for bad), by the friends that we choose.

Today's passage is the inspired and concise way to state this principle. Yet, Paul had to include the phrase "Do not be deceived" as a contextual highlighter, because we often get it wrong. We assume that the negative influence of worldly friends has little, if any, sway over the attitudes and actions of those who are spiritually strong. However, a brief survey of Scripture will show the fallacy of that assumption. Wasn't Barnabas negatively influenced by his friend Peter as recorded in Galatians 2:11-14? Weren't some of the apostles negatively influenced by the viewpoint of Judas as recorded in John 12:4 and Matthew 26:8?

Thus, one of life's greatest choices is the choice of friendship. Who will be our closest friends? Who will be in our inner circle? Whose ideas and actions will we learn from more than any others in this world?

Since we make these choices from an early age, we need help. Parents, God has entrusted you with every aspect of your child's development, and that development includes the wisdom of friend choices. We must view this responsibility with seriousness and sobriety. This week's series of devotionals will address the types of friends that our children should have. May we always be vigilant to teach and model this in our families.

Today, I will... *have a conversation with my children about friendships, influences, and the power of our choices.*

TUESDAY

Everyone Needs a Friend Like Barnabas

Today's Scripture: Acts 4:36-37; 9:27; 15:36-41

William Arthur Ward wrote, "Flatter me, and I may not believe you. Criticize me, and I may not like you. Ignore me, and I may not forgive you. Encourage me, and I will not forget you."

In Scripture, he is introduced to us as Joseph (Acts 4:36). But immediately Luke informs us that the apostles nicknamed him Barnabas, which means "son of encouragement." Once introduced in this way, he is mentioned another 27 times in the New Testament. To put that into perspective, Timothy is only mentioned by name 24 times. In other words, Barnabas becomes a key person in the spread of the gospel and in the strengthening of the early church. He was the kind of friend everyone wanted to have. He was loyal to those he loved, and he stood up for those who were doubted by others.

In today's three short texts, we have highlighted some of the selfless actions of this great friend. One's problems became his problems because he was a "supplier." He made people feel wanted when others didn't because he was an "includer." He reminded people that their mistakes did not define them because he was a "forgiver."

Parents, help your children to find friends like Barnabas. This world can be very difficult, and those in the world can be cliquish, judgmental, exclusive, and harsh. In childhood and adolescence, our children struggle with fitting in and finding their places. Friends like Barnabas are vital to their maturity and self-worth. These types of friends don't make our children vie for their approval, and they seek to include rather than exclude.

Today, I will... *talk to my children about the value of their friend choices. I will emphasize the godly traits of forgiveness, inclusiveness, and sacrifice. I will also model these traits so that my children know what to look for in their friends.*

Everyone Needs a Friend Like Nathan

Today's Scripture: 2 Samuel 12:1-12

For the Psalmist, the final illustration of a miserable life is a life wherein our friends shun us and our "companions have become darkness" (Ps. 88:18). Have you ever had a best friend become an enemy? Have you ever been mistreated by someone who had been your closest ally in life? If so, you can testify to the enteral value of having a friend that is true and real no matter the circumstance.

Nathan proved to be such a friend. Everyone, including our children, need friends with the loyalty and concern of Nathan. Friends like this will be committed to what is best for us, not merely what is comfortable. They will be focused on helping in our walk of faith rather than hindering that walk.

Nathan was a friend to king David. He wasn't David's best friend, but he was the best friend for a season in David's life. On two different occasions, Nathan dared to tell David that his decisions were not in keeping with God's purpose and plan. The first time was in reference to David's presumptuous plan to build God a house (see 2 Samuel 7:1-17). The second time was in response to David's lust-fueled sin with Bathsheba and against Uriah (2 Samuel 12:1-12). On this occasion, he was loving, wise, courageous, and truthful to expose David's sin and call for David's repentance.

Because we often sin secretly, willingly, and regrettably, we need someone in our lives to stand in our way. We need confrontation and loving rebuke. We need reminders of our inabilities and someone to highlight our shortcomings.

As our children grow and mature, they will be tempted to surround themselves with those who will soothe their wounds rather than expose their weaknesses. However, without friends like Nathan, our children might never see the magnitude of their sin nor the need to make it right in Christ.

Today, I will... *pray for my children to find at least one friend like Nathan—a friend who will lovingly correct them with Heaven in mind.*

THURSDAY

Everyone Needs a Friend Like Paul

Today's Scripture: Philippians 2:19-24

The growth and maturity of the New Testament church are predicated on cross-generational instruction and (either formal or informal) mentorship. You can't read passages like Titus 2:1-8 without considering the role that older women play in the life of younger women in the church and the role that older men play in the maturation process of younger men in the kingdom of God.

Sadly, in our attempts to meet the needs of various age demographics in individual churches, we often separate the younger from the older too often. They should share meals. They should worship together. They should serve shoulder to shoulder. They should be friends.

The apostle Paul understood the necessity of befriending and investing in the younger generation. Timothy understood the value of accepting that friendship and being trained by someone older with a wealth of wisdom, experience, and knowledge. Their story is not told in one single text but is sprinkled throughout the stories of Acts and the letters of Paul. The success of their friendship is highlighted by Timothy's ministry in Ephesus (1 Timothy 1:1-5). It is further highlighted by Paul's assessment of Timothy: "For I have no one like him, who will be genuinely concerned for your welfare. For they all seek their own interests, not those of Jesus Christ. But you know Timothy's proven worth, how as a son with a father he has served with me in the gospel" (Philippians 2:20-22).

Our children need to seek friendships and relationships with someone who is ahead of them on the journey. Someone who has insights they don't have. Someone who has wisdom they yet have gained. Someone who has perspectives currently unavailable to them simply because of inexperience. Maybe their "Paul" is a widow or widower in the congregation. Maybe he is an elder or an active deacon. Maybe she has raised all of her own children and now has time to invest in someone else's. Our church pews are filled with those who will be to our children what Paul was to Timothy.

Today, I will... *talk to my children about the need for spiritual mentors. I will pray that God opens doors to make these friendships a reality.*

131

Everyone Needs a Friend Like Jesus

Today's Scripture: John 15:13-15

Have you ever watched a movie and just knew how it was all going to play out? The script was predictable, and the plot was obvious. There was no suspense or even a moment of uncertainty. You knew how it was going to end. If so, maybe you predicted the last devotional topic of the week without even seeing the title. If we are going to teach our children about the type of friends they need, wouldn't Jesus be the top choice on that list?

Jesus was a friend to all, including those who others felt were not friend material (Matthew 11:19). At the point of his betrayal and arrest, Jesus even looked at Judas and said, "Friend, do what you came to do" (Matthew 26:50).

Jesus also explained what true friendship looked like in John 14:13-15. It is about sacrifice and service. Just hours after He explained this, He illustrated it by laying down his life at Calvary. He is the greatest friend you or I or our children could ever hope to have.

He is the embodiment of every characteristic we have considered this week. He has encouraged us as Barnabas did for those in his life. No one believes in us more than Jesus. He has warned us of our sins like Nathan did for David. He came to live, breathe, and talk directly to mankind about the depths of our sin. He is everyone's "Paul," and we're all his "Timothys." Jesus calls for all of us to walk with Him and to learn from Him (Matthew 11:28-30).

Parents, encourage your children to live like Jesus and to surround themselves with others who try to do the same.

As a friend, Jesus wants to hear about my struggles and makes every effort possible to alleviate them. As a friend, Jesus loves deeper and stronger than an army of supporters or family members. As a friend, Jesus is intentional and deliberate.

Today, I will... *pray for more young people to look and live like Jesus. I will pray that my children are included in that number.*

WEEK 23

Glorifying God In the Family

STEVE LUSK

What Does It Mean to "Glorify God?"

Today's Scripture: Matthew 5:13-16

As we explore "Glorifying God in the Family" it would be helpful to understand what it means to "glorify God." The word translated "glorify" often "signifies an opinion, estimate, and hence, the honor resulting from a good opinion" (Vine's Expository Dictionary of Old and New Testament Words, Thomas Nelson Publishers, 1997). Another form of the word means "to magnify, extol, praise" (Vine's, page 482). To "glorify God" means that we magnify Him or make Him prominent in our lives.

Notice some Scriptures which talk about glorifying God. In Matthew 5:13-16, Jesus says, "...let your light shine before others, so that they may see your good works and *give glory to your Father* who is in heaven." Mark records a miracle of healing that Jesus performed (Mark 2:1-12). When the man who was healed got up and walked away, the people "were all amazed and *glorified God...*" The apostle Paul wrote to the Romans saying, "May the God of endurance and encouragement grant you to live in such harmony with one another, in accord with Christ Jesus, that together you may *with one voice glorify the God and Father of our Lord Jesus Christ*" (Romans 15:5-6).

As we think in terms of glorifying or magnifying God, the questions may arise, "How can I make God 'bigger' in my life? Isn't God already big?" In one sense, we can never make God "bigger" than He already is. He's sovereign over all the universe! But we can be a kind of magnifying lens through which the world can see God more clearly. When I do good for others and praise God with my words, I am *glorifying* Him in my life.

Today, I will... *use words and do good deeds in order to be the lens through which others can see God more distinctly, giving Him all the praise.*

TUESDAY

A Family's Priorities May Glorify God

Today's Scripture: Luke 2:40-52

What is important to your family? Some families put emphasis on educational achievement. Other families pursue athletic accomplishments. Still others emphasize the value of involvement in politics or community service organizations. And some families place a high priority on the arts, such as painting, photography, drama, or musical performance. Each of these has benefit in the social, mental, emotional, and physical development of the children in our families. Certainly God may be glorified in our participation of any of these activities.

But to make God prominent in our families, we must prioritize the things that He values. As a boy Jesus went to the temple with His family and was later found to be asking and answering questions of the religious leaders there. When His parents asked Him about this, His response was, "Did you not know that I must be in my Father's house?" Later, the text tells us that "Jesus increased in wisdom and in stature and in favor with God and man" (Luke 2:40-52). His growth in every area of life was important, but even as a youngster, Jesus understood the value of prioritizing the things of God!

So what should we prioritize in our families in order to glorify God? A good place to start would be to gather with God's people to worship Him and understand more of His word, much like Jesus and His earthly family did. Does your family put gathering for worship or Bible study before other endeavors – ball games, music lessons, homework, or community events? How we spend our time speaks volumes about what we value. And if we are to value the things of God, we must put Him first.

A man asked Jesus which commandment was the most important. His response revealed His Father's priorities—love God and love fellow man (Matthew 22:34-40). As worthwhile as many pursuits may be, nothing compares to glorifying God by prioritizing these two commands before all else.

Today, I will... *glorify God in my family by pursuing the things that are of first importance to Him!*

Teaching the Bible in My Family Glorifies God

Today's Scripture: Psalm 119:11, 105

According to data from DataReportal, the average American spends 7 hours and 4 minutes looking at a screen every day. While this number may seem startling, there are a number of explanations for this—work from home, online schooling, virtual meetings, gaming, and social media—just to name a few. Some of these are worthwhile and even necessary, but others may be seen as unhelpful or harmful. This data is being offered, not as a blanket criticism, but as a challenge. Are there ways we can use our time, even screen time, to glorify God?

As much time as we spend in various pursuits (some of which could be construed as necessary), how much time are we spending in pursuing the will of God by reading and studying His Word? Can screen time be helpful in learning and understanding what God wants us to know and do? The answer can be a resounding "Yes!" (Note: These devotionals in this book are being produced via screen time!)

Screen time can be helpful by using online resources to read and study the Bible. But the point of today's devotional is this – are we spending any time glorifying God in our family by reading and studying the word of God? The Psalmist proclaimed, "Your word is a lamp to my feet and a light to my path" (Psalm 119:105). In our sometimes dark world, our families need the illuminating guidance that comes from the light of the word.

Psalms 119:11 says, "I have stored up your word in my heart, that I might not sin against you." How much time and energy is your family putting into "storing up" the word of God? Is there anything you could do that would benefit your family more than spending time reading, studying, discussing, and putting into practice the word of God?

Today, I will... *glorify God by spending time studying God's word with my family.*

THURSDAY
Praying with My Family Glorifies God

Today's Scripture: Hebrews 4:14-16

Many of us would never consider sitting down to a meal without offering a spoken or silent word of gratitude to God. Yet sadly, mealtime may be the only time that some families spend in prayer. When you take time to pray with or for your family, you are making God prominent in your family.

Did you know that Jesus, the Son of God, spent time in prayer? At least fifteen times in the Gospels (Matthew, Mark, Luke, and John) Jesus is said to have been praying, sometimes spending much time in prayer (See Luke 6:12). In addition to the example He set, Jesus also uses many occasions to teach about the importance of praying. If Jesus' aim was to glorify His Father (John 17:1) and He spent significant time in prayer, then we should glorify God in our families by emphasizing prayer.

Pray for members of your family by name. It is wonderful to hear your name being called before God's throne of grace! (See Hebrews 4:14-16). Have your children heard you call their name before God in prayer? Has your spouse, your grandchildren, or your grandparents heard the same? Have they heard you thank God for them or ask God to bless their lives?

When troubles come your way do you think to pray? "...do not be anxious about anything, but in everything by prayer and supplication with thanksgiving let your requests be made known to God" (Philippians 4:6). "Is anyone among you suffering? Let him pray..." (James 5:13a). Is prayer your family's default reaction to trouble?

It is easy to criticize leaders (and others) but do we also pray for them? Paul wrote to Timothy, "...I urge that supplications, prayers, intercessions, and thanksgivings be made for all people, for kings and all who are in high positions...This is good, and it is pleasing in the sight of God our Savior..." (1 Timothy 2:1-3). God is glorified when we pray for others rather than criticize them.

Today, I will... *glorify God in my family by spending time in prayer with and for them.*

Serving Others with My Family Glorifies God

Today's Scripture: 1 Peter 4:10-11

Jesus has been described in many ways. He was a carpenter's son. He was a teacher. He often called Himself the "Son of Man" (Matthew 8:20). Peter proclaimed that He was "the Christ, the Son of the Living God" (Matthew 16:16). But Jesus is also referred to as a servant (See Isaiah 53:11; Acts 4:27; Matthew 12:18). It is not a stretch to say that setting an example of serving others was one reason Jesus came to earth (Matthew 20:28). Among other things He washed His disciples' feet and miraculously served others in order to glorify God (See John 11:4, 40; 13:1-12). If Jesus was all about serving others, we can glorify His Father by serving others in our families.

There are many beneficial activities in which families may engage. Families can work together, study together, play together, or travel together. These may be enjoyable and memorable activities but perhaps nothing parents can do will make a more lasting impression on their children than engaging in service to others. And in the process of serving others, God will be glorified! "As each has received a gift, use it to *serve one another*, ...whoever serves, as one who serves by the strength that God supplies—*in order that in everything God may be glorified...*" (1 Peter 4:10-11).

We may serve by providing food, clothing, and shelter to those in need, visiting prisoners, sick, and shut-ins, providing foster care for children, comforting those who have suffered loss, writing notes of encouragement to those who may be discouraged, or doing many other good deeds. We do not do these things in order to put the spotlight on ourselves, but in order to be the lens through which our Heavenly Father is magnified. "...let your light shine before others, so that they may *see your good works and give glory to your Father* who is in heaven" (Matthew 5:16).

Today, I will... *seek to glorify God by serving others with my family.*

WEEK 24

Encouraging Young Men to Be Leaders

JERRY ELDER

Stand

Today's Scripture: Deuteronomy 6:7-9

My grandfather was a huge influence in my life. With only a third grade education, he could barely read, and he generally just signed his name. I don't think I ever saw him write a full letter. But, oh, what an influence!

The family would gather together on a Friday night at my grandparents' house. The kids would play in the yard; the adults would meet in the house, men in one room, women in another. Around dark, my grandfather would go outside and whistle really loud. All the kids and family would gather to the front porch. There, my grandfather would read out of his old leather bound King James Version Bible. Upon closing that Bible, he would look at my uncle, and ask him to lead the family in prayer. My uncle would lead some of the most beautiful prayers you've ever heard. I know he learned that from my grandfather.

My grandfather passed that down to our generation, encouraging us to follow the Lord. It was passed through our family, much like what we read in the old testament of the faith of Abraham, Isaac and Jacob.

In Deuteronomy 6:7-9, we read of Gods plan for man to pass down faith through future generations.

"You shall teach them diligently to your children, and shall talk of them when you sit in your house, and when you walk by the way, and when you lie down, and when you rise. You shall bind them as a sign on your hand, and they shall be as frontlets between your eyes. You shall write them on the doorposts of your house and on your gates." (Deuteronomy 6:7-9).

It is through this teaching that we have received, that we have developed our faith, that we have developed our love for an Almighty God. It is where we in our life take our stand that Jesus is our Lord and that Jesus is our Savior, our Redeemer and our Friend.

Today, I will... *remember where I have come from, and remember where I stand today!*

TUESDAY

Speak

Today's Scripture: Joshua 1:7

It was in a small church in Munford, Alabama, where a group of young men were taught the skills of speaking, song leading, and praying. I remember it as if it were yesterday. Brother Wilder would come to the Bible classroom and call out names to come and go with him. "Russell, Jeff, Keith and Junior, all of you boys come with me."

There we would go with him to a little small classroom barely big enough for all of us to fit. There he would hand us the old *Sacred Selections* songbook and tell us all to: "Turn to number eighty-two, 'Brighten the Corner Where You Are.'" We each would lead the first verse of that song as he would teach us how to project our voice, how to look at the audience and to remember the purpose of our songs. After a night of practice, he would say to us, "Now you boys be ready because next Wednesday night you are going to lead this to the congregation!"

Wednesday night would come and we would all sit down front. Then we would take our turn and lead the verse of the song that we had prepared. Announcing the number loud, standing up, and speaking up, we would lead our song. The congregation would praise us young men for the job that we had done.

When Joshua was given the responsibility over the children of Israel, there was no doubt of the pressure that he was assuming. Moses had delivered them out of Egypt and led them to the point of the promised land. There, Joshua was given these instructions:

"Only be strong and very courageous, being careful to do according to all the law that Moses my servant commanded you. Do not turn from it to the right hand or to the left, that you may have good success wherever you go" (Joshua 1:7).

Today, I will... *speak up for the Lord, knowing my voice is heard and my faith is seen! Speak up TODAY!*

141

WEDNESDAY

Submit

Today's Scripture: Psalm 46:10

"God gave you two ears, and one mouth. You ought to do twice as much listening as talking!" I have heard that statement many times in my life. I heard it from my mother, as we would talk about things that would bother me or when there was conflict taking place. Oh, it wasn't just from her that I heard those words. I heard them from teachers, preachers, friends, and the list could go on and on.

It makes sense. In the trials of life when the pressures get so strong, sometimes we just want to scream and be heard. What is it God tells us? "Be still, and know that I am God. I will be exalted among the nations, I will be exalted in the earth!" (Psalm 46:10)

God wants us to listen, even when it's hard in our life. He wants US to listen to HIM! When we listen, we are showing our willingness to submit to God. We are showing our willingness to do HIS will, to be obedient, to be faithful!

Submission can be hard; at least that's what we are told, but it comes from a perspective of the mind.

Do you love God? Do you love His Son? If you do, then submission is not hard. We want to do what the Father has told us to do and because we LOVE Him we submit to Him!

Jesus asked that question of Peter:
He said to him the third time, "Simon, son of John, do you love me?" Peter was grieved because he said to him the third time, "Do you love me?" and he said to Him, "Lord, you know everything; you know that I love you." Jesus said to him, "Feed my sheep" (John 21:17).

Jesus expects full submission to Him and to do the will of the Father. Above family, above friends, above self!

Today, I will... *submit MY life to HIM!*

THURSDAY

Success

Today's Scripture: 2 Timothy 2:15

How do you gauge success? Is it being at the top of the ladder in a business? Is it being a state champion in a particular sport? Maybe it's how many plaques you have on the wall for the number of years served in a particular work.

Success could be gauged in so many different ways. It seems that we live in a world where we all want to be successful.

But where does it start? As in anything, you have to start from the bottom. You can't start on top of a roof because you have to get to the top from the bottom and that requires a ladder. So many times in our world today, people want to start at the top. Many want to be the CEO of a company, or perhaps they want to have the highest paying job that took others thirty years to acquire.

I think about Paul in his letter to Timothy when he said: "Do your best to present yourself to God as one approved, a worker who has no need to be ashamed, rightly handling the word of truth" (2 Timothy 2:15).

As great as a worker that Timothy was, he was nothing without the help of his mother and his grandmother. He also relied upon others around him to help him grow in his faith. That is where Paul stepped in and actually called him his "true son in the faith" (1 Timothy 1:2).

Do we want to create great leaders in the world? How about in the church? Then we need to have those that mentor and guide people to be leaders. It is the elders, Sunday school teacher, the preacher, the youth minister. Yes, it takes these, but it also takes the CHURCH to help us all grow and to become successful.

Today, I will... *help someone along their journey to be successful in the Lord first; then that will help them to become successful in life!*

FRIDAY

Sustain

Today's Scripture: 1 Thessalonians 3:11-13

How do you do it? How do you keep living day by day, doing the same routine? Do you get bored? How do you sustain keeping your faith strong in the Lord every day?

When you think about the questions above, they apply to all of us, in our every day lives. We have routines, plans, and standards! Life can bring on a lot of things and we need to learn how to sustain ourselves through all of this.

I love the church at Thessalonica. The example of that church was seen throughout the entire region (Macedonia and Achaia.) In fact others wanted to be just like it! But what was it that made this church so special? You could see it in their actions! After Paul had sent Timothy to visit the church, he came back with an astounding report of how well this church was doing in loving the people all around! Paul was so excited about the work that he replied with this encouragement:

> "Now may our God and Father himself, and our Lord Jesus, direct our way to you, and may the Lord make you increase and abound in love for one another and for all, as we do for you, so that he may establish your hearts blameless in holiness before our God and Father, at the coming of our Lord Jesus with all his saints." (1 Thessalonians 3:11-13)

With all of the great work that this church was doing, Paul encouraged them to keep on keeping on, and then do more!

It's easy to get tired, frustrated, confused. But when we keep our faith strong in God and in His word and we live our lives every day showing faithfulness, we will be encouraged.

Pray. Study. Love. Put the fruit of the Spirit to work!

Today, I will... *SUSTAIN in living for the Lord...and even more!*

WEEK 25

The Family & Service to the Church

J.J. HENDRIX

The Main Thing Is to Keep the Main Thing the Main Thing

Today's Scripture: Matthew 6:33

My Grandfather, A.J. Hendrix, was a faithful, gospel preacher. He served as a preacher, conducted many gospel meetings, took part in church plants, ran a church camp, did mission work (Russia, India, and Honduras), created an evangelism technique that traveled the world, and most importantly, he loved his family. I remember being a teenager and seeing a plaque on his desk. It said (in big gold letters), "The Main thing is to keep the Main thing the Main thing." That plaque and those words resonated with me. Not only did he want to keep God his focus, but he wanted a daily reminder in the form of a plaque on his desk.

My Grandfather wanted to go to heaven and wanted to share the gospel all over the world and in many different ways. Most importantly, he wanted to be a good example to his family in his service. The example he left to me was to not just do the bare minimum. Do more. Look for new ways to serve God. My grandfather wanted to keep the main thing the main thing, and he did so by dedicating his life in many areas to serving the Kingdom.

In Matthew 6:33, Jesus said, "But seek first the kingdom of God and his righteousness, and all these things will be added to you." For us to keep the Main Thing the Main Thing, we have to seek God first. He has to be at the forefront of our minds. When I let my free time be consumed with seeking ways to serve the Kingdom, I will not only find ways to serve, but I will be an example of service to the Church and to my family.

Today, I will... *pray to God that I seek Him first and, in doing so, that I will be a positive example to my family and those around me.*

My Family Needs to See God as #1 In My Life

Today's Scripture: Colossians 3:23-24

Merriam-Webster's Dictionary defines example as "one that serves as a pattern to be imitated or not to be imitated." I have a responsibility to my family to choose to be a good example instead of acting as a bad example. I need to live as though God is important in my life. I have a great need for God and a great God for my need. God needs to be what drives my life and I need to serve Him to the best of my ability.

In Brother Paul Delgado's article, "What Really Matters", he touches on keeping our proper sight on service to God. Delgado emphasizes three characteristics for those well rooted in faith to Christ from Steven Garber's book *The Fabric of Faithfulness*. The first characteristic is a worldview that sees the Bible, Christ, and Christianity as being the answer and center of truth. The second characteristic is being surrounding with Christians that help stay centered on Him. The third characteristic is belonging to a congregation where the Christian life is embodied together by working together in service to God. If I work on these three characteristics, I can better be the example that my family needs to see in keeping God first.

In Colossians 3:23-24, Paul wrote, "Whatever you do, work heartily, as for the Lord and not for men, knowing that from the Lord you will receive the inheritance as your reward. You are serving the Lord Christ." If I want to serve God, I cannot just tell the children to study for the Bible Bowl while I watch the ball game. I need to serve God as I want my children and my spouse to serve God, and that should be as one who practices what he preaches. It does God no favors with my family if I say I love Him and then just go through the motions of worship to Him.

Today, I will... *be a good example. I will lead my family in the right direction by showing them that God is #1 in my life.*

Service to the Church Is a Family "Team" Effort

Today's Scripture: Ecclesiastes 4:9-12

"The family that prays together, stays together," is a famous quote that many have recited over the years. A family that prays together can have their minds focused and become a family that serves together. Many families take up hobbies that they can do together, be it art to skiing. Families can bond over things they do together as a unit.

I love the L2L (Lads 2 Leaders) program because it is not just a program for children, but a program for entire congregations. Alongside my children, I can fulfill the responsibilities of events like Good Samaritan (where you look for opportunities to serve), as well as things like Read the Word and Know the Books. Utilizing this congregational program, my family serves God and our local congregation as a team. There are other programs that only involve youth or only occur over a weekend, but this program allows parents to participate alongside their children in growing and serving together throughout the year.

I am reminded of the strength of working together when I think of the words of Solomon. He penned, "Two are better than one, because they have a good reward for their toil. For if they fall, one will lift up his fellow. But woe to him who is alone when he falls and has not another to lift him up! Again, if two lie together, they keep warm, but how can one keep warm alone? And though a man might prevail against one who is alone, two will withstand him—a threefold cord is not quickly broken" (Ecclesiastes 4:9-12). Teamwork really makes the dream work, and families that work together to serve God are stronger.

Today, I will... *choose to put God and the church before me. It is easy to be selfish, but I choose to be selfless and serve my God with my family.*

THURSDAY

Worship Is the Icing on the Cake

Today's Scripture: Hebrews 10:24-25

One of the favorite parts of any cake is the icing. It makes a sweet cake that much sweeter. The earliest documented case of "frosting" a cake occurred in 1655 and was nothing more than sugar, eggs, and rosewater. This concoction was applied to the cake and it stabilized in the oven, making a somewhat hard shell. Today, there are many ways that people "ice" a cake from glazes to buttercream. Food scientists can come up with unique ways to cover a cake to make it sweeter.

But, no matter how great the icing is, if the cake is bad, the whole presentation will be lacking. Unfortunately, many will view the totality of their service to God as attending worship services when worship is the icing on the cake. Worship is where we get to "kneel before the Lord, our maker" (Psalm 95:6). Worship is where we "offer up a sacrifice of praise to God, that is, the fruit of lips that acknowledge His name" (Hebrews 13:15). The Christian life is a delicious cake, worshiping the creator is the sweet icing.

If worship is the icing on the cake, Christian services IS the cake. Hebrews 10:25 states, "Not neglecting to meet together, as is the habit of some, but encouraging one another, and all the more as you see the Day drawing near." We have the blessed opportunity to come together to worship Him. But a proper emphasis should go on Hebrews 10:24, "And let us consider how to stir up one another to love and good works." Just that verse alone shows us there is more to the Christian life than sitting in worship. We have a responsibility to each other to help in times of trials and celebrate in times of gladness. That's what makes life so sweet, knowing you have a family that supports you and wants you to go to heaven.

Today, I will... *choose to live the life that God wants me to live. Our lives should be in service to God, and worshiping Him is what makes life sweeter.*

Choose Selfless Over Selfish

Today's Scripture: Romans 12:12

In the 1500's, Nicolaus Copernicus developed the heliocentric model. What is that you may ask? It is the notion that the Earth revolves around the Sun. Copernicus was not the first one who came to this conclusion as Aristarchus of Samos had come to the same conclusion in the 3rd century BC. This upset many people as they felt the earth was the center of the universe. Many people today feel that they are the center of the universe. We live in a society that wants people to indulge in personal pleasures, this creates a very self-focused society.

Christians need to have God as the center of their universe. This occurs when one thinks of others more than self. Inspired by the Holy Spirit, Paul penned, "Do not be conformed to this world, but be transformed by the renewal of your mind, that by testing you may discern what is the will of God, what is good and acceptable and perfect." (Romans 12:12). It is easy to be selfish, especially in a world that is full of self-gratification at every turn. If I put God and the Church first in my heart, I am being the proper example to my spouse, children, friends, and family.

While many refuse to believe that they are not the center of the universe, let us be more like Copernicus and Aristarchus in realizing that the world does not revolve around us, but we revolve around something greater. Those scientists thought it was the sun (and it is), but we as Christians can know that our lives should revolve around our loving God.

Today, I will... *make God the center of my life and do my best to serve Him and the church to the best of my abilities.*

WEEK 26

The Family & Service to the Community

PAUL CARTWRIGHT

Put on Your Shoes and Let's Go Do Some Mission Work

Today's Scripture: Deuteronomy 6:4-9

I spent many days with my grandparents in Palestine Texas. We lovingly referred to my grandparents as Mam-Maw and Pap-Paw, and we spent many days shelling peas, checking on the cows, and eating ice cream. Pap-paw was an elder in the Lord's Church, and he took his charge to "...shepherd the flock of God" (1 Peter 5:2a), seriously his entire career as an elder. I remember one day Pap-Paw came and said to me, "Put on your shoes, and let's go do some mission work", and I was confused. In my young mind, mission work took place in a foreign country, but that day I learned that mission work can, and should, take place in our own back yards. Our mission work took the form of bringing a cake Pap-Paw had baked to the home of a member of the Lord's Church who needed some encouraging. While we didn't have a Bible study that day, we did talk about the Lord, and we prayed for the well-being of the member we went to visit.

When I reflect back on that time, I am drawn to Deuteronomy 6:4-9:
> 4 Hear, O Israel: The Lord our God, the Lord is one. 5 Love the Lord your God with all your heart and with all your soul and with all your strength. 6 These commandments that I give you today are to be on your hearts. 7 Impress them on your children. Talk about them when you sit at home and when you walk along the road, when you lie down and when you get up. 8 Tie them as symbols on your hands and bind them on your foreheads. 9 Write them on the doorframes of your houses and on your gates.

My Pap-Paw taught me these truths without ever reading this passage to me, and it was some of the best training I ever received.

Today, I will... *put on my shoes and serve someone else in the name of the Lord.*

She Sleeps In a Bed Just Like You Do

Today's Scripture: Matthew 10:42

One December when our daughter was young, we went into the inner-city of Houston to pass out food and blankets to the people living on the streets. While we were passing out food and blankets a little girl who was roughly the same age as our daughter walked up to us. Our daughter gave her a blanket, and they exchanged pleasantries with one another. That evening while getting ready for bed our little girl wanted to talk about the new friend that she made that day. Our daughter wanted to know where her friend lived, and we shared with her that her friend didn't live in a home of her own, that she lived in a big room with many other people because they could not afford to live in a home of their own. "Daddy, does she have a bed?" As long as I live, I will never forget those words that came out of my little girl's mouth. Our goal that day was to teach our little girl how blessed she was, how to serve others, and doing so meant leaving our comfort zone to serve in the community.

My little girl took a giant step outside of her comfort zone that day to do something nice for someone in the name of Jesus Christ, and I could not have been prouder of her. Sometimes stepping outside of our comfort zones can be as simple as giving someone a drink of water.

Matthew 10:42 (ESV)
"And whoever gives one of these little ones even a cup of cold water because he is a disciple, truly, I say to you, he will by no means lose his reward."

Today, I will... *step out of my comfort zone to serve my community with my family.*

You Never Know Who You Will Meet While Knocking on Doors

Today's Scripture: Hebrews 10:24-25

In the early 1990's there was a nationwide campaign known as One Nation Under God. The goal of this campaign was for the Lord's Church to reach out to the community concerning the saving grace of Jesus Christ.

One congregation participated in a door knocking campaign utilizing their family units to reach the community. A father and son team knocked on the door of a house they were assigned to and began to share about the campaign as well as inviting the occupant to worship with them. The owner of the house thanked the father and son for coming by and then graciously informed them that his family were members of the same congregation. After sharing a good laugh at this situation and then departing from the home of their fellow member, the father and son shared a sobering moment when they both realized that the reason they didn't know this man was because he was not a frequent participant in worship services or other Church activities.

This teachable moment caused the father to share some thoughts from the Bible with his son, specifically from Hebrews 10:24-25:

> And let us consider how to stir up one another to love and good works, not neglecting to meet together, as is the habit of some, but encouraging one another, and all the more as you see the Day drawing near.

The good thing about this story is that it has a happy ending. The knock at the man's door served as a wakeup call, and while he still made his share of mistakes, the man began to take his relationship with the Lord and the Church more seriously. We all need a knock on our door from time to time, and like the man in our story, we need to make sure to answer.

Today, I will... *make my Church family a priority in my life.*

Rubber Gloves, Hairnets, & Feeding The Hungry

Today's Scripture: James 2:14-17

No one looks good in rubber gloves or hairnets; I believe that is something we can all agree on. Unfortunately, these are required fashion accessories when packaging food for the less fortunate people that need it desperately. All over the country families can join to package food that will be sent all around the world to help feed starving people. Our family has participated in several of these events, and each time we learn something new about the places the food is being sent and the people receiving it.

When we work together like this I am reminded of the need to take action to help those who are less fortunate as seen in the book of James.

James 2:14-17 (ESV)
What good is it, my brothers, if someone says he has faith but does not have works? Can that faith save him? If a brother or sister is poorly clothed and lacking in daily food, and one of you says to them, "Go in peace, be warmed and filled," without giving them the things needed for the body, what good is that? So also faith by itself, if it does not have works, is dead.

While no one looks good in rubber gloves and hairnets, the work that is done while wearing them puts our faith into action, helps us build a legacy of faith, and fulfills a need that would otherwise go unmet. I would encourage any family that is looking for a way to put their faith into action to consider feeding the less fortunate, even if it means donning rubber gloves and a hairnet.

Today, I will... *find a way to help the less fortunate by putting my faith into action.*

Christmas Wreaths & Headstones

Today's Scripture: 1 Thessalonians 5:16-18

Each December thousands of people assemble at national cemeteries across the country to place wreaths on the headstones of those who have given their lives in service to our country. This annual event is known as "Wreaths Across America." This event is open to anyone who wishes to participate, and it is encouraged that families participate in this event together. Participants are asked to place a wreath at the base of the headstone of the honored dead, to take a step back, to read the name on the stone out loud, and then to offer a prayer of thanks for that person's service and for those whom they left behind. The activity itself is rewarding and full of teachable moments for families, but the aspect that is the most moving is to stand back and watch the families of these brave men and women appreciate those who come out every year to place wreaths and say a prayer. Loss is never easy, but the prayers offered up on the behalf of those suffering loss can provide comfort like nothing else can.

The Apostle Paul believed in the power of prayer, he wrote about prayer in his letters to Christians, and we can learn a great deal from what Paul had to say about prayer.

> 1 Thessalonians 5:16-18 (ESV)
> Rejoice always, pray without ceasing, give thanks in all circumstances; for this is the will of God in Christ Jesus for you.

Wreaths across America is a somber occasion, but it is also a time when we can all pray like Paul instructed the Thessalonian Church and those prayers will bring peace to families who are grieving.

Today, I will... *pray for someone who is grieving, and I will reach out to them to let them know they have not been forgotten.*

WEEK 27

Making Your Home a Safe Harbor

JOHN McMATH

Lighthouse

Today's Scripture: Hebrews 3:4; Psalm 127:1

On a dark night, a ship's captain spotted faint lights in the distance. Right away, he ordered his signalman to send this message: "Alter your course 10 degrees south." Promptly a return message was received: "Alter your course 10 degrees north." The captain was angry that his command had been ignored, so he sent a second message: "Alter your course 10 degrees south—I am the captain!" Soon another message was received: "Alter your course 10 degrees north—I am seaman third class Jones. Immediately the captain sent a third message, knowing the fear it would evoke: "Alter your course 10 degrees south—I am a battleship!" Then the reply came: "Alter your course 10 degrees north—I am a lighthouse."

God, of course, is the source of light. The Bible refers to Him as our "light and salvation" (Psalm 27:1). The prophet Isaiah spoke of Him as an "everlasting light" (Isaiah 60:19). In the New Testament, the apostle John said that "God is Light" (1 John 1:5) and that Jesus is the "true Light which, coming into the world, enlightens every man" (John 1:9). Jesus Himself declared, "I am the Light of the world" (John 9:5b).

"For every house is built by someone, but the builder of all things is God." (Hebrews 3:4, ESV)

"Unless the Lord builds the house, those who build it labor in vain. Unless the Lord watches over the city, the watchman stays awake in vain." (Psalm 127:1, ESV)

Every home must set a course. The only way to make our homes safe harbors is to allow the light of God to set that course. As husbands, wives, parents, and children, light shines through us, but the origin of that light rests in God alone. We are merely lamps filled with His light and shining to the world around us.

Today, I will...*seek direction from the God in His Word and let His light shine through my actions.*

TUESDAY

Breakwaters

Today's Scripture: Ephesians 5:22-6:4

Man-made harbors will often require a breakwater. Breakwaters are massive, wall-like structures that partially enclose a harbor, protecting it from waves and currents. These breakwaters provide for smooth passage in and out of the harbor, often preventing unnecessary turbulence that can cause damage to boats or danger to passengers.

In his letter to the Ephesians, Paul seems to paint the picture of the husband/father as the breakwater of the home. Look at the amount of space giving instructions to the husband (six verses, 5:25-31) as opposed to the wife (three verses, (5:22-24). Not that one role is more important than the other, but each has his given responsibilities. Then, as Paul addresses parents (6:4), he focuses specifically on the father.

On our televisions and in our movies, the emphasis is quite different. The husband is the imbecile who needs his wife's guidance for even the most mundane tasks. The father is the buffoon who is easily duped by almost anyone, especially the children. Long gone are the days of Father Knows Best, My Three Sons, Leave it to Beaver, and even The Brady Bunch where the husband and father would offer sage advice and wisdom for life. The feminist movement took direct aim at the role of husband and father and has largely succeeded.

What we need in our homes is a restoration of Biblical manhood. It may not come with the swagger of John Wayne, but it is God's model for who we should be as men. Three words from Ephesians 5 point the way:
1. **Love** – "...love your wives, as Christ loved the church..." (Ephesians 5:25). This kind of love is the badge of our discipleship (John 13:35).
2. **Nourish** – (5:29) Such a love needs to be fed. The husband's arms should be a safe and uplifting place for his wife, as the father's arms should be for his children.
3. **Nurture** – A father is to bring his children up in the "nurture and admonition of the Lord" (6:4). Nurturing involves discipline and training — most especially in the "instruction of the Lord."

Today, I will...*as a husband and father, be the servant leader in the home God wants me to be. As a wife and mother, I will support my husband in every way I can to achieve success according to God's plan.*

159

WEDNESDAY

Calm Waters

Today's Scripture: 2 Timothy 1:5; 3:14-15

Behind the breakwater of a harbor, you may find sign which reads, "No Wake Zone." Inside the confines of a harbor calm and steady water is an absolute necessity.

You have heard the saying, "Behind every great man is a good woman." In yesterday's devotional we looked at the husband/father as the breakwater that protects the home harbor from the turbulent waters of the world. However, it is the wife/mother that can add real calm to the home.

"The word "wife" means "weaver," and it is she who weaves the many-splendored and variegated strands of love, femininity, respect, attractiveness, commitment, purity, attentiveness, understanding, industry, loyalty, and spirituality into the marital relationship" (Wendell Winkler, *The Man as Husband and the Woman as Wife; The Home as God Would Have It*, Elkins & Warren). Is there a sweeter term in the English language than the word mother? Abraham Lincoln is quoted as saying, "All that I am I owe to my angel mother."

Look at the trajectory and accomplishment in the life of Timothy because of the godly influence of his mother and his grandmother (2 Timothy 1:5; 3:14-15). Eli had two sons (1 Samuel 2-4), but their mother is never mentioned, and their lives were utterly tragic. Samuel, who had been dedicated to the Lord by his mother, Hannah, and left in Eli's care, grew and ministered to the Lord. The difference was, like Timothy, the influence of a godly mother.

Kittredge once wrote, "If we call him great who planned the Cathedral of St. Peter, with all its massiveness and beauty; if they call the old masters great whose paintings hang on monastery and chapel walls, is not she (the mother) great who is building up characters for the service of God, who is painting on the soul canvas the beauty and strength of Jesus the Christ?" Lord Shaftesbury wrote, "Give me a generation of Christian mothers and I will undertake to change the whole face of society in twelve months." Every harbor needs calm waters. Every home needs the calm, steady influence of a godly mother.

Today, I will....*honor my mother (living or dead) and encourage every young mother to pour the love of God into the lives of her children.*

Dredging

Today's Scripture: Hebrews 12:14

According to National Geographic, dredging, the process of removing sand and sediment from the bed of a body of water, is essential to maintaining a safe harbor. This process deepens and cleans the body of water. Our homes must be dredged of sin and contamination to keep them safe. This process is called holiness.

Holiness is a uniquely divine quality. It is absolute purity. In Isaiah's vision of God (Isaiah 6), the seraphim did not cry out, "Eternal, Eternal, Eternal" or "Wise, Wise, Wise" or even "Love, Love, Love" but "Holy, Holy, Holy."

But God requires us to be holy.

"I appeal to you therefore, brothers, by the mercies of God, to present your bodies as a living sacrifice, holy and acceptable to God, which is your spiritual worship." (Romans 12:1, ESV)

"but as he who called you is holy, you also be holy in all your conduct, since it is written, "You shall be holy, for I am holy."" (1 Peter 1:15–16, ESV)

Holiness is an essential quality for a godly home. If you are going to win the battle for holiness, you are going to have to win the battle in the most basic unit of society — the home.

To maintain holiness in our homes, our homes must have a *direction* —"train up a child in the way he should go" (Proverbs 22:6). Maintaining holiness will require *discipline*—"For the gate is narrow and the way is hard that leads to life, and those who find it are few" (Matthew 7:14, ESV). Holiness in the home will bring about proper *devotion*—"Hear, O Israel: The Lord our God, the Lord is one. You shall love the Lord your God with all your heart and with all your soul and with all your might. And these words that I command you today shall be on your heart. You shall teach them diligently to your children…" (Deuteronomy 6:4–7, ESV).

Today, I will... *"pursue holiness" (Hebrews 12:14).*

Anchors

Today's Scripture: Hebrews 6:19

Will your anchor hold in the storms of life,
when the clouds unfold their wings of strife?
When the strong tides lift, and the cables strain,
will your anchor drift, or firm remain?

We have an anchor that keeps the soul
steadfast and sure while the billows roll;
fastened to the Rock which cannot move,
grounded firm and deep in the Savior's love!
~ Priscilla Owens

In our world today, there is an all-out assault on the family. The divorce rate has skyrocketed. Latch key kids number into the millions. Conflicting and confusing messages come from every media source (television, movies, social media, etc.). When your family is being assailed from all sides, you need something to which you can cling. Whether it is a cleat at the dock, a mooring in the marina, or an anchor in open waters, you need something to steady the boat.

"We have this as a sure and steadfast anchor of the soul,
a hope that enters into the inner place behind the curtain,"
(Hebrews 6:19, ESV)

The late Mid McKnight identifies our homes as "Vestibules of Heaven." A home anchored in Jesus, our forerunner into heaven, will always hold in difficult waters. When the disciples were troubled in the middle of the Sea of Galilee, Jesus came to them walking on the water. By walking on water, Jesus showed His disciples that what appeared to be over their heads was already under His feet.

There is nothing—I repeat, NOTHING—that will come upon our homes that Jesus cannot handle. We must develop a pure hearted devotion to Him within our homes.

Today, I will...*turn to Jesus when things get confusing and difficult. I will hold on to the one anchor that will hold no matter what.*

WEEK 28

Beyond Children

JOHN MOORE

The Newfound Self

Today's Scripture: 1 Corinthians 6:17; Galatians 3:27

After children grow up and leave the home, it can cause a parent to go in search of a newfound identity. A life given to caregiving and childrearing can create an identity crisis for parents who have failed to see who they should be in the eyes of God. Some begin defining themselves by the way they look, or in the materials things they have acquired. We should never deny that "physical training is of some value" (1 Tim. 4:8, NIV), for we believe that our bodies are temples of the Holy Spirit (1 Co. 6:19–20). Paul disciplined his own body and kept it under control (1 Cor. 9:27), so there is a place in our Christian lives for proper care of our bodies. But, the desire to satisfy the void in our life by bodily exercise or through a newfound hobby can be become problematic. In our desire to care for our body as the temple of God, we might be tempted to think more highly of ourselves than we ought to think (Rom. 12:3). A preoccupation with diets and wealth can become a source of sinful pride.

Personal identity, worth, and true happiness must always be found in Christ. As much as we might love our children, our identity should always be defined through Jesus. Parents have been given a great gift (Ps. 127:3), but there is more to life than simply being a parent. As a Christian, we should desire to become absorbed in holy things and to clothe ourselves with Christ (1 Cor. 6:17; Gal. 3:27). Becoming like Jesus in all that we do and say should be our aim (Phil 2:5; 1 Peter 2:21). However, the blessing in this quest is as follows: Whoever will lose his life for Christ and the gospel will also find his life (Matt. 16:25). When one is baptized into Christ, new life occurs, and the old life is buried with Christ in baptism. The peace and security left behind because of sin are regained in the newfound life which Jesus gives.

Today, I will...rejoice in my life found in Jesus. He is my life (Col. 3:2-4).

Continue Your Influence

Today's Scripture: Matthew 5:16

Whether we like it or not, everyone has influence. From the time of our birth to the day of our death, we will in some way influence others. When a new baby comes into the family, he or she will influence the routine and habits of the home. Sleeping habits and daily chores will be one of the many habits a baby changes in our lives, but parents will exert the greatest influence of all. That influence, however, doesn't have to stop when children leave the safety and security of the nest. Our influence as parents continues well beyond the rearing of small children.

Let none of us be guilty of thinking that what we do and say goes unnoticed by our adult children. The apostle Paul revealed that "none of us lives to himself, and no one dies to himself" (Rom. 14:7). Children will continue to watch and observe our behavior, and in some cases we will have an even greater influence over them as adults. Sometimes our finest hour of influence can occur when our children become adults. Because our children don't reach their full developmental stage until they are between 18 and 21, they are often better equipped as adults to process the things we have been trying to teach them for years. Mark Twain allegedly (though this is largely unconfirmed) said of his father: "When I was a boy of fourteen, my father was so ignorant I could hardly stand to have the old man around. But when I got to be twenty-one, I was astonished at how much he had learned in seven years."

It is certainly true that our children will begin to think more carefully later in life about what we say. Our example then, of a Christ-like spirit, full of mercy and grace, will go a long way in helping our children grow closer to God. Jesus said we are "the light of the world" (Matt. 5:16), and that world most certainly includes our adult children.

Today, I will...be even more proactive in influencing my children, whether young or old, to love God.

WEDNESDAY

Prepare Yourselves for the Storm

Today's Scripture: James 4:13-14a

For my wife and I, 2020 brought the "perfect storm." Within the space of nine months, we faced several trials. We managed the stress of safely bringing home a group of forty-six travelers from Israel as Covid shut the world down. We fretted over the forced cancellation of a second trip and worried about attempting to protect those passengers' financial investments. We saw friends of ours pass away. We were by my father's side when he lost his battle to cancer in May, and then a dear friend and mentor passed away in September. In October, my mother sustained a massive stroke, and after several difficult days of struggle, she too left this life. Then, during Bible class one Sunday morning in November, I suffered a sudden cardiac event. Friends performed CPR and shocked me with an automated external defibrillator, and then it took EMS and doctors more than an hour to get a sustainable pulse. Two weeks in intensive care, the implant of an automated internal cardioverter defibrillator, and the use of antiarrhythmic medications have helped to produce for me and my wife a different way of seeing life. What we had thought might be the next beautiful season of our lives—"doing our own thing"—after raising our wonderful sons, turned into one of our greatest challenges.

Life can often catch us off-guard, and the best laid plans can sometimes end in trial or tragedy if we aren't prepared for them. Let none of us say that "today or tomorrow we will go into such and such a town and spend a year there, and trade and make a profit," for we simply do not know what life after family will bring (James 4:13-14a). Instead, let us say, "If the Lord wills we will live and do this or that" (James 15). Remember as well that you do not have to fear the storm, "though the earth be removed and cast into the depth of the sea (Psalm 46:1-3). Always remember, "If God is for us, who can be against us?" (Romans 8:31).

Today, I will...live in faith and prepare for the storm; for it will surely come.

God Is Faithful

Today's Scripture: Psalm 33:4

During the Greco-Roman period, an Egyptian child was thought of as having been approved or faithful when he had fulfilled his pious duties to his parents (Kittel 2:256). The idea of being faithful and approved was also used in the banking system of the ancient world. When coins were made, metal was heated and poured into molds and then allowed to cool. After the cooling process, the outer, uneven edges of the coin were shaved smooth. Some artisans, though, would shave extra amounts from their coins in order to keep back part of the precious metals for themselves. In contrast, those who placed only fully weighted money into circulation were known as genuine men of integrity and were considered trustworthy and faithful to the government.

As God's children, and as "empty nesters," we should always think of God as faithful. He will help us through the seasons of our lives. He, like a husband or reliable artisan, has been proven trustworthy and loyal. He takes care of His bride, the church, and sees to our needs. Psalm 33:4 says, "The Word of the Lord is upright, and all His work is done in faithfulness." Consider also these words, "He will cover you with His pinions, and under His wings you may seek refuge; His faithfulness is a shield and bulwark" (Ps. 91:4). The apostle Paul said, The Lord is faithful, who will establish you and guard you from the evil one" (2 Thess. 3:3). Moses commanded, "Therefore know that the Lord your God, He is God, the faithful God who keeps covenant and mercy for a thousand generations with those who love Him and keep His commandments" (Deut. 7:9). Many, many other passages make similar points that God is faithful to forgive, to help us during temptation, and that in faithfulness, His compassions fail not (1 John 1:9; 1 Cor. 10:13; Ps. 119:90; Heb. 10:23; Lam. 3:22-23).

Today, I will...*praise God for His faithfulness, and take comfort in knowing I am His.*

Digging Deeper

Today's Scripture: Hebrews 6:1

I love my children and have always been concerned about their physical well-being, no matter their age. Now that they are adults and have lives of their own apart from our care, we aren't as apprehensive about their safety nor their physical development. Now that they are grown, they are able to care for themselves. They are physically and emotionally mature, able to identify dangerous situations and can likewise tackle complex problems. We communicate as adults. Our conversations are deeper and involve discussions about higher and loftier things. We often talk as friends, and there are many things that I am now learning from them.

As a parent there is no greater joy than to know that your children walk in the truth (2 John 4) and especially to observe this as they grow older. But, this deeper level of interaction will not occur by accident. You as a parent must be intentional to help them develop and grow, and YOU must grow and develop as well. Spirituality demands maturity: maturity which considers both the deeper, more complex things about God and His nature, along with the demonstration of His virtues in our lives. Spiritual infancy is acceptable, but only for a while. Without being haughty, prideful, or arrogant, there is a time when we must "leave the elementary doctrine of Christ, and go on to maturity" (Heb. 6:1).

There are individuals who have been Christians for years, who by now should be teachers, but they are still only able to digest the milk of the word (Heb. 5:12-14). To be sure, the milk of the word will always be needed to nourish, but a mere elementary understanding of the gospel should never be the end target for Christian growth and development. As parents we must make certain that our lives are governed by the precepts of God and that we are seeking to feast upon the meat of the word, with a view of scripture that leads us to weightier matters (Matt. 23:23).

Today, I will...*be intentional about leading my family into spiritually deep conversations.*

WEEK 29

Single and Church Family

JON PODEIN

I'm Single, Not Broken!

Today's Scripture: Ephesians 5:15-16; Psalm 34:5

On the 14th of every February, we celebrate what is considered one of the most polarizing holidays on our calendar. Valentine's Day has become a commercialized day that is an exciting time to celebrate love between individuals. However, while many of our friends fill their social media accounts with pictures of dates, chocolates, flowers, love notes, and gifts, to the single person, it can become a time of shame, regret, and confusion. If you are a single individual reading this, there has likely been a good-intentioned brother or sister in Christ that has enthusiastically encouraged you to enjoy your season of "dating Jesus" while waiting for the "one" for you. After all, "it is *not* good for man to be alone," right? Thus, unintentionally leading the one that is single to feel and perhaps ask the question, "What is wrong with me?"

If you are single, let me explain what is wrong with you... absolutely nothing!! I understand that in our culture, especially within the church, there is a relentless drive to elevate marriage as a more "holy" or desirable position than singleness. However, that does not mean that a single person is any less valuable to God or more ineffective in their service to Him. You and I, regardless of our marital status, are on a path that our faith takes us along and it is our trust in that journey that allows doors of opportunity to open in our walk with the Lord. In fact, singleness can offer a "freedom of time" that allow for more moments to grow deeper in our faith and walk with God while serving others. Perhaps Paul had his singleness in mind when he reminded the Ephesians to "make the best use" of their time (Eph. 5:16). Singleness isn't a curse or a sign of brokenness! Rather it is season to take advantage of the opportunities that God places before us.

Instead of viewing singleness as a burden or something to be ashamed of because of someone's marital status, let's remember what David said in Psalm 34:5, "Those who look to him are radiant, and their faces shall never be ashamed." As we look to God, we can place our confidence in Him and be assured that He knows what is best for us within His time.

Today, I will...*embrace my singleness as an opportunity to grow closer to the Lord and to do His will during this season of my life!*

TUESDAY

What Does It Mean to Be Single?

Today's Scripture: Joshua 3:5; 1 Corinthians 7:32-34

Just before the Israelites were about to cross the Jordan river, Joshua told the people to "Consecrate yourselves, for tomorrow the Lord will do wonders among you" (Joshua 3:5). Every one of us have been called to consecrate ourselves to God. To put it simply, to consecrate means to set apart for a particular reason. We can consecrate anything by setting it aside to be used only in particular circumstances and we have been called as believers to set our lives apart to be used by God. So, what does all of this have to do with being single? Everything!

First, we must realize that being single does not mean being able to be "footloose and free." Neither does it mean to be one who is searching for a mate just looking to get married. In fact, being single means that you are a complete person, separate and distinct, with the ability to function alone. In other words, you are a single individual that is distinctly and uniquely one. This means you can function alone, stand alone, think alone, choose alone, go through alone, and ultimately, know God alone.

To be single has more to do with our individual relationship to God, than it does with our marital state. Paul told the single members of the Corinth church that they should be "anxious about the things of the Lord" (1 Corinthians 7:32). For centuries, marriage has been lifted up as the state of condition that every man and woman should aspire towards, and anyone who does not marry, has somehow failed to attain the utmost in life. However, the first responsibility of every person is to mature himself in Jesus Christ. Everyone must develop a love for God and the things for God on a single basis whether he is married or not. If we can't spend alone time with God, we won't be able to spend alone time with an individual.

As a single person, you have opportunities before you that are unbelievable. Being single requires a different perspective. It is not your preparation time to get married one day. Being single is your time of perfecting who you are as a person chosen by God to do great things. It's your time to pursue knowing who God is and knowing the things of God.

Today, I will...*consecrate myself to the Lord and to dedicate my life to Him, whether single or married.*

Help! I Don't Want to Be Single!

Today's Scripture: Philippians 4:6-7; 2 Corinthians 13:5; Ecclesiastes 2:26

One of the main reasons relationships fail is because most people tend to rush to get together with someone without ever taking the time needed to get to know one another well first. If you happen to ask one of them why did they rush into forming a serious relationship or get married with their partner, you'll likely get the same answer: "I just didn't want to be single anymore." The problem with saying, "I don't want to be single" is that it equals saying, "I don't want to find a good partner" However, wrapped up in this phrase are three sentiments that can fit every Christian, but especially the single Christian.

First, when you're in a hurry, you make bad choices! Have you ever gone into a clothing store or a bookshop when you were in a hurry? I already know the answer …you haven't. Because, to buy something as simple as a pair of jeans, you need to look at your choices, try them on, and then decide if you're going to take them home. So, if you need to take some time to pick a piece of clothing, imagine how much time you need to pick the right partner. When we rush, we become anxious, and Paul encourages us not to "be anxious about anything" (Phil. 4:6) but rather we are to pray. Not only does prayer align our heart and motives with God's, but it also helps us to slow down and think through decisions with more clarity and wisdom.

Second, if you don't feel comfortable with yourself, you won't feel comfortable in a relationship! Usually, the reason people desperately need a partner to be happy is because they have a problematic relationship with themselves. Being single often means you'll have to spend a lot of time alone. Therefore, time alone equals time to think, and time to think equals self-reflection. And self-reflection means that you might learn some things about yourself that you're not going to like. So, instead of facing your flaws, regrets, and fears, you prefer to find a partner who will occupy your mind and provide you with confidence and reassurance. How many times does Paul pleads with us to "examine ourselves" (2 Cor. 13:5)? It is this self-reflection that allows each of us the opportunity to dig down and truly address challenges that we may have within our personal lives.

Finally, don't count on a spouse to make you happy! The problem with saying, "I don't want to be single anymore," most of us mean, "I don't want to be sad anymore." We count too much on other people to make us happy and we think getting into a relationship will solve all our problems and will make us finally feel better about ourselves. But that's not at all how things work. You can be in a relationship with a kind, gentle, giving partner, and still feel unhappy. On the other hand, you can be single and feel cheerful and fulfilled. Solomon wrote, "For to the one who pleases him God has given wisdom and knowledge and joy" or happiness (Ecc 2:26). In reality, true happiness can come only from within and with our relationship with the Lord.

At the end of the day, it's perfectly natural to want to be in a relationship. After all, love makes the world go round, right? What's not okay, however, is to count on a relationship to make you happy. That comes from God and His love toward us!

Today, I will... *allow myself to self-reflect to bring about needed changes in my life and I will strive to find my happiness in the Lord and not lay that responsibility on another person.*

Being Single in the Church...Don't Forget About Me!

Today's Scripture: 1 Corinthians 12:12-26

When I was asked to write for this series about singleness, the first thought that came to my mind was to ask myself, "How I could write something on this topic that could be beneficial for fellow Christians who are married to understand what it is like to be a single Christian in today's church?" It does not take a sociology degree to realize that young adults are choosing to delay getting married, in some instances well into their 30's. In addition, with the divorce rate in the United States still hovering around 50% as well as individuals that have had their spouse pass from this life, many have also joined the single community. And, they are in our church buildings every worship service and Bible study.

Would it surprise you that in a 2019 survey that over 45% of Christian singles feel devalued, like an outcast, or in a lesser life stage at church because they are single? Or that a staggering 94% of single Christians report that their local congregations don't address their needs as single people or issues of singleness and don't understand them? I guess that shouldn't surprise us too much since so much emphasis in church life is placed on married couples with children, the family unit. Think about how our Bible classes are structured and titled: Young or Middle Marrieds. Even many congregational mottos that I have seen are "family focused." Honestly, I have probably preached 1 sermon on singleness (sadly, usually at retreats for singles) for every 50 that focused on married or family life and relationships. And the reality is these are all things that need our attention and focus.

I am reminded of Paul's description of the church as a body in 1 Corinthians 12 and how, like our bodies, it is made up of various members that have their very own unique function that allows it to run efficiently. We each have our role in the church regardless of if we are single or married, whether we have children or not. It is interesting in verse 21, Paul makes the observation that the eye cannot say to the hand or the head to the feet that "I have no need of you!" I know that is an idea that would be so far from our minds within the church to say out loud, but there are times we can make certain segments of our local bodies feel this way by our actions and structures. Whether it is a single young professional, or a single parent that recently went through a divorce, or a single widow or widower coming to worship alone for the first time in years, or the happily married couple with their children... we each are part of the body of Christ, each with a special role in God's Kingdom!

Today, I will... *will strive to remember that every member of my local congregation is valuable and will reach out to remind them just how important they are to God and the church.*

Playing Your Part as a Single In The Church

Today's Scripture: 1 Corinthians 7:7-8

If you ever go into a bookstore, and you look for books on living life, you find all kinds of books on being a husband or wife, on how to raise your children, on parenting in a godly way, and so forth. But you rarely find any books on living life well as a single. I think that happens because in our society we place a high value on the institution of marriage, but in doing so, we relegate single people to the "back of the bus" and leave them wondering what role they have in the church. Now granted, often there are more families in a local congregation than singles, but that doesn't mean that we exclude them from fellowship. However, even if unintentionally, that is often what happens. For the single person, it becomes hard to live that way for long without questions of "Have you met anyone yet?" or "When are you going to think about getting married?"

In 1 Corinthians 7:7, Paul equates singleness to that of a "gift" and if I am honest with you, I have often jokingly asked, "Is this a gift that I can give back?" After all, what good is being single anyway? I believe that Paul is saying that if you are single, consider some of the advantages of remaining that way. However, that challenge is that whatever situation we find ourselves, we too often focus on the negative aspects of it. Married people do it and sometimes say, "Oh to be single and free from the responsibilities." Singles do it and say, "Oh to be married and find that completeness that God wants to give through a spouse." We need to think about the advantages of whichever situation we find ourselves. And if you are single, there are some advantages.

Singles get to use their gifts to serve others more. According to 1 Peter 4:10, by serving others we serve the Lord, and this is why God has given us all that we have. He gives us our talents and abilities to serve others. He also gives us time to serve, and we need to be wise stewards of our gifts and our time because those who have less time in some areas may have more time in other areas to serve. And truthfully, service can take on many forms and include various interactions for the single individual than for those who are married and will never be able to pursue.

Finally, as the church, we need to be ok with this too!! We need to help those that are single to continue to be incorporated into the life of the church. If you are a married member within your congregation, invite a single person you know over for dinner. Integrate them into your activities, and work at helping singles feel a part of the body in the church.

Today, I will...use my time, gifts, and abilities to serve God in ways that others may not be able to serve.

WEEK 30

Staying Together in Difficult Times

MARCUS McKEE

Don't Be Surprised

Today's Scripture: 1 Peter 4:12

Remember vinyl records? Those wonderful thin black discs? Each record had an "A" side and a "B" side. The "A" side had the hit song and the "B" side some lesser-known song that wasn't played very often, if at all. Isn't that how life is—a record playing the songs of a person's life with an "A" side and "B" side? Most of the time we only hear the "A" side of someone's life song (or 'see' it on social media). It's usually an amazing hit! It's about an amazing family, the world's best spouse, the most beautiful, extremely intelligent, and talented children. It's a song that tells about a life so magical everyone hears Mickey Mouse singing "It's a Small World" in the background. However, everyone's life has a "B" side – the song about relationship difficulties, financial struggles, depression, health issues, and messy family dynamics. Often the song is so bad that it takes all our strength to listen to the end.

When difficult, even devastating, times happen, it can take all we have to just tie a knot on the end of our rope to hang on! It is during those times that our perspective can make a profound difference with how it affects our family. Peter wrote in 1 Peter 4:12 to not be surprised when the storms of life come our way. Realizing that life happens to everyone, we can go from asking God, "Why me?" to, "Give me strength and insight to endure and glorify you, Oh Lord." When we have the right perspective, we are able to resist a self-defeating attitude that can easily creep upon us. The right perspective helps us take actions and formulate plans to help our family stay strong while our "B" side song is playing.

Today, I will...*instead of asking "why me," I will ask God to grant me insight and strength to endure when the "B" side songs of our family life are being played.*

Be Strong and Courageous

Today's Scripture: Joshua 1:9

When Joshua was assuming leadership of Israel from Moses, it had to have been one of the toughest challenges of his life. Joshua was Moses' assistance for 40 years, but now he was going to be "the man"—talk about a stressful time! Think about this: He was tasked with leading God's chosen people, which was no easy task, even for Moses! He was taking over for one of, if not the greatest leader in history, a man who was a big deal to God (Numbers 12:1-9). Joshua was going to lead people who, on their best days, had shown themselves to be difficult to please and who could turn on a leader quickly. This was a monumental task! God told him he would be leading them into the promised land and told him to be strong and courageous. Joshua didn't go hide by the baggage; he faced this challenge head on and stepped up to lead!

Research by psychologists shows that when an individual faces his issues head on, he will develop courage and other attributes that enable him to effectively deal with those issues. When that "B" side song is being played, we can be tempted to not deal with the issue or issues which only creates more problems and is especially damaging to our families. The LORD told Joshua that He would be with him just as He was with Moses, and He has promised us that He will never desert us (Hebrews 13:5). When those tough times come, we can handle them because our God gives us strength and a spirit of "power and love and discipline" (2 Timothy 1:7). It is very important that our family sees us handling life's challenges with the strength that comes from God so they can have confidence that we will survive those challenges!

Today, I will...ask God to help me face my challenges head on with the strength and courage that only He provides!

Navigation Matters

Today's Scripture: Psalm 119:105

One of the most inspiring stories of survival is that of Sir Ernest Shackleton and the *Endurance*. After their ship became stuck in pack ice in the Weddell Sea, Shackleton and his crew survived for over 2 years in some of the harshest conditions on the planet. Their story is a great example of turning a "B" side song of life into a hit through patience, tenacity, and determination. Amazingly, they survived numerous challenges including a harrowing 720-mile boat trip on the open ocean from Elephant Island to a whaling station on South Georgia Island. Shackleton took 4 men with him to traverse some of the most inhospitable seas in the ocean in a small 20-foot boat. They were able to make it to their destination due to the excellent navigation skills of Frank Worsley. Without his ability to navigate correctly, they would have never made it to South Georgia Island and would not have rescued all the men.

Being able to navigate is a critical skill necessary for helping our families survive the storms of life, and our God has provided us with the tools we need to do just that. When Joshua took over for Moses, God instructed him to meditate on His Word day and night and to not turn from the right or the left (Joshua 1:8). David over and over again wrote about the importance of knowing God's Word in order to survive the trials of life. God gave us a handbook for life, but it doesn't do us any good if we never use it or open it up. If Frank Worsley had never learned to navigate the seas by the stars and 'dead-reckoning,' then 27 men would have perished. When we learn how to use God's Word, then we will be able to navigate the storms of life and get our families to safety!

Today, I will..._look to God's Word to be the lamp for my feet and the light for my path._

A Job for Everyone

Today's Scripture: Ecclesiastes 4:9-12

When things started to become bleak for the crew of the *Endurance*, their leader, Sir Ernest Shackleton, kept them busy with day-to-day tasks to ensure everyone contributed to his survival. To get our families through life's "B" side challenges, we must involve them and let them contribute! When life's toughest challenges come, we are better equipped to survive as a family versus a single member of the family. Every person on the crew of the Endurance had a role and a job which kept him busy and helped him to feel valued and needed.

During the "B" side times, family members especially younger ones, can feel left out and unsure of what is happening which can cause anxiety. While there will be differences in the type and amount of information provided to a family member, each one can be given a job even if it is small and seems inconsequential. Ever seen a 3-year-old "help" her mom? She is proud and prancing around like a rooster because she is doing something to contribute—she is a "big-girl." She may even tell you about what all they did and how big of a part she played! Think about the difference this type of attitude would make for each family member when going through difficulties. When we have a role and job to fill, we are in the loop and active which keeps us focused on solutions and not problems. We feel valued when we can contribute to the family. A 3-strand cord is not easily torn apart, but we must weave all those strands together for their strength.

Today, I will... *ask God to open my eyes to ways I can involve each family so they can contribute and feel valued.*

Focus On the Eternal

Today's Scripture: 2 Corinthians 4:16-18

After surviving for almost 2 years in the frozen wilderness of Antarctica and then barely making it to South Georgia Island, Sir Ernest Shackleton and his men still had to traverse over 32 miles of dangerous ice wilderness with glaciers and mountains. It could have been easy for them to give up, but Shackleton and Frank Worsley were not men to give up until they had spent every breath in their lungs. Shackleton, Worsley, and Crean trekked 36 hours without rest until they at last made it to the whaling station at Stormness. Sometimes, it takes that type of "don't ever give up" spirit to carry us through a "B" song of life with our families intact. The question is, "How do we keep going when things seem to keep knocking us down and things for our families seem hopeless?"

In 2 Corinthians 4:16-18, the Apostle Paul explains how he doesn't lose heart when he is being afflicted in every way. He says he is being renewed day by day because he isn't focused on the situation—the temporal things—but on the eternal things! In multiple letters, Paul describes the terrible persecutions he was experiencing to provide his readers with hope! Throughout those 2 years Ernest Shackleton didn't allow set back after set back cause him to take his focus off of the goal: getting his men home. His attitude bred confidence and hope in his men which ultimately led to everyone being rescued. Similarly, Paul's ability to survive his experiences provided hope for his readers to endure their situations. When we don't give up during difficult times, we will develop endurance and perseverance (James 1:2-4), and our ability to keep going will inspire hope in our families and enable us to survive our "B" songs of life.

Today, I will...*ask God to help me focus on the external things so that I don't give up!*

WEEK 31

Patience in The Family

DAVID MORRIS

MONDAY

Rethinking Patience

Today's Scripture: Galatians 5:2223

"Patience is a virtue." Or so we are told. Yet everything in our society screams otherwise. We have fast food, fast drivers, and fast schedules. Our phones train us to have short attention spans and heighten our anxieties. We seem to live in a culture that promotes impatience.

Considering our fast-paced lifestyles, why is patience thought of as a virtue? Why isn't telling others to hurry along and get out of our way the real virtue?

Well, could it be that each of us realizes there are moments when we need others to be patient with us? When others show patience toward us, even if it is just the simple act of letting us merge into a line of traffic, we recognize this as an act of kindness.

In the same way, Paul recognizes patience as an act of kindness that grows out of something great. In Galatians 5:22-23, Paul writes that "the fruit of the Spirit is love" and includes "patience." Interestingly, the word "fruit" is singular. Some scholars believe the fruit of the Spirit is therefore the first thing listed, "love," and that love can be described in eight different ways which includes "patience."

Seen in this light, patience is an outgrowth of our love toward others. This is an important way to rethink patience. It is intimidating to think of trying to be more patient in our fast-paced world. But if we begin to see patience as a concrete way to demonstrate love, we will begin to see how being more patient is possible.

Too often we allow our stress to boil over and burn our relationships with our spouse and children. But if we begin to see patience as a tangible practice that shows love toward them, it becomes an intentional act that allows us to demonstrate how much we really treasure them.

Today, I will...begin to think of patience as an expression of love toward my family. I will pray that God will give me a mindset to lovingly practice patience in the home.

Defining Patience

Today's Scripture: Exodus 34:6

If we practice patience as an expression of love toward our family, it will be helpful to spend some time meditating on the real meaning of patience. In defining patience, let's look to Scripture.

One of the most important texts in the Old Testament is Exodus 34. Here, Moses encounters Yahweh. The Lord descended in the cloud and proclaimed His character to Moses this way: "The LORD, the LORD, a God merciful and gracious, slow to anger, and abounding in steadfast love and faithfulness" (Exodus 34:6). One of the key ways God describes Himself is "slow to anger." This Hebrew phrase is 'erek 'appayim and could be translated "long nosed." This means that it takes a long time for God's "nostrils to flare" and become angered. Did your parent ever call out to you using your first, middle, and last name? You knew that they had flared nostrils, and their patience had run out.

This phrase, "slow to anger," is repeated often and usually describes God's character. It is vital for us to see that Old Testament writers defined patience in terms of the very nature and character of God. Since God is patient, He does not treat us in the way that we deserve. He is patient toward His children.

In the New Testament we see the same theme. Peter wrote, "The Lord is not slow to fulfill his promise as some count slowness, but is patient toward you, not wishing that any should perish, but that all should reach repentance" (2 Peter 3:9). Paul called God the "God of patience" (Romans 15:5). He also noted that Christ displayed "His perfect patience" (1 Timothy 1:16) in saving him.

God's desire and ultimate goal for His people is that we would see His patience, His "longsuffering" (KJV), His "slow to anger" character, and allow that character to become the inspiration for our own lives.

Today, I will...*look to God's own character to define patience. Pray that His patience toward me would be the example for the patience I show my family.*

WEDNESDAY

Examples of Patience

Today's Scripture: 1 Samuel 1:2-20

So far, we have thought of patience as an expression of love and looked to God's character to define patience. Today, let's meditate on four examples of Godly patience.

Abraham waited for decades for God's promise of a son (Genesis 12:1-9). His example of patience is imperfect. He attempted to force the promise to come true through his own plan (Genesis 16:4), resulting in much heartache. Imagine waiting to become a father, only to see yourself becoming old. But Abraham endured, believing God would fulfill His word.

Jacob loved Rachel. He labored for her hand patiently for seven years, only to be deceived into working seven more (Genesis 29:23-25). But Jacob did what he believed was necessary because he loved her deeply.

Joseph grew up the favored child in a dysfunctional home. His jealous brothers sold him into slavery. But Joseph remained faithful to God and patiently endured many struggles. How many times through those years did he think about their betrayal? But when Joseph, by God's providence, ascended to power in Egypt, he was reunited with his brothers and extended forgiveness to them.

Year after year, Hannah prayed for a child. "She was deeply distressed and prayed to the LORD and wept bitterly" (1 Samuel 1:10). She patiently endured the taunting of a rival and the years of yearning for a child. When God blessed her with a son, she dedicated him to the service of the Lord.

We need to be reminded that God is with us, even when we do not understand our circumstances. Like Abraham, maybe you find yourself advanced in years, waiting patiently for God's help. Like Jacob, maybe you find yourself in a marriage situation that requires much patience and work. Like Joseph, maybe there is family tension that requires a soft word. Like Hannah, maybe you find yourself waiting for a child. Our challenge is, in every circumstance, to wait patiently and trust.

Today, I will...*look to the examples of Scripture and pray that God will grant me the same faithful endurance.*

Developing Patience

Today's Scripture: James 1:2-4

Have you ever been shaving and, as you look in the mirror, see your father looking back at you? As I get older, sometimes I see a resemblance to my dad. Maybe it is the way I walk, or in something that I say. In some way, hopefully good, children are supposed to bear evidence to who their father is. If that is true, then it is our heavenly Father who defines the patience that His children are to show others. Biblical patience is therefore defined as a steadfast, enduring, longsuffering continuance defined and demonstrated by the very character of God Himself.

The question then is, how is this patience developed? The answer is not easy to hear. God's will is that we would be "conformed to the image of his Son" (Romans 8:29), bearing the family likeness of His Son. That conformity and resemblance can only be achieved through patiently enduring suffering and trials.

James writes, "Count it all joy, my brothers, when you meet trials of various kinds, for you know that the testing of your faith produces steadfastness" (James 1:2-3). Our patient God creates patient children developed in the experience of trials. This means we develop the family likeness through experiencing wrongs we cannot make right, bearing injustices that we cannot immediately fix, and difficulties we cannot remove. The bad news is, then, that patience is only developed in the arena of suffering, enduring, and waiting. But the good news is that we can "count it all joy" because, having endured, we become "perfect and complete, lacking in nothing" (James 1:4).

The benefit that we receive from trials is largely dependent upon how we look at them and the way we handle them. One person may respond in such a manner that they are increasingly bitter and angry and disengaged. Another, facing the exact same circumstance, finds that the circumstances point to the reality and presence of God in their lives.

Which will you be?

Today, I will...*strive, through trials, to become more like Christ.*

Displaying Patience

Today's Scripture: Ephesians 4:32

In looking at patience, we have noticed that patience can be an expression of love as we look to God's own patient nature for inspiration. We looked at Biblical examples of those who practiced patience and learned that patience is developed through trials.

It has been said that you are either coming out of a trial in life, enduring a trial right now, or you are heading into a new one. All of us experience suffering. All of us are mistreated. Paul's instruction in the face of this is to "clothe yourselves with compassion, kindness, humility, gentleness and patience" (Colossians 3:12).

There is an old illustration that says we are to be like the weather-beaten sailor. His face is bronzed from the sun and tough as leather. No one reaches that condition by staying on the shore. Most of us would say, I don't want to go out on the sea of life because it's turbulent, so I'll stay in the tranquility of the harbor. But without the experience of the storm, our faith becomes weak and can fade.

The patience developed in the storms of life lead us to be longsuffering toward others. And one of the most obvious ways we display patience is through forgiving offenses. It is not the only way patience is shown, but it is certainly one way.

Do we ever have a reason to extend forgiveness within the setting of the family? Mark Twain famously said when a child becomes a teenager you should put him in a barrel and feed him through a hole in the lid. Family is often the place where we need most to offer forgiveness.

Paul wrote that we are to be "kind to one another, tenderhearted, forgiving one another, as God in Christ forgave you" (Ephesians 4:32). Patience allows us to create peace in the midst of arguments. "A hot-tempered man stirs up strife, but he who is slow to anger quiets contention" (Proverbs 15:18).

Today, I will...*pray that Godly patience will lead me to practice forgiveness and reconciliation.*

WEEK 32

Loving What You Have

KEITH PARKER

Complaining About Buns

Today's Scripture: Philippians 2:14

Have you ever tried to eat a chili dog on a hamburger bun? Don't! But if you try, grab a fork.

We were, at my house, out of hot dog buns, So my wife had the bright idea of serving my chili dog on a hamburger bun. After expressing my disappointment about the bun choice, she said, "Be happy with what you have."

We live in a world that is filled with dissatisfaction. We gripe and complain about everything under the sun. It may be the food that we eat, the clothes we wear, the cars we drive, the houses we live in...or our families.

Complaining (even about food) is not a new thing in any sense of the imagination. It's as old as the Old Testament. Remember the Israelites? The children of Israel came to the Desert of Sin. And, you guessed it, in the Desert of Sin, they sinned. The whole community grumbled against Moses and Aaron, "Would that we had died by the hand of the LORD in the land of Egypt, when we sat by the meat pots and ate bread to the full, for you have brought us out into this wilderness to kill this whole assembly with hunger." I love Moses' response: "Your grumbling is not against us but against the LORD" (Exodus 16:8).

We used to sing the song, "Oh, be careful little tongue what you say." Why? "Because the Father up above is looking down in love. Oh, be careful little tongue what you say." When we gripe and complain, we are complaining against God. What we say is a reflection on the Father above, the giver of every good and perfect gift (James 1:17). Paul put it like this: "Do all things without grumbling or disputing" (Philippians 2:14).

Today, I will..._live without griping and complaining. I will love what I already have...even if it's hot dogs on hamburger buns._

TUESDAY

Where Are the Nine?

Today's Scripture: Luke 17:11-19

Many years ago, Jesus was on his way to Jerusalem. As he came to a certain village, ten men who had leprosy met him. The lepers began to beg, "Jesus, Master, have mercy on us." When Jesus saw them he said, "Go and show yourselves to the priests." As they went, they were cleansed.

Question: Do you remember how many of them were thankful? Think about it. Don't answer too quickly. How many of the lepers were thankful that they had been healed? One? You say, "One"? I don't think so. Oh, I know only one came back and thanked him. He threw himself at Jesus' feet and praised God in a loud voice. But I'm convinced that all ten of them were thankful. There's no way that you could have lived with such an awful disease like leprosy, instantly be healed, without being thankful. All ten of them were thankful, but only one came back to say "thanks." You see, there's a difference in being thankful and in giving thanks.

The Bible teaches both. In Colossians 3:15 Paul said, "And be thankful." Two verses later, Paul wrote, "And whatever you do, in word or deed, do everything in the name of the Lord Jesus, giving thanks to God the Father through Him." Colossians 3:15 says to be thankful. Colossians 3:17 says to give thanks.

What about our families? In Colossians 3 we read about our familes (read verses 18-21). Most of us are thankful for our mates, but when was the last time we expressed our gratitude? Husbands, have you sent your wife flowers or candy to express your thankfulness? Have you hugged your kids and in their presence thanked God for their lives? Children, have you cleaned house for your mom or washed your dad's car just to show him the depth of your love? We're thankful, but how do we give thanks?

Today, I will...*express my gratitude to someone in my family. I will give thanks for my family and what I already have.*

189

Cancer, COVID, Crashes

Today's Scripture: Acts 21:5

Read Acts 21:5. Observe four facts. Let me help you: "When our days there were ended, we departed and went on our journey, and they all, with wives and children, accompanied us until we were outside the city. And kneeling down on the beach, we prayed..." First, notice the people: "They all, with wives and children, accompanied us." Second, notice the place: "outside the city...on the beach." Third, notice the position: "And kneeling down." Fourth, notice the purpose: "We prayed." On a beach close to the city of Tyre, the disciples with their families (wives and children) bowed their bodies (and their hearts) to God in prayer. You've heard it said, "Families that pray together, stay together." Here's a beautiful example of that.

For many months (and even years) I have prayed that the Lord would keep my family from three things. First, I have prayed that he would keep us from cancer. A few weeks ago, we found out that our son has cancer. Second, I have prayed that the Lord would keep us from Covid 19. Even as I write this, my wife is at home struggling with Covid. Third, I have prayed that the Lord would keep us from crashes (serious auto accidents). I leave Thursday of this week to go preach in the state of Ohio. I'm a traveling preacher and I have prayed a lot for safety (Is this the week that God will say "no" to this request?).

I'm convinced that God answers every prayer that we pray. Sometimes He answers, "Yes" (I like this answer). Sometimes He answers, "Wait" (This one is a little bit harder to like). Sometimes He answers, "No" (I don't like this answer). But when God's people pray, great things happen (James 5:16).

You know what I love? I love the fact that God knows best. He cares for me...even when he says, "No."

Today, I will..._gather my family and thank God for all the answered prayers._

THURSDAY
Mom and Dad

Today's Scripture: Proverbs 23:22

The wise man said, "Listen to your father who gave you life, and do not despise your mother when she is old" (Proverbs 23:22).

My wife and I lost both of our dads about nine years ago. They served as elders in the church of Christ. They were good men filled with wisdom. We miss them everyday.

After my father-in-law died, Sandra (my wife) wrote about her dad: "Daddy was a great spiritual influence on his family. He led nightly devotionals with everyone taking turns reading scripture after dinner. The family would gather around the bed on our knees each night before bedtime in prayer. Daddy conducted many home Bible studies, often using the Jules Miller filmstrips. As a result many were converted. He had a passion for mission work. He went to Africa, Argentina, Canada, and coast to coast. He was also involved in a jail ministry. Daddy was a member of the West Huntsville Church of Christ where he served four years as a deacon and as an elder for 19 years." A good man, indeed!

Although our dads are gone, our mothers are still living. My mother just turned 90. My mother-in-law is 92. Although they both have their health challenges, we are grateful that they are still here. My grandmother (my mother's mom) lived to be 105. Who knows? Our moms may still be around for another 10 or 15 years. As was said about Timothy's mom and grandmother (2 Timothy 1:5), our mothers have displayed sincere faith.

Perhaps you've lost a significant someone in your family. Perhaps a grandfather that you respected. Maybe a mom that you loved. Even a brother or sister that you "looked up to." Do yourself a favor. Go to someone in your family who is still living and say the three beautiful words: "I love you." Although you can't communicate with the dead, you can express your love to the living.

Today, I will...*say to someone in my family, "I love you."*

Seeing the Good

Today's Scripture: Luke 15:11-24

Although Jesus never refers to the boy of Luke 15 as "the prodigal son," that's the way that we know him. Luke 15 is mentioned in a sermon or a Bible class, and we say, "Luke 15? Let's see. Oh, yeah, I remember. Luke 15 is the story of the prodigal son." We call him a "prodigal son, a sinful son, a rebellious son."

But, you know something, I can see some good in him. First, the son of Luke 15 didn't blame others. He didn't blame others that he ended up in the pig pen. He didn't blame his mama, his daddy or his older brother. He didn't say, "Mom and dad, you know why I ran away? It's my brother's fault. Get on to him." We often want to shift blame, don't we? We often want to point fingers at somebody else.

Second, the son of Luke 15 didn't beg. He said, "I have a healthy body and a good mind, and I'm able to go to work." Do you remember the kind of work that he did in that far country? He fed hogs. He slopped the pigs. He realized, "If a man doesn't work, neither should he eat." He didn't depend on a government handout.

The point? He's a bad and rebellious kid, but I still see some good in him. And, brethren, isn't that what we ought to be able to see in the lives of others and in the lives of our family members? The good instead of the bad? Paul put it like this in Philippians 4:8: "Finally, brothers, whatever is true, whatever is honorable, whatever is just, whatever is pure, whatever is lovely, whatever is commendable, if there is any excellence, if there is anything worthy of praise, think about these things."

Today, I will..._go to a member of my family and express the positive. I will "brag" on him or her. I will tell the person what I love about him._

WEEK 33

Teaching Our Children to be Kind to Others

DAN HAMMITT

A Loyal Love Manifested in Action

Today's Scripture: Micah 6:8

The prophet Micah gets right to the point of what God requires of His people, "He has told you, O man, what is good; and what does the Lord require of you but to do justice, and to love *kindness*, and to walk humbly with your God" (Micah 6:8).

The principle word used to express kindness in the Old Testament is *chesed*, which means "a loyal love that manifests itself not in emotions but in action." Kindness is a steadfast love that maintains relationships through gracious aid in times of need.

So, how do we teach our children to be kind to others? One way is to raise our children to be aware of others, confident in who God created them to be, and so thankful for their blessings that kindness will naturally flow from who they are, not just something they do. It's that simple, right? Well, not so much.

Our children will one day encounter the same problem we all face, our sinful nature. They will fall short of God's glory and fail to be aware of others, or confident in their own skin, or thankful for their blessings. Because of this, they need someone to teach them how to develop a heartbeat of kindness.

Shaping and nurturing a child's heart to be kind requires an intentional focus on cultivating the spirit of kindness within their core being, not just focusing on outward actions. It's planting the seed of awareness of others and their needs. It's planting the seed of confidence in who they are as God's creation. It's planting the seed of being thankful for the blessings that God bestows upon them. The result will be a heart firmly planted in the rich soil of kindness.

Today, I will...*focus my attention on developing a heart pattern of kindness within my children.*

Do Unto Others

Today's Scripture: Luke 6:27-31

"And as you wish that others would do to you, do so to them" (Luke 6:31). The "Golden Rule," as so many like to call this instruction from Jesus, demonstrates an act of kindness that only comes from our Father in heaven. Treating others, the way we would want to be treated, is so simple. It makes perfect sense. But that doesn't make it easy to follow.

Jesus gives this instruction while talking about loving your enemies. He's telling us that it doesn't matter what someone else does to you. Love them. Be kind to them. Choose kindness every time.

Whenever our children complain about something a friend said or did that upset them or hurt their feelings, we will often tell them that we can't control what others say or do. We can only control our words and actions. So, choose kindness every time.

But what does kindness look like? Well, Jesus seems to be telling us that whatever you would want someone to say or do in a situation, do or say just that. In its correct context, the "Golden Rule" is a concept that is rooted in divine love which bears all things, believes all things, hopes all things, endures all things.

Treating others in the same way that we would like them to treat us is a Christian principle that is rooted in Godly love which is poured into our lives from above—and God's love never, never fails.

Today, I will...*develop a spirit of kindness deep within my heart so that I will easily choose to treat others the way I want to be treated.*

Being a Good Neighbor

Today's Scripture: Luke 10:30-37

Of all the freedoms we experience on this side of eternity, freedom from sin is by far the most valuable. Jesus once said, "Truly, truly, I say to you, everyone who practices sin is a slave to sin. The slave does not remain in the house forever; the Son remains forever. So if the Son sets you free, you will be free indeed" (John 8:34-36). The freedom Jesus offers is freedom from everlasting guilt and shame. To those who trust and obey, Jesus offers freedom to know God, love God, and to serve God.

That is the essence of the amazing story we find in Luke 10. A lawyer asked Jesus this question, "What shall I do to inherit eternal life?" Jesus replied, "What is written in the Law? How do you read it?" The man replied, "You shall love the Lord your God with all your heart and with all you soul and with all your strength and will all your mind, and your neighbor as yourself" (Luke 10:27). Jesus told him he was correct, and that if he did these things, he would have eternal life.

But wanting to justify himself, the lawyer asked, "Who is my neighbor?" Jesus answered him by telling the story of the Good Samaritan. One day a man was walking along the road and was suddenly robbed, beaten, and left for dead. A couple of people passed by and ignored him, but when a Samaritan man came upon him, he stopped and helped him. He had compassion on him.

Whatever his motivation, the Samaritan man chose God's way of kindness along the road that day. He saw this man in need and knew that he had the resources to help him. He chose kindness over fear, busyness, and indifference. He modeled what it means to be a good neighbor.

When our children recognize their blessings and power to help others, they can reach out in kindness and be a good neighbor.

Today, I will..._be a good neighbor and show kindness to those in need._

Kindness Is Best!

Today's Scripture: Proverbs 3:3-6

The Bible is full of promises upon which we can build our lives on. These promises come from God and are for all of us to read and follow. These promises will never change and will never fail. One promise that God gave us is that if we trust in Him in all areas of our lives, He will direct our paths: "In all your ways acknowledge him, and he will make straight your paths" (Proverbs 3:6).

But before God makes this amazing promise, He gives us the key to developing kindness in our hearts: "Let not steadfast love and faithfulness forsake you; bind them around your neck; write them on the tablet of your heart" (Proverbs 3:3). The translation "steadfast love" is actually the principle word used to express kindness in the Old Testament, *chesed.*

When we surrender our lives to God and put on the fruit of kindness, He will not only lead us down the right path but the best path for our lives. He will lead us towards the best outcome in our studies, our friendships, our dating lives, our marriages, our families, our finances, and our hopes and dreams.

Choosing kindness will not always be the easiest or most popular choice for our children, but it is the choice that will lead them to what is right for their lives and what's best for them.

Today, I will...*put on the virtue of kindness and allow God to guide my steps in how I live my life so I can experience the best this side of eternity has to offer.*

Setting Wide Margins

Today's Scripture: 2 Corinthians 8:9

There's an amazing story in the Old Testament that captures the impact kindness can have on one's life – the story of Ruth. Ruth makes the decision to remain with her mother-in-law after the death of her husband and wants to do her part in helping them survive. So, she makes a request of Naomi, "Let me go out into the harvest fields to pick up the stalks of grain left behind by anyone who is *kind* enough to let me do it" (Ruth 2:2).

Naomi agrees and Ruth ends up in the fields of Boaz. Boaz notices Ruth and makes this kind gesture by allowing her to gather grain in places that were traditionally off limits. But then Boaz reaches a whole new level of kindness when he gives this command, "Let her gather grain right among the sheaves without stopping her. And pull out some heads of barley from the bundles and drop them on purpose for her. Let her pick them up, and don't give her a hard time" (Ruth 2:15-16).

Here's what I see in Boaz's kindness: He was willing to set wide margins with his kindness. What areas in our children's lives can we set wide margins for kindness? Here's a few possibilities:
Time – make time for others; don't get so busy that you don't have time for unexpected moments of kindness.
Talents – use your resources (mind and abilities) to benefit others.
Forgiveness – extend forgiveness with wide margins to yourself and others. The Law said three times; Peter suggested seven times; Jesus said seventy times seven.

If you still need motivation, consider Paul's words, "You know the generous grace of our Lord Jesus Christ. Though He was rich, yet for your sakes He became poor, so that by His poverty He could make you rich" (2 Corinthians 8:9). Why set wide margins in our kindness? Because Jesus Christ set wide margins in His kindness and grace for us.

Today, I will...*set wide margins in my kindness.*

WEEK 34

Teaching Our Children About Dating

STEVE BAILEY

Attraction

Today's Scripture: Proverbs 18:22; Proverbs 19:14

A recent online article reminded me of my younger days. The author stated there are five stages of dating. I readily admit that now that I am "older" I did not know the five stages of dating I am about to share. The five stages of dating are attraction, reality, commitment, intimacy and finally, engagement.

Many years ago, I heard a preacher say in a sermon regarding Christian marriage, and it seemed so obvious at the time, "We tend to marry the people we date!" That statement is amazing, isn't it? If we could just teach our children that every person he or she dates, could possibly be a mate, it would weigh heavily on the fact one could eventually marry that person and be committed to them for the rest of their lives. In essence we are saying to our kids, "Don't go out regularly with anyone you could not see yourself married to for the rest of your days."

The first idea of dating for most people is attraction. Sometimes it is personalities that match. Attraction is often the first stage of dating. It happens ever so innocently. A teen meets another at a church function. Or perhaps it happens at a school function such as a football game, or concert. There is that glance or moment at the serving table and smiles and kind words are exchanged. A little small talk takes place; a phone call is made, or cell numbers exchanged, and the possibility of a date now becomes closer to happening.

The dating relationship is one that could go on weeks or even months. Then as the newness of that person wears off, one or the other person may want to see and date other people. Let's face it—it happens. The adage that says, "Love at first sight," may be just "lust" at first sight. That is the time to back off. That is not what Christians do. The world sadly teaches differently. There are boundaries for Christian boys and girls. This dating period is a time of deciding if a boy or girl wants to move ahead in the relationship.

Proverbs 18:22 (ESV) He who finds a wife finds a good thing and obtains favor from the Lord.

Proverbs 19:14 (ESV) House and wealth are inherited from fathers, but a prudent wife is from the Lord.

Today, I will..._not only instruct my children about the seriousness of dating, but I will let them know I am praying for them in the dating relationship._

TUESDAY

Reality

Today's Scripture: Proverbs 27:15; Proverbs 31:10

The second phase of dating is called reality. In this arena, one quickly begins to see the person that is being dated is either just what they are looking for, or they begin to see the other person's fault(s). These faults can vary from a small idiosyncrasy to a major "jump off the page" flaw that screams, "I do not want to be with this person again!"

This realization is really a blessing. Seeing that you are no longer interested in that person is really a blessing in disguise. It is better now to find out than to make a lifelong mistake.

What could some of these glaring flaws be you ask? Thanks for asking. The crowning quality of all is that the person you are dating does or does not share your belief in God, Jesus, and His Church. There must be a firm foundation on which to build. That foundation between a boy and a girl must be built on the commonality of God. Many people have made the mistake of saying, "I will convert him or her." Then later they may find themselves going to worship services alone for 50 years. The time to find out if you have anything in common about God is NOW, not later.

Perhaps inviting your date to worship services, Bible class and teen gatherings is a good place to start. A boy or girl who does not like being around other Christian teens, probably will not enjoy being in worship service with men, women, teens, and babies who love God. Better to find out now than later. Reality is just that. It is getting real with one another. It is the pure truth of who a person really is or if he or she is an imposter. It is better to find out today than twenty years from now.

Proverbs 27:15 (ESV) A continual dripping on a rainy day and a quarrelsome wife are alike.

Proverbs 31:10 (ESV) An excellent wife who can find? She is far more precious than jewels.

Today, I will...*impress upon my children the importance of dating and eventually marrying a Christian. With God's help I will do this.*

Commitment

Today's Scripture: Hebrews 13:4

Today's word in dating is Commitment. Once you get past the attraction and reality stage, next comes the "C" word. It is a ginormous word called commitment. This aspect of dating often means that each person has made it known that they want to date each other exclusively. This in times past has been known as "steady" dating, and I believe it still is called going steady.

During this time the male and the female have grown accustomed to the other's personal flaws and strengths, likes and dislikes. Love has a way of hiding these flaws. It often leads one to overlook a major flaw. Love can keep the other person from seeing the flaws of the other. Either way it is important to know by now if a person dearly loves The Lord, His Church and His People. If this is the case, there is common ground on which to build. If this truth is not recognized by now, perhaps each person will need to "take off the rose-colored glasses" and see the other as they are. One needs to know if it is necessary to stop the relationship knowing that they will either break the heart of their "steady" or they will break the heart of God. It is better to know now, rather than later. I have been told many times in counseling, "I just did not see it" or they said, "I refused to acknowledge the flaw."

The world will tell you that with commitment, you can just live together and see if it works out. That is diametrically opposed to what God wants. Many young people today assume sex outside of marriage is "just sex," and there is nothing to it. That is wrong. The world has cheapened the act of sex and the institution of marriage. Christians are not like pigs...they don't "wallow like pigs" in the lust of sex before marriage.

It is maybe in this phase of dating that some long-range plans could be talked about. The future is coming; perhaps it is good to discuss the future and see where this relationship is going.

Hebrews 13:4 (ESV): "Let marriage be held in honor among all, and let the marriage bed be undefiled, for God will judge the sexually immoral and adulterous."

Today, I will...pray for my children to see clearly what God wants for them in their lives. My prayer will be for God to be the center of their lives.

THURSDAY

Intimacy

Today's Scripture: Genesis 1:27

Intimacy is often a difficult topic to speak about with your son or daughter. The idea of intimacy is, however, a fact. There is no denying that we all want intimacy. The human body craves intimacy. God created the human body to have that want or need. We must recognize our boundaries as Christians.

Intimacy is defined as: the state of being intimate. A close, familiar, and usually affectionate relationship. Webster goes on to say, as if to assume, that all affection will lead to intimate sexual activity such as intercourse. It certainly does not have to come to this, especially in dating…and should not.

Christians know that the sexual act between a man and a woman is reserved only for marriage. It begins with a mother and father teaching their children when they are young that this is the way God wants it to be. They further teach that sex is reserved for marriage and only marriage. Just because Hollywood movie stars, many books and novels describe it as something different, simply does not make it right.

God is all about purity. The greatest gift a man or woman can give to their mate is their virginity on their wedding night. It can be a gift they have been working on and saving for their mate. The wedding night will be a gift that no one else has opened or shared.

The world does not march to the steps of a Christian, but the record of many shows the land covered with the carnage of disappointment, lack of trust, and flashbacks of multiple relationships. It must grieve God as He sees what mankind has done with His marvelous plan and creation.

The scriptures teach that each of us has been made in the image of God either male or female. "In the image of God he created them; male and female he created them" (Genesis 1:27 ESV).

Today, I will…*pray for my children to find the right mate. I will pray that they will keep themselves pure for marriage.*

Engagement

Today's Scripture: Ecclesiastes 4:9-12

Engagement is the final stage of dating. This ought to be the greatest time of the dating experience. Once true love is found and acknowledged, the logical step, if both parties are ready, is to announce that they are engaged to be married.

The date for the wedding can be set, and wise plans are put into action for the ceremony. There is now no doubt that this couple loves each other, sees "eye to eye" on spiritual matters, financial matters, and sexual matters. The couple is ready to "shout it from a mountain top" that they are in love with each other and are ready to make a lifelong commitment to each other.

To say that a lot of decisions must be made, is an understatement. A year-long engagement is perhaps the normal time frame. Some people opt to marry sooner. There are many decisions and choices that must take place in just a short while. Ask God for wisdom during this time.

The culmination of dating leads to marriage. Little girls dream of a big church wedding. Men dream of the ever-lasting love of finding the one for life. This does not happen unless a great deal of effort is used in planning and preparation.

When a couple is engaged, do not be surprised that something is hiding "beneath the surface of d;ating" and raises a few bumps in the road. Many a marriage has been put off or cancelled all together during this time period. But wise dating and being open with each other is the key. Praying, planning, and asking God for guidance will help insure a good marriage.

The perfect marriage is not to be found. But a marriage can be worked into perfection by God if good sound dating is experienced.

Ecclesiastes 4:9-12 (ESV): "Two are better than one, because they have a good reward for their toil. For if they fall, one will lift up his fellow. But woe to him who is alone when he falls and has not another to lift him up! Again, if two lie together, they keep warm, but how can one keep warm alone? And though a man might prevail against one who is alone, two will withstand him—a threefold cord is not quickly broken."

Today, I will...*pray again and again for my precious children to find a Christian mate.*

WEEK 35

Dealing with The Loss of a Child

JEFF JENKINS

The Lord Is My Shepherd

Today's Scripture: Psalm 23:1-4

The sweet singer of Israel understood what it was like to have a child pass away. There is no way we can be certain that when David penned the twenty-third Psalm he was referencing the death of his child. Yet these words are some of the most comforting thoughts ever written to soothe the broken hearts of parents who have lost a child

"Even though I walk through the valley of the shadow of death, I fear no evil, for You are with me; Your rod and Your staff, they comfort me" (Psalm 23:4). Any child of God, who has walked down into death's valley and seen a child pass away, senses the peace from God that passes all understanding (Phil. 4:7). Many who will read these thoughts have been in that dark valley. Some have recently made this journey, while others walked through that dark valley many years ago but still struggle with navigating life.

One of the lessons all of us learn who have traversed this valley or who have attempted to provide counsel for others, is that no two journeys are the same. As well, we will be more helpful to one another, when we realize that what "works" for one person cannot serve as a uniform answer for everyone.

In the meantime, may I share just a few thoughts, some general, some more specific, that have been helpful for me and others. Please understand that I do not by any stretch of the imagination believe I've figured this out. As anyone who has journeyed this path will understand, we continually search for ways to handle the pain of loss. I would sincerely love to hear from others who have endured time in the valley and seen a child pass away and who would be willing to share what has been most helpful for them.

Today, I will...*allow God to shepherd me through the ongoing journey of death.*

We Are Not Alone

Today's Scripture: Deuteronomy 31:6

Remember that you are not alone. One of the great promises in Scripture for all of God's people is that we do not have to walk this life alone. We read repeatedly that the God we serve is "present." You have to love these precious words from the wise King Solomon. "Trust in the Lord with all your heart and do not lean on your own understanding. In all your ways acknowledge Him, and He will make your paths straight" (Pro. 3:5-6).

The promise that God gave to His wandering people is very applicable to those of us who are traveling in uncharted waters. "Be strong and courageous, do not be afraid or in dread of them, for the Lord your God is the One who is going with you. He will not desert you or abandon you" (Deut. 31:6).

In addition to the promises from God that He will not leave us alone, Christians are blessed to be surrounded by an army of God's special people to hold us up in our difficult days. It is beautiful and overwhelming to be strengthened by God's family from around the world. Calls, letters, cards, emails, messages, visits, kind acts from Christians literally around the world will be one of the greatest blessings to the lives of those who lose a child.

My conviction is that when we are enduring what is without a doubt one of the most challenging seasons of life, we will be stronger by surrounding ourselves with people who love us, who care deeply for us, and who we enjoy spending time with from day to day. Included in this group would be our physical family. We would also include our spiritual family, and our closest group of friends who will be our champions, our heroes, during this difficult time.

Today, I will... *thank God that I am not alone.*

We Can't Control Everything

Today's Scripture: Proverbs 3:5-6

Some things are just out of our control. One of the few things I don't enjoy about flying is the feeling of not having control. I'm a typical man. We like to be in control—at work, in our family, of the remote control, of our vehicles, our pets, our family, and even our health. As these words are being typed, I'm in the air returning from visiting some dear friends. Our flight was delayed four times because of weather. We will arrive safely at DFW three hours later than our ETA!

We sat on the tarmac for about an hour. When I texted my family and friends to give them an update, they all said basically the same thing. They said, "Be safe and fly safe." My thought was, "I don't have any control over whether I am safe on this flight. And, if I were the pilot, we certainly wouldn't be flying safe!!"

But then then something comforting happened. The pilot came on the loudspeaker and said, "We are going to take off folks, sit back and relax, don't worry about a thing. We're going to take good care of you!" And my entire feeling about the flight changed immediately.

No one chooses to lose a child or wants a child to pass. I know I didn't. We pray that our children will be safe. We pray that they will be healthy and happy. We do everything that we know to do as far as our part is concerned. But we all know that we don't have power over what can ultimately take place, other than pray and use the best wisdom we can use.. We are not in control. If you trust God, I'm certain that you prayed for your child for months, or years, but they didn't recover. So, what do we do?

Today, I will...remember that God is in ultimate control.*

Recognize the Value of God's Word

Today's Scripture: 2 Corinthians 1:3-5

Someone has calculated more than 7,000 promises in the Bible. Many of these "exceeding great and precious promises" provide great comfort during the most difficult seasons in our lives. When we are hurting, we would do well to study Psalm 119. Each of the twenty-two divisions of this great Psalm remind us again of how valuable God's precious Word is to those of us who are walking through the valley of the shadow of death. The Word of God is written in part to bring us comfort, and when we study it prayerfully, indeed it does just that.

There are several excellent books available that will help us with outstanding practical advice for dealing with grief. However, in my heart I do not believe there is anything that has ever been written that will help us more than the Word of God, produced by our loving Father. "Blessed be the God and (because He is the Father of our Lord Jesus Christ, (who bids all who are heavy-ladened to come to Him), (because He is) the Father of mercies (lovingkindness) and (because He is the) God of all comfort, (because He is the God) (because He uses us to bring comfort to others) who comforts us in all our affliction so that we will be able to comfort those who are in any affliction with the comfort with which we ourselves are comforted by God. For just as the sufferings of Christ are ours in abundance, so also our comfort is abundant through Christ" (2 Corinthians 1:3-5).

Today, I will...*allow God's Precious Word to calm my heart.*

Recall the Importance of Worship

Today's Scripture: 2 Samuel 12:20

Recall the importance of worship. Long before I begin my personal journey through this dark valley, it seemed astounding to me to see how many Christians would turn away from worshiping God when they were encountering pain in their lives. After years of attempting to assist others and enduring various seasons of pain in my own life, that astonishment has only increased.

It is not my intent to be insensitive in any way, but anyone who believes that staying away from the worship of God when he is struggling with life is sadly mistaken. We do not need less of God when we are hurting, we need more of Him.

When the man after God's heart believed that his child had died, he enquired of his servants, "Is the child dead?" When they responded that the boy had died, Samuel records the Kings response. "So, David got up from the ground, washed, anointed himself, and changed his clothes; and he went into the house of the Lord and worshiped" (2 Samuel 12:20). If you have endured the loss of the dearest on earth to you, I would plead with you not to stay away from worship, but rather respond in the way that David did.

Being in God's House with God's people, lifting our hearts to Him in worship has a way of calming the most burdened hearts. My God help us to never lose our desire to worship Him and be surrounded by His Family.

Today, I will...*remember to spend time in God's House with God's people*

WEEK 36

Helping Children To Be an Influence Rather Than Being Influenced

CHRIS McCURLEY

MONDAY

Be a Mirror!

Today's Scripture: Genesis 1:26-28

"Then God said, 'Let us make man in our image, after our likeness. And let them have dominion over the fish of the sea and over the birds of the heavens and over the livestock and over all the earth and over every creeping thing that creeps on the earth.' So God created man in his own image, in the image of God he created him; male and female he created them. And God blessed them. And God said to them, 'Be fruitful and multiply and fill the earth and subdue it, and have dominion over the fish of the sea and over the birds of the heavens and over every living thing that moves on the earth." (Genesis 1:26-28)

God established His authority over the family by His mere creation of it. Why did He create family? We, us, were made in the image of the Almighty God. He created US, male and female, in His image, in the image of the trinity. That's who the "US" is. When God said, "Let US make man in OUR image, He was referring to the Father, the Son, and the Holy Spirit. That's the US. We were made in their image, and our creation defines the purpose of our family. God said, "Let us make man and let us make man like us—male, female, offspring, family—let us make them to look like us." From the very beginning the goal was for man to be a mirror. We were made to be eikons. Eikon is the Greek word for "image," and it involves two main concepts—representation and manifestation. We are to be mirrors. Mirrors that reflect the image of the US who created US. The goal of family is to be a visible portrait of God, and that was the goal from the very beginning.

Today, I will...do my best to reflect the image of my Creator to my children. I will strive to be a proper example for them to follow.

Be a Cage Builder!

Today's Scripture: Psalm 127:1

Psalm 127:1 reads, "Unless the Lord builds the house, those who build it labor in vain."

Every house has a builder. There are a lot of builders, but far fewer craftsmen. A lot of folks can throw up a structure, but the number of people who can construct a solid, well-built, well-designed, flawless home is rather small by comparison. In fact, when it comes to a spiritual house, there's only one true craftsman. Our Lord provides the materials, He provides the plans, and He supplies the power.

All too often, however, there's a sewer line that brings unfiltered filth into our homes, which brings up a question, "What kind of cages have you built in your house?" Is there a cage around your television? The computer? The video game system? Your schedule? Your activities? Building a godly home is going to require us, as parents, to be cage-builders. God's blueprints demand that the home be built according to code, and part of that code includes building cages, marking off boundaries, and building fences, so that Satan doesn't have a direct pipeline into our home. The apostle Paul wrote, "But put on the Lord Jesus Christ, and make no provision for the flesh, to gratify its desires" (Romans 13:14).

When you make provision for something, you supply it. We cannot allow a supply line of immorality into our homes. That doesn't mean that we must throw out the computer, throw out the television, or throw out the video games. It doesn't mean we have to shut ourselves off from the outside world for fear of being tainted. It simply means that we must build a cage around the things that have the potential of supplying our home with unrighteousness. It means that we must lock the door to Satan. It means that our home should function as a fortress of solitude from the world.

Today, I will...build cages and draw boundaries around the things that have the potential to drive a wedge between my family and God.

Be a Shooter!

Today's Scripture: Psalm 127:3-5

An elderly man suffering with Alzheimer's was living in a nursing home. Every Sunday afternoon, his daughter and son-in-law would bring the grandchildren to the courtyard of the facility to meet their grandfather. The longer this ritual continued, the feebler the man got. He grew more and more confused to the point that he couldn't remember names and couldn't find his way back to his room. Still, every Sunday he was there, in the courtyard, waiting to see his precious family. One Sunday his daughter asked, "Daddy, do you know what day it is?" He didn't. She then asked, "Daddy, if you don't know that it's Sunday, then how did you know to meet us out here today?" The man replied, "I just come out here every day and wait for you."

Fathers love their children. As a father myself, I would go to the ends of the earth to make certain that my children's needs were met. Any father worth his salt will pour himself into being the best dad he can be. A good father loves his children and wants what's best for them. A godly father, however, seeks a higher goal. The godly father loves his children so much that he raises them with an eternal mindset so that, one day, his family will enjoy a wonderful reunion in heaven.

Psalm 127:3-5 reads, "Behold, children are a heritage from the Lord, the fruit of the womb a reward. Like arrows in the hand of a warrior are the children of one's youth. Blessed is the man who fills his quiver with them! He shall not be put to shame when he speaks with his enemies in the gate."

Children are like arrows, and what do you do with an arrow? You shoot it. If our children are like arrows, then the best thing we can do is shoot them. We don't actually shoot them. We aim them at the proper target. What's the proper target? Heaven. That's the bull's eye. We should aim them and release them toward the target. We don't get points for getting close; therefore, we've got to make it count.

Today, I will..._cherish my children as the precious gift they are by praying for them and modeling Jesus to them._

THURSDAY

Be a Child Who Makes the Father Proud!

Today's Scripture: Ephesians 6:1-3

Mark Twain once said, "When I was a boy of fourteen, my father was so ignorant I could hardly stand to have the old man around. But when I got to be twenty-one, I was astonished by how much he'd learned in seven years."

By and large, young people are not keen on authority. As a rule, they don't like being told what to do, especially by their parents. They dream of a day when they can live life on their own terms. But God had a plan when He designed the family. He knew that obedience to the heavenly Father begins with obedience to earthly parents. The earthly home prepares us for kingdom living. The home is where it all starts. Notice what Paul writes in Ephesians 6:1-3, "Children, obey your parents in the Lord, for this is right. 'Honor your father and mother' (this is the first commandment with a promise), 'that it may go well with you and that you may live long in the land.'"

Notice that Paul is addressing children in his letter to the Ephesians. When the church received a letter, they would gather to hear it read to them. This means that within this assembly there were children seated next to their parents, listening to this letter being read. What these children heard were three things: (1) Obey, (2) Honor, (3) Prosper.

Paul wasn't laying it all on the parents. Although parents are ultimately responsible for raising their children in the nurture and instruction of the Lord, the child plays a pivotal role in his own upbringing. It's a two-way street, which is why Paul takes the time in his letter to speak directly to the children.

God designed the home. He is the architect, and things function best when every member of the household fulfills their God-given responsibility. Godly parents model this to their children in their faithfulness to the Heavenly Father.

Today, I will...*make it my mission to live out my God-given role within my family and encourage the other members of my household to do the same.*

215

Be a Dripping Faucet!

Today's Scripture: Deuteronomy 6:4-9

"Hear, O Israel: The Lord our God, the Lord is one. You shall love the Lord your God with all your heart and with all your soul and with all your might. And these words that I command you today shall be on your heart. You shall teach them diligently to your children, and shall talk of them when you sit in your house, and when you walk by the way, and when you lie down, and when you rise. You shall bind them as a sign on your hand, and they shall be as frontlets between your eyes. You shall write them on the doorposts of your house and on your gates (Deuteronomy 6:4-9).

In the past, I surveyed Deuteronomy Chapter 6 and surmised that I need to carve out so much time each day to read the Bible with my kids, pray with them, do a devotional, etc. That was the takeaway, or so I thought. But the more I read Deuteronomy 6, the more I see it like a faucet that is dripping rather than one that is being turned on and off.

Moses is speaking to people who bowed down to idols in the past and who will bow down to idols in the future. He's reminding them that the God who chose them is the God they must choose every single day. God also expects faith to be handed down. Parents are responsible for fostering faith in their children. God intends for faith to take the lead in the family. There will always be other tasks to tend to and other duties as assigned, but God is not scheduled, and faith is not a category.

This is a long-haul endeavor. It's a daily dripping. At the time Deuteronomy was written, there weren't copies available to everyone, so memorization was essential. That's why Moses exhorts the people to keep these words on their hearts. It wasn't just about head knowledge. It was about heart action. For the parents to properly teach these things to their children, they had to first write it on their own hearts. The children needed to see that their father and mother served God. They needed to see passion from their parents because we cannot expect more from our children than what they see in us.

Today, I will...take advantage of and even create opportunities to talk to my children about God, Jesus, and what it means to be a faithful Christian.

WEEK 37

Making Your Home a Haven of Happiness

PAUL SHERO

The Phone Is Off the Hook

Today's Scripture: Deuteronomy 24:5

"'When a man is newly married, he shall not go out with the army or be liable for any other public duty. He shall be free at home one year to be happy with his wife whom he has taken'" (Deuteronomy 24:5).

God tells Israel that family is more important than military or business. How would such an idea work today?

When Patsy and I were young and the girls were little, our life was busy. We were overbooked. The church was growing, and I was the preacher. Many times family events got trumped. Then we came up with this idea. Some nights we declared the evening Shero Fun Night. We took the phone off the hook so whoever called would hear a busy signal. That is exactly what we were "busy." Not everyone liked this, but my family did. On that evening we ate our favorite food, played games and were an uninterrupted family. One game the girls really liked was "Little House on the Prairie." We lit oil lamps, turned out the lights and played table games.

Today the phone goes with us. But we could turn it off for a little while. I was told one time that "good" is the biggest enemy of the best. We let a lot of "good" things crowd out the best things. How many times are you one of those people? I'm not saying "Little House" is the answer but setting aside uninterrupted time for those important to you is the answer.

Find it. Carve it out, be ruthless but get it. *Plan it.* Make a plan as what you want to do. *Guard it.* Nothing can take this time. *Protect it.* Stay on track. Don't let the devil creep in—no multitasking here. *Reflect on it.* Ask yourself how the time went and what you could do to make it better.

More thoughts: Time, when it passes, can never be regained and our family is the only thing God gives us that we can take to heaven. Remember the conduct side of your report card. Remember the one that said "using time to best advantage?" How is your conduct grade?

Today, I will...*put family first ahead of work. I will find the time for family only events.*

TUESDAY

Because Our Home Is Holy

Today's Scripture: Hebrews 13:4

"Let marriage be held in honor among all, and let the marriage bed be undefiled, for God will judge the sexually immoral and adulterous" (Hebrews 13:4).

When God takes anything for His personal glory, He sets it apart and sanctifies it for His use. This process is called holy. Since God created marriage, He intends for it to be holy. Jesus used this truth, "But from the beginning of creation, God made them male and female" (Mark 10:6). Why does the fact that the home is holy make it a haven for happiness to be set apart means you belong? This is such good news. Our home belongs to God. My wife belongs to me. I belong to my wife. Our children are not just children they are our children. Their parents are not just some adults in the house! We are their mother and father.

This belonging brings confidence and peace in our lives. It means we are not drifting without a place or purpose. We are a Christian home, holy to God and holy to one another. We are not alone. This brings unspeakable joy to me in this chaotic world. When my home is a holy place to God and to each other, we have confidence. This produces peace. Coming home is a pleasure. Our mind is able to rest and reflect on our day. Having a holy family and home means our home is an honest place. A truth zone if you will. Everywhere you look you see and hear lies. But in your home you find honesty, sincerity and truth. This produces resolve and a clear vision of where you are and where you are going. Because we are a family set apart by God, we are sanctified. This means we are forgiven. Home becomes the place where we begin again.

When your home is filled with forgiveness, truth, peace, love, purpose, and belonging, it also becomes a place of joy. Happiness abounds when you start for home and you smile. When bed time would come, my mother would say, "Let's choose up sides and go to bed." Then she would look at my dad and say, "I choose you."

Today, I will..._choose to make myself set apart for God in my family._

The Dream

Today's Scripture: Ephesians 5:31-33

"'Therefore a man shall leave his father and mother and hold fast to his wife, and the two shall become one flesh.' This mystery is profound, and I am saying that it refers to Christ and the church. However, let each one of you love his wife as himself, and let the wife see that she respects her husband" (Ephesians 5:31-33).

Most of my dreams are nonsense, but every now and then I wake up with a smile.

The best dream I ever had was this: In my dream I am waking up in my bed many years ago. I was a young husband in Oklahoma. Our children were little girls, and Patsy was my young wife. I knew somehow I had been able to go back in time. My beautiful young wife somehow knew she had been sent back as well. No one else not even our children knew we had been sent back. What a wonderful day we had. We ate breakfast together and played with our girls. We were afraid to leave the house for fear that dream would end. We called my mother and father and had a nice talk. I told them how much I loved them. We read to the girls and even went fishing. We played games and talked and laughed. Patsy cooked our favorite foods. In those days they were all inexpensive but we ate like kings. After the girls went to sleep, we stayed awake since we knew this day would end when we fell asleep. We talked laughed, loved and promised we would do better. We even said if we were still here tomorrow we need to buy some Walmart stock.

I think of that dream often. On that day, in that dream I stayed on the important stuff. Back here on planet earth, I don't always concentrate as I should. My mind stays full of less important matters, and for my negligence I am poorer. You know, I could choose to have a perfect day any day.

Today, I will... *do my best to make today a day to dream about.*

THURSDAY
When Trouble Comes

Today's Scripture: Proverbs 15:1, 4, 18; Galatians 6:1

If two or more people get together it will not be long before you have a disagreement. The question is: "Will the disagreement be resolved in a good way?" It is even more important if this group is a family. There is no trouble like family trouble. We know each other. We know each other so well. We know our sins and where the "soft spots" are.

The pain that comes out of these disagreements can be intense. Recovery can take a long time. We must ask ourselves "What do I want to happen? Do I want to win or correct a wrong? Do I want to hurt or to heal? Do I want to tear down or build up?"

If we want to correct the problem, God has instructions for us.
1. "A soft answer turns away wrath, but a harsh word stirs up anger" (Proverbs 15:1). We know how quickly an argument can grow. Solomon says to keep your voice soft and your words kind and the anger will shrink. But when your words are loud and sharp the heat turns up quickly.

2. "A gentle tongue is a tree of life, but perverseness in it breaks the spirit" (Proverbs 15:4). When we enter the conversation with a gentle spirit and with gentle words, we build up our loved ones. But when we are harsh we break their spirit.

3. "A hot-tempered man stirs up strife, but he who is slow to anger quiets contention" (Proverbs 15:18). When you bring fiery words, the controversy grows. But when you show restraint and control your temper, the argument cools down.

4. "Brothers, if anyone is caught in any transgression, you who are spiritual should restore him in a spirit of gentleness. Keep watch on yourself, lest you too be tempted" (Galatians 6:1). If what we really want is to restore and heal, we must be spiritual as we go through this process of restoration. We must be gentle.

Today, I will...be gentle in word and attitude. I will be soft in my presentation and build up instead of tear down.

A Family Story

Today's Scripture: Deuteronomy 6:20-21

"When your sons asks you in time to come, 'What is the meaning of the testimonies and the statutes and the rules that the LORD our god has commanded you?' then you shall say to your son, 'We were Pharaoh's slaves in Egypt. And the LORD brought us out of Egypt with a mighty hand" (Deuteronomy 6:20-21).

When our girls were little and bedtime came, there were always stories. Books were read and stories told. They loved them all, but there was one kind of story they always wanted—family stories. You know, stories about their people, stories that happened before they were born. Like when Patsy and I met or even before, like when we were children. They couldn't get enough of them. Some they memorized and wanted them retold. A new one was always welcomed. They demanded that they be true. Names had to be given: historical settings were required, and the connections to them were a must. They would start something like this: "When I was a little boy before your Uncle Bo was born, my great grandfather came to see us at Christmas." I would have to explain he was my father's grandfather.

They would smile as they focused the story they were about to hear. Sometimes I would see them counting on their fingers how many great great greats there were. These stories were not only fun to tell and hear—they were important. They fixed their lives to a family. These stories helped us understand that this family thing is not temporary. We actually belong, and this gives us perspective in any immediate trouble or pleasure we are facing. We even made up a song (our song) about the Sheros. It started, "Oh once there were two Sheros." As we sang, we added the girls, cousins and even pets. We split the names Shero into two parts. One half of us sang, "Sher-" "Sher-," and the other half answered "-ro" "-ro". It was loud and silly, but we were stuck tightly together. We were after all "The Sheros." Stories are powerful, especially true ones.

Almost every Old Testament sermon was a family story. They were a big part of making our home a "haven of happiness." Now every Sunday those girls come eat lunch with us, and they bring their children with them. Some Sundays we even have a great grandson at the table.

Today, I will...*tell my children a story about our family and our God.*

WEEK 38

The Family And Evangelism

GRAHAM McDONALD

Raising Cain: Child of Creation

Today's Scripture: Psalm 145:8-9

"The hand that rocks the cradle," it is said, "is the hand that rules the world." A parent's influence has a profound impact on the life commandments a child will carry with him into adulthood. When raising a family that knows and respects God, there is every effort in the home to help children understand and love God; there is an encouragement to become a person who loves and honors God.

When Eve gave birth to Cain, she began the first human family on earth. As Genesis 4 continues, it does not go at all well. Cain murders his brother and becomes "a fugitive and a wanderer" (Genesis 4:12). In a single day, Eve lost two of her sons. Christian parents want the very best for their children, and the best should be Jesus. It doesn't always go as planned. Our children may not murder each other, but they won't always make righteous choices. As Christians, what are we supposed to do when our children reject God, especially if after becoming Christians themselves they later abandon Him?

God's reaction to Cain is an important message for us—He responds with grace. Cain is not forgiven of his sin because he is unrepentant. Yet, God made provision for him. He was not executed for his crime (Genesis 4:15); he would marry, have a family, and he founded his own community (Genesis 4:17). His descendants domesticated livestock (Genesis 4:20), invented musical instruments (Genesis 4:21), and forged tools of bronze and iron (Genesis 4:22). Cain was a child of Creation before he was a child of God. Even when he rejected God (Genesis 4:16), he wasn't rejected entirely. Instead, God took care of Cain materially. The spiritual blessings were gone, and no one expects to see Cain in heaven. But God still loved him even though he did an abominable thing.

Today, I will..._pray for my wayward children and remember that I have a responsibility for them that does not end if they reject God._

TUESDAY

The Children of Israel: God's Steadfast Love

Today's Scripture: Romans 5:20-21

A family counsellor today may rightly say that Jacob had a dysfunctional family. Jacob defrauded his brother, was defrauded by his uncle, had two wives and two concubines, and had numerous children with four women. His oldest son, Reuben, slept with his father's concubine, Bilhah (Genesis 35:22). Sons two and three (Simeon and Levi) killed the men of Shechem (Genesis 34). His sons conspired to lie to Jacob that Joseph had been killed (Genesis 37:31–32). So, yes, a dysfunctional family.

Dysfunctional is an appropriate word for the human family. God is the Father, but the children are up to all sorts of wicked deeds: fraud, fornication, infidelity, incest, violence, murder, etc. Yet, God still loves us. It's a bit mind-boggling at times.

Jacob never stopped loving his children. For sure, he was thoroughly miffed with them at times. Reuben, Simeon, and Levi fell out of favour with their father it seems, but they were still his children. They still received a blessing from him before he died (Genesis 49:3–7).

The grace of God towards humanity is amazing (Someone should write a song about it!). His grace though is more than spiritual. He had a plan to redeem us, and He sent His Son to achieve it. Yet, in the meantime, the sun still rose on both the evil and the good (Matthew 5:45). Even those who once loved Him, but turned away from Him, are still cared for by Him. God remains righteous. He created us, so He ensures that earth and its goodness can provide for our daily needs. He offers us redemption through His Son. If we reject that offer, or even if we accept it but then abandon it, we remain created in His image. His grace and love will impact our lives.

Today, I will...*pray that my family learns God is always wanting the very best for them in this life but especially in the next.*

Judah: The Man Who Changed God's Mind

Today's Scripture: Psalm 78:67–68

Judah is an unlikely hero. It was his idea to sell Joseph into slavery (Genesis 37:26–27), and he married a Canaanite woman, Shua (Genesis 38:1) with whom he had three sons (Genesis 38:2–5). His sons weren't much better than their dad. Er was wicked so God killed him (Genesis 38:7), and Onan disgraced the Levirate tradition, so God killed him too (Genesis 38:8–10). When it came time for Shelah to fulfil the Levirate obligation, Judah reneged on an earlier promise (Genesis 38:11, 14). After being widowed, Judah went looking for the illicit companionship of a woman (Genesis 38:12, 15–16, 18).

Not exactly role-model material for our young men was Judah. However, that's not the whole story. When Judah discovers that Tamar was pregnant, he wants her burned (Genesis 38:24). Then, he discovers that she is pregnant with his child (Genesis 38:25–26) and declares Tamar to be more righteous than he was (Genesis 38:26). Of all the sons of Jacob who behaved wickedly, Judah is the only one who is singled out as demonstrating repentance. This is beautifully illustrated by his intercession for Benjamin and Jacob (Genesis 38:18–34). His dysfunction was abandoned, and he was more like the God of Heaven in his love and grace.

People change. We don't always see it, and we don't always want to believe it, but people can change. Today's rebel may become tomorrow's hero. That is certainly true of Judah. At first, he is making terrible decisions just like Reuben, Simeon, and Levi. In the end, he recognizes righteousness and becomes a righteous person. We must remember Judah when our children behave contrary to what God teaches or abandon their faith. God never wrote him off. Judah didn't escape God's wrath against sin (his two sons were killed by God), but he wasn't forsaken by God either. Indeed, from Judah would come the Redeemer of all mankind (Genesis 49:10).

Today, I will..._ask God to provoke my children to see His righteousness and learn repentance from it._

THURSDAY

Onesimus: More than a Slave

Today's Scripture: Philemon 15-16

When a slave ran away from his master in the Roman Empire, it was an exceptionally dangerous choice being made. While by New Testament times there was progress in the rights of slaves, they remained the property of their master and cruel punishments could be exacted by the master and the authorities. It was even a crime to harbour a runaway slave, so Paul sending Onesimus back to Philemon was the right thing to do (Philemon 12–13). Whatever it was that motivated Onesimus to leave Philemon's household, he ended up with Paul. In turn, Paul converted Onesimus who became a brother in Christ—to Philemon as well as Paul (Philemon 10, 16). In Philemon 15, Paul hints at the providence of God, and that Onesimus ran away to find Paul and learn the gospel. "Perhaps" is the word—we don't know for sure.

When we love God and manifest that love of God for our household to see, we can never fully comprehend the impact that has on those who are closest and dearest to us. When our children grow up and decide against becoming a Christian or leaving the home having been baptized and then deciding to leave their faith, it may baffle us as to what went wrong. Sometimes, nothing did. Christian parents do their best for their children to make the path straight and obvious for them, but the children don't always make the right choice.

The Bunyoro of Uganda has an expression, "A child belongs to not one parent or home." We are more familiar with the proverb, "It takes a village to raise a child." Sometimes, someone else makes a difference in helping our children obey the gospel. For whatever reason, Onesimus left the household he had known to risk everything in the world only to discover God's love when he came to a familiar face.

Today, I will...*pray that my hope is stirred that someone else may have the opportunity to help my children love Jesus and be faithful to God.*

Being Barnabas: Seeing What Others Miss

Today's Scripture: Acts 9:27

Barnabas loved God. He was a Levite with all the responsibilities that entailed within the Jewish community. He obeyed the gospel and cared for others (Acts 4:36–37). Barnabas was active in the Lord's church because he loved God. Barnabas was a gospel preacher (Acts 11:21–22). When he and Paul (still called Saul at the time) undertook their first missionary journey (Acts 13:2–3), Barnabas is named first, probably because he was the lead in the team (cf. Acts 14:12 where he is mistaken for Zeus, the king of the gods). Barnabas was active in the saving of souls. Barnabas was the one who brought Saul to the apostles (Acts 9:26–27). Given Saul's recent history with the church, it is understandable why the church was reluctant to accept Saul into fellowship. However, Barnabas loved God and that meant even loving our enemies (cf. Matthew 5:44). Are we surprised that Barnabas means "Son of Encouragement" (Acts 4:36)?

Barnabas saw in John Mark the potential that Paul didn't (Acts 15:36–41). It would be unfair to blame Paul for refusing to take John Mark, but as he had demonstrated to Paul in Jerusalem, Barnabas was ready to take risks by being a mentor to the rejected. Perhaps Paul appreciated Barnabas' wisdom later in his ministry (cf. 2 Timothy 4:11).

Everyone needs a Barnabas, and each of us needs to work at emulating Barnabas. Our children may not respond to our encouragement to obey the gospel, but they may respond to someone else's. We may be discouraged by our children's lack of faith or reluctance to stay faithful, but it doesn't disqualify us from being encouragers of other young people who need a mentor. Barnabas saw grace at work in people and was an active participant in helping that grace grow and flourish into salvation in Christ.

Today, I will..._pray for my children that they obey the gospel, and I will pray for the children in other families that I may encourage them to love Jesus and become Christians._

WEEK 39

Balancing Our Time

BILLY SMITH

Determine Your Priorities

Today's Scripture: Ephesians 5:1-20

During his presidency of Freed-Hardeman University, Dr. E. Claude Gardner would often remind his faculty and students, "Everyone has the same twenty-four hours each day; it is what we do with those twenty-four hours that makes the difference." How true—words of wisdom from a life well lived and filled with accomplishment.

As people who are looking forward to eternity, nonetheless, we live with the reality of time, both its demands and restraints, its limits and potential. Do we have too much to do? Yes! Do we have enough time? The common answer is "No!" Yet, we seem to do what we want to do, often accomplishing the least important tasks instead of the most. This coupled with the natural tendency to laziness and idleness requires that we learn the invaluable lesson of balancing our time, or as Paul expressed in today's text, "Making the best use of the time, because the days are evil." In Poor Richard's Almanac, Benjamin Franklin observed, "Do you love life? Then do not squander time; for that's the stuff life is made of."

The place to begin for making the most of our time is in determining our priorities, our goals and objectives in life. Too many have no concept of where they are headed or where they want to go. Contrast this with the seven-year-old young man I met recently who boldly exclaimed, "Someday I am going to be the president of Freed-Hardeman University!" I am not betting against him; in fact, I am praying for him.

When we determine what we want to be and what we want to do with our life we eliminate the trivial and focus on the values, virtues, and skills that will get us there. The process may be long, but we must learn to balance what we can and cannot be, what we must and must not do, where we go and where we dare not go. Our loving example is none other than the Lord Jesus, who made the most of each day in His three-year ministry, who knew precisely the mission that only He could complete: "For this purpose I was born and for this purpose I have come into the world – to bear witness to the truth" (John 18:37).

Today, I will...*make the most of my time by more effectively and faithfully determining my priorities for this life, and far more importantly, for my life to come, to the praise of God.*

TUESDAY

Dedicate Your Life to the Lord

Today's Scripture: Psalm 90; Romans 12:1-2

"So teach us to number our days that we may apply our hearts to wisdom" (Psalm 90:12). This is among the wisest counsel the Bible offers, since our days on the earth are few, in comparison to eternity. The very best use of our time is found in fully dedicating ourselves to the Lord. Paul could not have expressed it better when he urged the Romans, "To present your bodies as a living sacrifice, holy and acceptable to God" (12:1). If I have made God the priority of my life, then everything I am and all that I have is dedicated to Him: "Seek first the kingdom of God and His righteousness" (Matthew 6:33). How may this be accomplished?

First, dedicate yourself to God's word: "Your word is a lamp to my feet and a light to my path" (Psalm 119:105). Earlier the psalmist had asked, "How can a young man keep his way pure? By guarding it according to Your word" (119:9). Two verses later he states, "I have stored up Your word in my heart that I might not sin against You" (119:11). Not only must we make time to read the Bible daily, but we must also digest the word, coming ultimately to a comprehensive knowledge of Scripture. It will forever be true that "faith comes by hearing, and hearing through the word of Christ" (Romans 10:17).

Second, dedicate yourself to God's will: "My food is to do the will of Him who sent Me" (John 4:34a). The Lord proved that to be true in both the agony of Gethsemane (Matthew 26:36-46) and the absolute anguish of Golgotha (Matthew 27:32-50). Notice that both settings are bathed in prayer. So, too, are our lives spent in earnestly seeking God's will for our decisions, choices, and activities. We must make time each day, and often many times a day, praying for God's guidance, wisdom, and forgiveness. When we fail to pray, we rob ourselves of the greatest power in the universe. "Ere you left your room this morning, did you think to pray?"

Third, dedicate yourself to God's work: "...and to accomplish His work" (John 4:34b). As members of the Lord's church, we are all ministers, servants, and laborers. When time challenges us to forget our priority and fill our schedules with the fleeting things of this life, we must remember our calling, and find our place in serving both the Lord and people. We are faithful worshipers, yes, but we are also effective workers in the kingdom of God. Our mission is the same as that of Jesus, clearly stated in His visit with Zacchaeus: "For the Son of Man came to seek and save the lost" (Luke 19:10). There is and can never be a higher calling, and you and I are given the precious and noble task of doing all we can, in as many ways as we can, to all the people we can, for as long as we can.

Today, I will...re-dedicate myself to a life of learning the word of God, of seeking His will through the privilege of prayer, and to doing His work while it is yet day, to His honor and glory, and to the salvation of souls.

WEDNESDAY

Develop Your Gifts

Today's Scripture: 1 Corinthians 12:12-26; Romans 12:3-8

"Having gifts that differ according to the grace given to us, let us use them" (Romans 12:6). Gifts, or abilities and skills, are developed over time and involve a number of factors, from our intelligence to our physical strength, to our emotional stability, and to our spirituality. We are the products of both nature and nurture. That is, each of us is born with some natural talent while other abilities are acquired through preparation, performance, and perseverance. Not everyone can be a scholar, physician, artist, athlete, author, musician, or scientist, but everyone has an individual contribution to humanity's common good.

This is the point Paul is making to the churches in Rome and Corinth when he compares members of the church, and their function, to members of the human body that perform the function for which God created them. While his instruction applies primarily to the use of spiritual gifts unique to the first century church, the principle remains the same for our natural gifts in the twenty-first century church.

First, we are to know what we can do for the Lord: "Think with sober judgment, each according to the measure of faith that God has assigned" (Romans 12:3). While we must not think too highly of ourselves as God's servants, neither are we to think too lowly of ourselves, leaving the Lord's work for others to do.

Second, we are to accept what we can and cannot do for the Lord: "We have many members, and the members do not all have the same function" (12:4). A careful self-analysis of our abilities, along with the commandments of God, helps us realize not everyone can serve as an elder, deacon, evangelist, worship leader or Bible school teacher. There is so much more that constitutes the work of the church. We must find and accept our place of service.

Third, we are to recognize God has given each of us a gift, a talent: "Having gifts that differ according to the grace given to us" (12:6a). With the abundance of talent residing in every congregation, we dare not envy what someone else can do but gladly rejoice in what God gives us to do!

Fourth, we are to use our gift in contributing to the Lord's work: "Let us use them" (12:6b-8). In this special text Paul gives seven distinctive examples of how the church works through the collective abilities of her individual members in carrying out the Lord's mission. In doing so, he encourages us to make the most of our time as we develop and use our gifts.

Today, I will...*continue to develop the gifts God has given me, the abilities, talents, and skills that will enable me to better manage my time and my life in His service.*

Discipline Your Habits

Today's Scripture: 1 Corinthians 9:19-27

"I do not run aimlessly…but I discipline my body and keep it under control" (1 Corinthians 9:26-27). Life takes time. To receive the most from life we must learn how to balance our time, from the most important to the least important. After one's devotion to God, the Bible, and the church, our greatest investment of time must be with our families. And this takes planning, prayer, and discipline.

A twelve-year-old boy asked his father, an attorney, "Dad, how much do you charge for people to visit with you for one hour?" Puzzled, the father answered, "$300." A few weeks later, the boy showed up at his father's office, having made an appointment. His explanation was, "Dad, I have been saving $300 so that you can spend one hour with me." Had I been that father, I would have been crushed by my son's sincere indictment. I can only hope that father took his son into his arms and repented of his negligence in tears. What follows is a tried-and-true program of time management:

First, begin the practice of using a notepad, or computer page, for planning each day of the week. *Second*, on the left-hand column of the page, divide the day into half-hour (or hour) increments. *Third*, on the back of the page, or another computer page, list everything you need to accomplish today. *Fourth*, put in the half-hour (or hour) increments the things you need to accomplish in the order of importance, including family time. *Fifth*, now that you have planned the day's work, work the plan!

This may be painful at first, but after a few days, planning will become a disciplined habit and a part of you. If you stay with it and not give up, you will arrive at the point where you cannot go into a day without a plan. The plan will actually become fun as you see yourself accomplishing more, and consequently, enjoying life more. Time is a gift from God and when used wisely, leads to a balanced life of achievement and enjoyment; the abuse, misuse, and waste of time is at best unfortunate and at worst sinful. "He dies for lack of discipline" (Proverbs 5:23).

Today, I will…*begin a program of planning for each day, from the most important things to accomplish to the least important. I will remember to focus on both the Lord and my family.*

FRIDAY

Define Your Destiny

Today's Scripture: Hebrews 11

'Set your mind on things that are above, not on things that are on the earth" (Colossians 3:2). The most important thing in life is going to heaven. An outstanding student leader gave the opening address to his evangelism club. In an unforgettable statement, he said, "There is nothing in this life that is worth missing heaven for." That includes a person or persons, possessions, position, power and prestige.

Hope is defined as "desire with the expectation of obtaining that which is desired." If we desire something without expectation, it is not biblical hope; if we expect something that is not desired, neither is that what the Bible describes as "a living hope" (1 Peter 1:3). However, when we desire something with the realistic expectation of receiving it, that is hope. The hope of heaven for the faithful child of God defines who he is, what he is about, and that for which he longs. This heavenly hope is what the Hebrews writer describes as "the anchor of the soul" (6:19), sustaining us through the storms of life until the Lord brings us safely home.

There are sixteen names specifically mentioned in Hebrews 11 as people whose faith was based on their hope of heaven: "They desire a better country, that is, a heavenly one. Therefore God is not ashamed to be called their God, for He has prepared for them a city" (11:16). They understood, as must we, "This world is not our home." Did they live long lives, raise families, and perform great deeds? Yes! But their focus remained on their God and their eternal destiny. You and I have known, and know those today, whose names would appear in an expanded version of Hebrews 11. They lived by the same faith, obeyed from the same heart, and served with the same purpose as those who lived in the long ago, who are commended by the Spirit of God as examples for us to emulate as we journey to that eternal city.

The best description I have heard of a spiritual person is someone who is "heaven-minded." There is no question, among those who know him best, about his character, his focus, his priority, his vision, his mission, and his eternal destiny. May we strive with everything that is within us to be such a person, people who recognize that time is fleeting, who understand the "times" in which we live, and who plan accordingly for that great day that is coming. "Come, Lord Jesus" (Revelation 22:20)!

Today, I will...resolve as a child of God to use the time He has given me wisely, to do all the good I can, to all the people I can, in as many ways as I can, for as long as I can.

WEEK 40

Putting God First

DAVID SHANNON

Putting God First in Marriage

Today's Scripture: Genesis 2:24; Ephesians 5:31

Holy matrimony is made up of two individuals who put God first. "First" speaks to order. Not second, but first. Consider the creation. "In the beginning God created." He created us (Genesis 1:27), therefore, we are the creation, and He is the Creator. He was first and has authority (Isaiah 45:9). God continued to create by bringing into existence the institution of marriage. Marriage was engineered by God's creative perfection on day six in the garden. How do we apply this order to our daily life? How do we put God first in marriage? Consider our imperfection and God's call for us to be holy (1 Peter 1:15). It is in marriage we learn much about love, service, mercy, patience, and forgiveness. Putting God first in marriage will multiply the opportunities for self-denial, loving others as ourselves, and putting God's will before our own.

Consider also the mystery of marriage mentioned in Ephesians. By God's design, there is no other earthly relationship wherein we become one, except for our place in Christ's body, the church. It is sobering to think we become one with God. This union was described using the same verse to describe the origin of marriage in Genesis 2:24. In Ephesians 5:31-32, the inspired message quotes the Genesis account of "the two shall become one flesh." The unity of becoming one with Christ is likened to us becoming one with our spouse. These two relationships should not be fractured. Holy matrimony is when a husband and a wife's union with Christ shapes every moment of their marriage. It is the highest of callings and the deepest of unity. It is not easy to fully comprehend, but it is one of the greatest mysteries a person has ever lived (Ephesians 5:32). Let's say together: God first for my family. It is not a statement declaring our merit but a cry of dependency on God, knowing it is all that matters to my family.

Today, I will...*ponder the importance of the authoritative origin of marriage, remembering Jesus' words, "What God has joined together" (Mark 10:9). I will strive to allow my unity with Christ to permeate all that I am in my home in light of the great mystery.*

Putting God First in Marriage and Not Children

Today's Scripture: Genesis 2; 4

In the order of creation, the natural conception of children and the uniqueness of the parenting relationships are interesting to observe. In Genesis, by God's design, it is within the committed marriage relationship that children are to be conceived and nurtured. What a gift to children, but what a responsibility to parents! Parents must deny themselves and place God first. Parents must deny themselves and place their marriage and their spouse as a priority.

Let me ask you a question. When is the first time parenting is mentioned in scripture? I've asked this to hundreds through the years at parenting seminars. Rarely, if ever, did anyone answer correctly. The usual guess is Genesis 4. But actually, the first time parenting is mentioned in the Bible is in Genesis 2:24 in the context of children leaving home. God expects parents to raise children to leave. Children enter this world 100% dependent, but through training, instructions, and experiences, children are to develop into responsible Christian adults who can navigate life.

Now let's think about the parents again. God created a framework for parenting. The beautiful, profound framework of marriage is becoming obsolete in our country. We must understand that the world will never follow God's plan for sexuality, parenting, and marriage. Even those who only wear the label of Christianity will not. The fleshly temptations are too strong for the mildly committed. Only those who put God first will follow this unique and powerful home design. In God's plan, the man and woman are devoted to God first and committed to the institution of marriage second to create the best environment to raise a child. If the parents value or choose the child above God or marriage or spouse, the order is confused, and the foundation of parenting is weakened. Simply put, the foundation of parenting is two layers. The first layer is two parents who are committed to God. The second layer is two parents who are committed to each other. This is the place to raise godly children (Malachi 2:15).

Today, I will..._meditate on how different the world would be if every child born this year had two parents who were committed to God first and to God's design of marriage second._

God First in Giving

Today's Scripture: Proverbs 3:5-10; 1 Corinthians 16:2;
2 Corinthians 9:7-10

You probably love this passage, "Trust in the Lord with all your heart, and do not lean on your own understanding. In all your ways acknowledge him, and he will make straight your paths" (Proverbs 3:5-6). These verses call us to place our trust in God and not ourselves. Now that the writer of Proverbs has established this principle, what do you think will be the topic he addresses next? Giving. If giving is about anything, it is about trust! He continues, "Honor the Lord with your wealth and with the first fruits of all your produce" (Proverb 3:9). We have the freedom to spend and give our money as we think best, or we could trust in the Lord and lean not on our own understanding.

What is God First giving? The Proverb writer teaches this as a way to honor God. God does not accept second fruits or afterthoughts or what is left. Paul taught the same while instructing the first-generation Christians. "On the first day of every week, each of you is to put something aside and store it up, as he may prosper, so that there will be no collecting when I come" (1 Corinthians 16:2). When? The first day of the week. Who? Each of you, not just the wealthy or mature adults. Give? Lay something aside. How much? Give as you have prospered. Giving began with a tithe, or 10%, in the old covenant. This is a good percentage to start with today, but each one must decide for themselves. The importance of a percentage is that it is a natural way to give based on how much you have prospered, which is the teaching.

Consider this illustration. A person made $100 and gave $10. The following week he prospered $500 and gave $10. In the third week, he made $1,000 and gave $10. Each week he was a giver. But this person did not give as they had prospered. Giving is to spring from a heart of gratitude because the person has paused to count their blessings and give accordingly. With cheerfulness, let us give back to God first, trusting He will continue to provide (2 Corinthians 9:7-10).

Today, I will...*commit to taking time on Saturday evening to count all the financial ways God has prospered me this week and cheerfully give to God on Sunday.*

God First Versus Materialism

Today's Scripture: Matthew 19:16-22; 1 Timothy 6; Matthew 6:24, 33

The rich young ruler was a promising young man who was religious, moral, and respectful to his family. Yet, there was one area he was not willing to place God first - his possessions. Imagine if he had looked at Jesus and said, "Don't make me choose between you and my money; I'll choose the money." While he did not say it, he did do it. The temptation to not put God first is so great that Jesus continued his teaching by saying a rich man entering heaven would be more difficult than a camel going through the eye of a needle (Mathew 19:23-24).

How hard is it for you to put God first? The last chapter of 1 Timothy is challenging on this topic. Notice these powerful teachings:

- Be Content: Godliness with contentment is great gain (vs 6). Which do you value most: contentment or possessions?
- Think Big Picture: What is beyond your money and possessions? Eternity. "For we brought nothing into the world, and we cannot take anything out of the world" (vs 7).
- Who or What do You Love: "For the love of money is a root of all kinds of evils. It is through this craving that some have wandered away from the faith and pierced themselves with many pangs" (vs 10). So simply put, God first or money first? One brings peace and the other pain.
- Who Takes Care of You: Do you think money will take care of you? Be honest. Only God can provide for you, so trust in Him and not in riches (vs 17).
- Share: Don't try to keep it all; share it (vs 18).

Jesus preached about growing anxious over daily necessities reminding His audience that God is their provider. He concluded by saying, "But seek first the kingdom of God and his righteousness, and all these things will be added to you" (Matthew 6:33). Jesus was saying God first. Before this, he told the audience that a person could not have two masters (Matthew 6:24). He said you could not serve God and money. We must choose whom to put first.

Today, I will...*honestly consider whether I find my identity, comfort, or trust in my money, possessions, or God.*

239

God First in Your Love

Today's Scripture: Matthew 22:34-40; Romans 5:8; Matthew 26:39

The lawyer asked Jesus a difficult question. Which commandment is the greatest? Could there be one that is greater than the other 612 laws? Jesus answered, "You shall love the Lord your God with all your heart and with all your soul and with all your mind. This is the great and first commandment" (Matthew 22:37-38). In other words, love God first.

The second commandment is about loving others and ourselves. Jesus continued to teach that all other commandments could be understood and obeyed through these two laws. For example, loving God first will lead us to love our enemies and "pray for those who persecute you" (Matthew 5:44). Loving God first demands we deny ourselves. That is why Jesus said, "If anyone would come after me, let him deny himself and take up his cross and follow me" (Matthew 16:24). Do you know what prefaced this teaching? Jesus had just predicted his death to Peter, and Peter said he would not allow this to happen. Jesus called Peter Satan and explained to him that his actions came from a human perspective and not God's perspective. Let's recap this for application. If I put God first, my love for God will cause me to view everything and everyone from the perspective of "What is God's will?" We often say, "This is what I would do." Let us instead be quick to see what God would have us do.

Jesus not only commanded this love but demonstrated it on the cross (Romans 5:8). In the Garden of Gethsemane, Jesus dreaded the cross and prayed for another way. Because of his love for God first, he finished his prayer with the words, "Nevertheless, not as I will, but as you will" (Matthew 26:39). So Jesus denied His self-will and demonstrated His love for God by dying on the cross. Some have said, "I am not being genuine to God if I do things for Him I do not want to do." Well, I am thankful that Jesus did. One of the most challenging parts of putting God first is putting me second.

Today, I will...*list three ways I have failed recently in denying myself to place God first. Today I will love God by putting Him first in these areas.*

240

WEEK 41

When a Family Member Fails

RALPH GILMORE

Don't Use Proverbs 22:6 As a Weapon

Today's Scripture: Galatians 6:1-5

The Proverbs are generally true and sometimes always true. But Proverbs 22:6 is a passage that is inspired but only generally true. How could Abraham, David, Samuel, Jacob, and most other Old Testament characters have been blessed by God even though they had children who failed? When a child fails, regardless of the age of the child, either you or someone you know may try to use Proverbs 22:6 ("Bring up a child in the way he should go; even when he is old he will not depart from it.") as a spiritual weapon to try to behead you spiritually. That approach to interpreting the passage is unwarranted, unchristian, and unhealthy. If that interpretation is correct, consider this scenario: If my child fails, I failed; if I fail, my parents failed; if my parents failed; their parents failed; etc. Surely that interpretation fails.

At the time of your child's spiritual failure, your positive stance should be that it is not about you, but it is about the one who fails. I remember a time when I tried to resign from my work at Freed-Hardeman University and at the Campbell St. church of Christ because of problems with one of our children. Instead, the president of FHU and the elders at Campbell St. stood by my wife and me. It made all the difference. At times like this, a strong support network will help you through. Galatians 6:1-5 is helpful to study. There are two different words that are used for "burden" in this passage. One word refers to the burden or emotional load that one is expected to bear. The other word refers to an overload as in a beast of burden upon which too much load has been placed. You and God can handle the load you are expected to bear as well as an overload that you have. It does seem that bad things often happen in threes—i.e., three things to deal with at once.

In dealing with the child involved, you should listen if you expect to be heard. Watch carefully the tone of your voice as well as the time and the way the matter is approached. Consider how Jesus would handle it. Don't beat yourself to death over a misinterpreted passage.

Today, I will...seek to find some serenity in the prayer bearing its name. O God, Grant me the serenity to accept that which cannot be changed; courage to change that which can be changed, and wisdom to know the difference.

242

TUESDAY

Love Is Aways Right; Enabling Is Always Wrong

Today's Scripture: 1 Corinthians 13:13

Love is indeed always right (1 Cor 13:13), but enabling is always wrong. It may be difficult for you to define until you are in the middle of a situation in which the difference is imminently clear. This may be true when a child, or spouse, is spiritually failing. So, first we will talk about love. You probably know what I will say next. Express love openly in your family. My wife's family was better at this than the way I was brought up. Our family genuinely loved each other. I am only talking about how love is expressed. I have learned that saying "I love you" is almost never a bad thing. Your children almost always need to hear it. Your spouse definitely needs it.

However, in this devotional I want to spend more time on being an enabler which, by definition, generally describes someone whose behavior allows a loved one to continue self-destructive patterns of behavior. We must try to emulate and teach emotional intelligence to each other in the family. In this context, it means to teach that we all have choices to make and to handle our emotions in an intelligent way. Yet, when we are choosing poorly, we may need to suffer the consequences of our actions. When my wife and I have tried to manipulate situations in order to "exempt," as it were, our family members from consequences, it has generally not turned out well. Of course, you should always be there for your children with spiritual, emotional, and if necessary financial support during the time of failure. However, your well-intentioned actions might at time be enabling your family member in need to continue their destructive behavior. At that point, it is time to find other ways to help that do not enable. Paul implies in 2 Thessalonians 3:10-15 that the Thessalonian Christians who were working and were giving financial support to those who were not working (as they thought the resurrection of Jesus was coming any day) was such an enabling occasion (Please refer to Romans 1:32 and 2 John 11 for other applications of this enabling principle.). We did find other ways to help our children during times of crisis, but we did struggle with finding the balance.

Today, I will..._love deeply, but I will try to learn that love applied improperly is not love. Please help me, O Lord, in my family to learn to apply love properly and to love genuinely._

Do the Next Right Thing

Today's Scripture: Proverbs 21:2-3

When trying to unscramble eggs or herd cats, there are so many variables involved that I feel emotionally paralyzed when trying to help a family member or myself in times of crisis. In the failure of any of my family members, it is sometimes true that I have also failed first. What do I do? I learned from attending Alcoholics Anonymous that I should do the next right thing. I can't think about doing the next one thousand right things, but I can focus on one right thing. If it is the right thing to do, then do it as soon as possible. This may include getting counseling for yourself and other family members. When one family member fails, it affects the entire family unit.

Solomon says in Proverbs 21:2-3 that "Every way of a man is right in his own eyes, but the Lord weighs the heart. To do righteousness and justice is more acceptable to the Lord than sacrifice." Verse 2 rightfully emphasizes the motives of my heart first while verse 3 emphasizes my actions stemming from good motives. This same idea is reflected when Samuel addresses the failing of King Saul to fully obey the Lord in 1 Samuel 15:22.

During a family crisis, these principles apply. I have had to prayerfully examine the motives of my heart first. I remember a time when I acted as though my own reputation as a Bible faculty member at Freed-Hardeman University or as a preacher for the Campbell Street church of Christ was more important than my daughter(s). I have repented of this. I should allow others to think what they will about me, but I will always try to help a family member headed toward spiritual oblivion. With this adjustment in my priorities, I was in a better place to help my family and to help myself. Moments like these assist parents to understand each other better and to be on the same page when threats to the family arise. After God, the family is always first. From this perspective, I now am in a position to "do the next right thing."

Today, I will...*try to do the next thing that is right in Your eyes. I will try to hear Your voice when my family needs me the most. Please help me to follow righteousness.*

THURSDAY
Let Go and Let God

Today's Scripture: Ephesians 3:20

I am sure you have heard the expression "Let go and let God" before. Although it is a principle that may be useful in the event of a family crisis, or failure, it can be misunderstood. For instance, it could imply one's own uselessness in what happens in one's life. What if somebody said, "I don't think I will study for the exam. I will let go and let God." To put it in perspective, before I let go of whatever it is and let God do whatever He chooses, I must first do all that I can to help the family member who is failing.

I should not attempt to hand it over to God when I need to be involved in the outcome of the crisis myself. "Control" is a funny word—often an illusion, a mirage, or a utopian wish. Sometimes I think I am in control when I am merely kidding myself. As a parent, I have had to learn this in difficult ways. When Joyce and I first became parents, it was in the '70s. During this era, a basic cultural value was that you should make your children mind. Unfortunately, sometimes making a child mind was thought as controlling the child. I have since came to understand that I never actually "controlled" my children; I just often modified their behavior. Only I am in a position to control myself. This is also true of each person (Romans 14:12).

I came to understand that there is a limit to which I can exert influence on my children's behavior. I never actually controlled them. When my wife and I had exhausted all we knew to do in a family crisis, we had no option but to "let go and let God." We did not have a choice at that point. (She was God's child anyway. By the way, she now has decades of sobriety and God claimed His own, but the action was among the hardest I have ever faced.)

Proverbs 16:9 reads, "The heart of man plans his way, but the Lord establishes his steps." Paul's prayer for the Ephesians in 3:20 pleads, "Now to him who is able to do far more abundantly than all that we ask or think, according to the power at work within us." Sometimes, let God do it.

Today, I will...*seek to allow You to be in control of my life as I freely give my life to You. Help me to know my limits.*

245

Wait Patiently for the Open Door

Today's Scripture: Psalm 27:14; 37:7; 38:15; 52:8-9

I remember nights when I was driving around town at 4:00 in the morning trying to find a child who had missed curfew. I don't know what I was thinking. Did I think that I would embody the "cave man" stereotype and drag her by the hair back into the family? Let me briefly survey some principles that might be more productive for you if you have a family member failing.

Look for teachable moments in the life of the family member who is failing. The recovery will not happen on your time, but on theirs—more specifically, if it does happen it will be in God's time. A teachable moment is a moment during which they are reaching out to you. You may need to listen carefully, but they will probably be there. Jesus would say this was a moment of their being "poor in spirit" (Matthew 5:3). It is crucial at this juncture that you know your family members well. The better you know them the better you may recognize teachable moments when they come your way.

Next, you need to prepare yourself to receive them back. If it is an addictive disorder or an emotional disorder, be ready with the information handy concerning places to get treatment and/or counseling. Be prepared mentally about what the arrangements will need to be at that point. Are they to be in your house? If so, under what conditions? You need to be the prodigal father who acted decisively when his son returned (Luke 15:20-24). You must be ready to forgive (which means to "put it aside").

Finally, you need to trust God during this time more than you ever have, perhaps (Proverbs 3:5-6). The motif of "waiting on the Lord" is most famously mentioned in Isaiah 40:29-31, but it also occurs in Psalm 27:14; 37:7; 38:15; and 52:8-9. It must really be important. The Hebrew word most often used for "wait" means to "hope in" or "hope for." The hope is definitely there. Don't surrender your hope to anything or anyone who would try to take it from you unless it is obvious that no hope is left. Hope is there for you. Grasp it lovingly.

Today, I will..._wait patiently on You. I will not give up hope which dwells in You forever. Help me when I cannot see it._

WEEK 42

Letting Our Children Go

MYRON BRUCE

Starting Out

Today's Scripture: Psalm 121:8

Every morning we prepare ourselves for a new day. And as we do, we ask the questions: What will I wear? Where will I go? Who will I encounter? With so many questions of "Who, what, and where," the one answer we DO know, is that there is much to be done. So, are you ready to face the day? Are you ready to answer the questions?

Parents know that this is a personal responsibility. From day one each parent knows there's a unique responsibility to prepare their child for the day, a task we must take seriously. With that in mind, I hope these next few studies will direct us toward not only facing the day, but preparing to "let our children go." While you may have all the answers to facing your day, will your children be as confident? Are you convinced that your children have the necessary tools/answers before you let them go?

In the 121st Psalm, the psalmist asked a question that most parents ask in light of raising their children, "I lift up my eyes to the hills. From where does my help come?" Certainly, the Christian can attest, as the psalmist continues, that my help "comes from the Lord..." But do we teach that to our children? As we are letting them go, are they confident in their faith to look to the One who can answer their questions and calm their fears?

This world will deceive and distract us as we go out and face each day. We know it's inevitable and we know that eventually the day will come when we let our children go. The question to answer is simply: Into whose hand will you let them go? Keep in mind, there is One who is guarding our going out and our coming in.

Today, I will...open my heart in prayer before I open my door to the world.

TUESDAY

More Than a Song

Today's Scripture: Proverbs 4:4

Most any child will recognize, perhaps even sing, the iconic line from one of our the most popular children's movies…

"Let it go, let it go!" By no means do I promote the movie or the song, but I do think we need to continue considering the idea of "letting go."

We understand that this life is filled with difficulties and hardships. From the moment we enter this world, struggles surround us. Some feel it more than others, but we all have trying times. Perhaps the most painful is separation, that point when we come to the fork in the road and know it's time to let go of what we have held so close to our hearts. The loss of our loved ones to death is a given, but that's not the only time we must let go.

Parents who are blessed with children watch them grow from the totally dependent toddler to the independent, sometimes confrontational, young adult. But even then, as they grow into maturity and strike out on their own, we come to understand that we must let them go. For some it's not a problem watching them back down out of the drive and head off into their future. We know it's what must happen: they are off to the next stage of life. But that doesn't keep us from shedding a tear or two. Maybe it's the fact we see the past 18 years driving away, and from my experience…I have to say it's hard to let go.

But letting go is a reality. And, if we're honest with ourselves, this can also be a joyous occasion when we know their destination. Remember to teach God's word and embrace Solomon's instruction as he writes; "Let your heart hold fast my words; keep my commandments and live…" (Proverbs 4:4).

Today, I will…_pray for peace and guidance as I come to appreciate and accept the day I'll "let it go…let it go."_

249

The Right Side

Today's Scripture: Psalm 124:1

Do you remember, as a child, being on the playground or in the park with your friends and choosing sides? Remember the summer days on a baseball diamond, pulling together our teams. The self-appointed captains would step in front of the line of eager athletes and begin their draft. Each of us would eagerly wait for our names to be called to see whose team we would be on. Without question, we all wanted to be on the winning side. And a captain who knew what to do would choose the fastest, strongest, and smartest players to be on his team. I recall after winning a game someone might say, "If we didn't have _____ (fill in the blank) on our side, we would have lost." It's important to put strong people around you, but how much more important is it to have the right captain? Someone who knows how and what to do to win!

King David understood this principle and wrote about it in the 124th Psalm, "Had it not been the Lord who was on our side..." Moms and dads also know it's important to place the right people around their children. With the ever-present realization that one day we will "let them go," our objective is to equip the ones we love with the right team, or better yet, the right "captain."

Abraham Lincoln is credited with having said to a military advisor, "My concern is not whether God is on our side, my greatest concern is to be on God's side...for God is always right."

We will one day let our children go; are we doing everything we can to ensure that they are on God's side? We have the choice of either being with Him or not. It is our decision. Just remember, He is the captain and when we obey and follow His Word, we win.

Today, I will...*ask the question "Am I on the right side?"*

Humble & Kind

Today's Scripture: Matthew 23:12

Having children is truly a blessing from God. But the childhood years don't last long. They grow up, just as you had hoped and planned, but now what? Some parents celebrate their long-lost freedom while others mourn the change, and fall into a great depression. Still others fall apart and fall away. Things are different for sure, but this article isn't intended to address the 'empty nest' as much as it is to focus on the idea of letting them go.

Every parent asks the question, "Am I ready for them to leave home?" But perhaps we should be asking, "Are THEY ready to leave home? Have I done the right things, have I given the proper advice and pointed them 'in the way he should go?'" (Proverbs 22:6). We do what God calls us to do as parents, and then we pray for their safety and for the decisions they will make. To be honest, there's not much more we can do!

Take a moment and read these two scriptures…

"Do nothing from selfish ambition or conceit, but in humility count others more important than yourselves. Let each of you look not only to his own interests, but also to the interests of others." (Philippians 2:3-4); "Be kind to one another, tenderhearted, forgiving one another, as God in Christ forgave you." (Ephesians 4:32)

Tim McGraw made famous a country song in 2016 that echoes the sentiment of these two texts—the premise and foundation of being humble and kind. How does this apply to "letting our children go?" What can we take away from a secular song? In my opinion, it's the very core of how we should raise our children to live in this world. God's word is the foundation of our lives, and we must search for ways to aid our children as they go forward.

Today, I will…*follow Christ's example, focus on Him and strive to be "humble and kind."*

FRIDAY

Before Letting Go...Help Them Grow

Today's Scripture: 1 Peter 2:5

The past few days we have considered the inevitability that our children will grow up and that we will eventually let them go. But before we leave this tender topic, we need to establish an imperative truth. Through God's direction, we must let our children go. But there's more value when we come to the realization that we must let our children grow so they'll be ready to go. They will never be prepared to "go" until we encourage them to "grow."

Paul's letter to the young preacher, Timothy, is a solid reminder that we must stay strong in our faith as we face this wicked, evil world. In the third chapter Paul writes, "...evil people and imposters will go on from bad to worse, deceiving and being deceived. But as for you, continue in what you have learned and have firmly believed, knowing from whom you have learned it and how from childhood you have been acquainted with the sacred writings, which are able to make you wise for salvation through faith in Christ Jesus" (2 Timothy 3:13-15).

Raising our children in the Lord is how we can let them go with confidence towards their future. For most of us, it's not easy watching our children grow up and move away. We certainly feel the void that is left when we let them go. But that void will be filled when we remember that our children have been "acquainted with the sacred writings..." Keep praying for them and hold fast to them even as they transition in this life.

As we consider letting our children go, it's of utmost importance that we focus on their growth. Let's practice Hebrews chapter 10 and "... consider how to stir up one another to love and good works."

Today, I will..._encourage my children with God's word and pray for their faithfulness._

WEEK 43

When I've Lost My Spouse

DEAN MILLER

Who Am I?

Today's Scripture: Genesis 1:26-27; Acts 17:26-28

When you were half of a whole, but the whole no longer exists—who are you? Previous to the death of your spouse, you were someone's wife or someone's husband. Who are you after the dearest on earth to you has passed away? That's an identity crisis! To make matters worse, the reality is it's a coupled world. You are no longer coupled. Where does a misfit fit? When a spouse dies, the marriage has ended (Rom. 7:3-4; 1 Cor. 7:39). Social awkwardness becomes a major challenge. It is natural to question personal identity when you are involuntarily single.

Marital status is important in contemporary culture. Professional appointments and various important documents expect a box to be checked: single, married, divorced, widowed. After checking "married" for years, now it is "widowed." Miriam Neff wrote, "I don't like the word and still will not check that box to identify myself" (*From One Widow to Another*, p. 11).

Should widowhood define someone? Should any marital status define anyone? Marital status is important, but should it define a person? Marital status is a part of who a person is, but does not define a person.

The identity that matters most, who we really are has to do with relationship--with God. "Then God said, Let Us make man in our image...So God created man in His own image: in the image of God He created him; male and female He created them" (Gen. 1:26-27). "And He has made from one blood every nation of men to dwell on all the face of the earth...in Him we live and move and have our being...'For we are also His offspring'" (Acts 17:26-28). The Creator defines the creation. The creature (every one of us!) exists in the image of God. That's what makes us special! That's our identity!

Today, I will...*refuse to permit life circumstances to define me and, instead, focus on my identify as an image-bearer of the Almighty.*

Grieving Is a Family Member

Today's Scripture: Psalm 61:1-2

When we have lost a loved one, we grieve. That's the natural reaction of human beings to loss. People matter. They are among the best of God's blessings. The loss of a spouse is an unparalleled loss. It is the only relationship in the Bible described as divinely joined together into "one flesh" (Matthew 19:4-6). Think about the amount of time and all the experiences that deepen that bonding. Think of the unique intimacy that has been shared. Learning to live with that loss begins with deeply grieving as long as needed.

The loss of a beloved husband or wife is overwhelming. It is a good time to embrace the spirit of the psalmist: "Hear my cry, O God, listen to my prayer; from the end of the earth I call to you when my heart is faint. Lead me to the rock that is higher than I" (Psalm 61:1-2). In the darkness of grief, the "Father of lights" can bless us with every good and perfect gift needed to meet the daily challenges (James 1:17). After all, He knows what we have need of even before we petition Him (Matthew 6:8).

When our spouse dies, may we never forget that others have suffered loss, too. Others in the family are grieving, too. Somebody has lost a parent or a grandparent. Somebody may have lost a child, a sibling, or an aunt or uncle. Grieving is a family affair, yet each member of the family may react to the loss differently. Like fingerprints, grieving is uniquely individual.

The apostle Peter directed husbands to "live with your wives in an understanding way" (1 Peter 3:7). When a family has suffered loss, it is critically important for everyone to try their best to interact with one another "in an understanding way." Family members may say and/or do things that are hard to understand. Effective family grieving requires a lot of love (1 Corinthians 13:4-8a).

Today, I will..._choose to genuinely grieve my loss and practice loving others while they grieve their loss in their way._

Be Patient with Yourself

Today's Scripture: 2 Peter 3:9

William Bridges wrote a book about embracing life's most difficult moments. It's titled, *The Way of Transition*. As an expert on the topic of transition, as a world-renowned lecturer on the subject, as a leader in helping businesses navigate transitions—life forced him to deal with a very personal transition. His wife, Mondi, died at the age of 57 (after 37 years of being together). He wrote in this book:

> Loss was such a complex experience! Layer after layer of meaning. No wonder that, in dream and memory, mourning sent you back over the ground again and again. No wonder mourning took so long…No wonder that people who make a change without mourning the loss of the past usually find it confronting them later on, down the road. No wonder that it takes more than a ceremony to lay someone to rest (p. 64).

Our grief-illiterate culture does not feel comfortable with the subject of loss and its impact. We don't talk about it. So, when we do suffer loss, we are likely not equipped to deal with its impact effectively. Loss is one of life's harshest blows, especially when it's the loss of a beloved spouse. It can make us feel like we are going crazy. But we're not, we are—in a word—grieving.

Sometimes in life we can be our harshest critic. We question ourselves. Why are we not handling this situation better? Why are we so lethargic? Why are we crying at the drop of a hat? Why are we not thinking clearly? Shouldn't we be in better shape by now?

Our Father in heaven is patient toward us (2 Peter 3:9). His abundant patience was in full display while Noah's ark was being prepared (1 Peter 3:20). That's a lot of patience! Patience is a part of the fruit of the Spirit that should be growing in our lives (Galatians 5:22-23). Recovery takes time…lots of time.

Today, I will…strive to be patient with myself, just as God is patient with me.

Growing Gratitude While Grieving

Today's Scripture: James 1:17; Matthew 6:25-34

Everybody is blessed. Blessed beyond measure. Blessed beyond merit. Richly blessed! The Source of the abundant blessings is our giving God. "Every good gift and every perfect gift is from above, coming down from the Father of lights, with whom there is no variation or shadow due to change" (James 1:17). In His infinite awareness and goodness, our loving Father in heaven provides His children's every need (Matthew 6:25-34).

Even though everyone is blessed far beyond mere needs, gratitude is not always an easy characteristic to possess. As one hymn suggests, there are times when "the burdens press and the cares distress, And the way grows weary and long." It's when trouble comes that we are not at our best. We are not our normal self. Our perspective can be distorted. The burdens of life can even blind us to blessings. Personal circumstances can be so bad, even the best of us may see nothing but troubles (Job 14:1).

When we have lost a marital mate, much has been lost: companionship, plans, intimacy, etc. The burden of spousal loss and the intimidating grief journey is exhausting. It can be the heaviest burden of life. The daily challenges of living with horrific loss tempts a person to focus exclusively on trials. The reality is, though, blessings always outnumber and outweigh burdens (always!). We may not see that, at times. We may not feel that way—but it's true.

What one of us has not taken our health for granted? When does a person appreciate their health? When they have lost it! Think back on all those years of trouble-free health. The burden of sickness can deepen gratitude.

I lost my wife on Christmas morning. In my deep grieving, my gratitude grew exponentially. I paid a dear price to more sincerely appreciate over 40 years of marriage. I certainly see life differently now. I am deeply thankful that I had her in my life and see now I am still being blessed because of her.

Today, I will..._choose to count my blessings—even when I am burdened._

The Need

Today's Scripture: Romans 15:13

"I need Thee, O I need Thee; Every hour I need Thee!"

The word "need" is a strong word. It is different than words like "want," "hope," "prefer," etc. A need is a necessity. Something we cannot live without. It reflects recognized dependence.

When life is good, we do not always recognize what we need. Our lives are moving forward in a well-established direction. We have a routine. We like our life. However, reality this side of eternity is not always pleasant. It can be more than challenging—it can be horrific. When I've lost my beloved spouse, the pain can feel intolerable and life may seem hopeless. Just getting up out of bed and putting one foot in front of the other is a daily grind. We feel empty. We may even question whether life is worth living.

One of the potential blessings of trials is how they can help us see our need more clearly. Desperation can bring us to our knees. It can help us appreciate the fact we need the Lord. Prosperity doesn't do that, but adversity can. Losing the dearest on earth to us (and having to live with that loss every day and every night!) is about as adverse as life can get.

Edwin White wisely observed, "When we reduce life to its essentials, only one thing is needful—to have God." That is a fundamental truth, but not always embraced until life gives us something awful, something we would never choose for ourselves. If there would ever be a time we might clearly sense our desperate need for God, it would be when our spouse has died.

Our Father in heaven is love (1 John 4:8). He knows what is going on both within us and around us (Acts 1:24; Hebrews 4:13-16). He "comforts us in all our affliction" (2 Corinthians 1:4). He is "the God of hope" Who can fill us "with all joy and peace in believing" (Romans 15:13).

Today, I will...*recognize my only real need and passionately pursue intimacy with my heavenly Father like I never have before.*

WEEK 44

Sports and Spirituality

CHRIS PRESSNELL

MONDAY

I Pitched This Sunday And Jesus Got Shut Out

Today's Scripture: Psalm 122:1

Regardless of how we feel about it, sports have become a major part of our society. As a former college tennis player and current high school tennis head coach, I understand the commitment that an individual has to make if he/she wants to be successful in the sport he/she choose to play. The impact of this is also felt by those who are closest to us, our family members. How many weekends have been devoted to sports' schedules? How much time has been committed to these games and practices? How much money has been spent on these activities? How many brothers and sisters have had to log the hours at a venue to watch a sibling in action? To be honest, the expectations we place on our children or even the expectations that they place on themselves require this kind of diligence and sacrifice. What would happen if we directed this much attention to spiritual things and the church? Have your children had to miss Bible class or worship for sports? Has the desire to be the next Tom Brady or Freddy Freeman denied us the next Abraham or Paul? Unfortunately, too often sports have become our idol. I have seen this happen and quite frankly to my shame have been guilty of it myself in the past.

So what's the answer? First, we need to establish a priority system. Paul in writing to the Colossians reminds them that Christ is their life (Colossians 3:4) not travel ball. May we remember that He should be our life also and not be lured into the hollow thrill of worldly fanaticism. Second, establish some parameters that are absolute. For our family growing up, missing worship service with the Lord's people was not an option. It has been my observation that the ball team is given preferential treatment while God and His people are the ones expected to accept the absenteeism of the Christian family.

Today, I will...decide that from now on God and His people will take precedence over recreation and entertainment. Furthermore, Father, please forgive me when I have allowed this to happen.

TUESDAY
Tennis and Testimony
Today's Scripture: 1 Corinthians 9:22-23

Although our family loves playing and watching sports, we were always taught to think of sports as a means to an end. The real end was not how it would benefit us individually but how it could be used as a means of showing Christ to others. Again, I haven't always done that to the extent that I wanted but hopefully I have succeeded more often than not. I want to share an example today and one in tomorrow's devotional of how being involved in sports has given me spiritual opportunities. Please understand that when I share these experiences I am not intending to toot my own horn. God is the one who opened these doors and to Him goes all the glory.

About 11 years ago in Syktyvkar, Russia, I was given the privilege of teaching at a Bible School. Three weeks of classes during a northern Russian winter in February meant a lot of time indoors. I asked about going to a gym to get a little exercise. My translator mentioned that around the corner was an indoor tennis facility. TENNIS!!!! That's right in my wheelhouse. I connected with the local pro, and we set up a hitting session. We hit it off (no pun intended) immediately and he invited me to come back to the club, free of charge, every night for the duration of my trip. Additionally, he set up tennis matches for his members with me. Curious about my tennis acumen, several members of the church and Bible school asked if they could come watch. While there, one of the Russian players asked the preacher of the church why I seemed so happy and was so nice. Apparently, his experience with other Americans had not been so pleasant as he found them to be rude and arrogant. He wanted to know what the difference was. The preacher informed him that I had Jesus Christ in my life and THAT makes all the difference in the world.

Today, I will..._allow the joy of being a Christian to be seen in whatever activity I am doing._

WEDNESDAY

Back to School

Today's Scripture: Luke 16:8

"...For the sons of this world are more shrewd in dealing with their own generation than the sons of light" (Luke 16:8). If you consider the ability of the sons of this world to market sin and peddle their filth then you really do have to tip your caps to them. They have people believing that the Bible should be ignored and that unrighteousness is the way of truth. Sadly, many Christians have done little to combat the dismissal of prayer from school or Bible morality in classrooms aside from complaining about it to others who take the same resigned approach. It is time for us to don our thinking caps and consider how we can turn the tide of moral erosion and debased mindsets in our communities and schools.

In July of 2018, the superintendent of a local school system contacted me about a job. Due to my history with tennis, she wanted me to become the head varsity coach of their high school program. Although honored to be considered, I initially declined recognizing the tremendous time and effort that kind of commitment would require. But, just to gauge her reaction...I told her that I would pitch the coaching job to my elders if she would grant me one concession. Intrigued, she asked, "What do you want?" I told her that I wanted to teach Bible in her high school. Concerned about potential litigation she asked, "How would we do that without legal ramifications?" "Oddly enough," I said, "in Alabama, Bible classes are state approved curriculum." Yes, you heard that right!!! They are taught in every state college and university as Humanity Religion courses. Since most high schools offer dual enrollment courses, an individual with a Master's Degree in Bible can teach these classes. To my excitement the superintendent said, "Let's do it." I went to my elders with this proposal and to their credit, wisdom and love for Christ they said, "You have to take that job." The rest is history. These jobs at the high school have given me amazing access and exposure to an enormous number of people.

Today, I will...*look for creative ways through sports to expose people to God.*

262

Love Actually Does Mean Something To This Tennis Player

Today's Scripture: Romans 12:9-10; Philippians 2:3-4

One of my favorite things about tennis is that until you become a big time star, playing in big time events, you have to referee your own matches. That's right, with the exception of maybe golf, tennis is a sport where there are no on the court officials for the competition. Each player is expected to judge whether his opponents shots are in or out and make the call. Tennis players are also taught that if the ball lands on the line it is in, and if you can't be 100% certain that it is out then you should play the ball like it was 100% in. This requires that the competing players be fair, honest and in some cases accommodating with each other. For example, if a ball from another court rolls onto your court then you need to call a "let" (kind of like a timeout) to make sure both players are not distracted or injured. The point is to be replayed even if you were in the winning position at the time. The server is graciously granted a first serve to restart the point even if the point initially began on a second serve. Occasionally, you experience a player that likes to cheat or act like a jerk, but for the most part the players behave with grace and sportsmanship. Rarely, have I ever had to step in and referee a contentious match where one of the players requested a line judge because of multiple bad calls.

I have often thought about this kind of consideration when it comes to the church. Wouldn't it be wonderful if we gave our brothers and sisters this kind of treatment? To not say that what they did was out of bounds until I know for certain? When it comes to love, instead of it meaning nothing to a tennis player, it really means to a Christian what I Corinthians 13:7 intends: I give you the benefit of the doubt.

Today, I will...*be more honest, fair, gracious and loving to my neighbors, family, and church.*

Fight the Spiritual Battle To the End!

Today's Scripture: Acts 20:22-24

Our son, Cade, was a very good athlete. Over the years he won trophies in baseball, basketball, and tennis. He even received a full college scholarship to play tennis. But my proudest moment as a father in regards to his athletic endeavors did not come in a victory but in a loss. It was the last match that he would ever play as a high school tennis player. As a junior, he had made it to the finals of the Alabama 6A state championship and lost in a very close match. As a senior, he was once again the region champion and headed to the state championship. This time, however, his draw would pit him in the semifinals against a player that had transferred from Florida. After a close first set, the young man took control of the match. It was obvious on that day that defeat was inevitable. This young man, being a sophomore, would go on to win the state title three years in a row. I will never forget the final point. I can not tell you how many strokes were hit between the two of them because there were so many. Despite the looming defeat, Cade chased down every shot. He ran and fought until the moment the other player finally hit a winner. He never quit and never gave up.

I confess that tears welled up in my eyes at the conclusion of the match-- not because I was disappointed that he lost but because I was so proud of his attitude and effort. I remember thinking about having this kind of determination and dedication in spiritual matters. In Acts 20:22-24, Paul knew that he was going to be exposed to uncomfortable circumstances and eventually death for his faith in Christ, but, he was not going to quit his mission. In this life, we may not always be victorious in every spiritual battle we face. We are going to be surrounded by hate, sin, and disappointment. BUT DON'T EVER GIVE UP!!!!

Today, I will..._determine to put on my spiritual armor and get back on the battle field for my King._

WEEK 45

Helping Our Children When There Is a Divorce

BRYAN McALISTER

MONDAY

Speak the Truth in Love

Today's Scripture: Malachi 2:8-16

In 1971, a seminal work was produced by Judith Wallerstein and collaborators. *The Unexpected Legacy of Divorce* detailed the aftermath of divorce on children. For 25 years, the study followed selected children from scenarios deemed "ideal" for divorce to occur. The families were as "normal" and as "mainstream" for the times as any could be. 25 years later, these kids, now adults, reported their conclusion of divorce's impact: "Personal relationships are unreliable." Well before 1971, the description offered for divorce came with these words, "Divorce [...] covers his garment with violence" (Malachi 2:16). Most translations provide the divine commentary, "I, the Lord your God, hate divorce." It's akin to our hate of cancer, disease, or death. We see the pain brought to the lives of those we love. No one comes out unharmed, not even God.

This week, as we travel a difficult road of reality for our families, check a few road signs along the way. The circumstances of divorce are as varied as the people who experience it. Still, there are some truths which can help.

Honesty, spoken in love, brings freedom and growth (John 8:32, Ephesians 4:15). Whatever discomfort, unpleasantness, or betrayal were experienced by the parents, the children likely did not suffer these things, at least not directly. Maybe the parents attempted to shield their kids from their conflict. If they managed to do this with any degree of success, the kids wrestle with compounded confusion. Truth is, if you're lying awake at night wondering what went wrong, chances are, so are they.

Children will blame themselves. Be honest, how often have you accepted blame for something beyond your control? Listen to their reasoning for believing so. Listening is not the same thing as affirming. Often we want to end a line of conversation, before it ever unfolds, because we already disagree with the conclusion. Kids may need to say out loud what is ultimately distorted in their mind and heart, before it can be aided and altered.

Today, I will... *pray for courage to speak the truth of divorce to my children, and to permit them to speak the truth of what they are feeling. I will pray for the strength to move with them through their feelings, and not just away from their feelings.*

TUESDAY

KEEP Speaking the Truth in Love

Today's Scripture: John 8:31-36

Devoted parents want to take pain from their children. On the surface, this appears comforting. However, when a heart, even a young heart, is not allowed to experience and express pain, the opportunity to gain resilience, courage, and strength is lost. Instead, we become burdened, less capable, and weaker because we were not allowed to grow through our hurt.

Jesus spoke of a vastly different separation in John 8:31-36. Still, the imagery is clear. When Jesus spoke of separation, it was *confusing* (vs. 33). They *created* meaning from what He spoke. These words were *contradictory* to what they had always believed. In many ways these are perfect descriptions of what thoughts can be experienced by children, learning the news of divorce. How can we help?

Combat the confusion with an honest conversation about what is or will soon take place. If possible, both parents and children should be present. While circumstances may vary, seeking Christ in the moment for the sake of caring for their child is a much nobler task. Demonstrating a cooperative spirit for the welfare of your children, while being honest about a hard life moment, will communicate to them their value. Use this time to inform, not cast blame or hurl insults.

Consider the truth of how things will change. It can be helpful for children to know what their new routine will be. The reality of not regularly seeing both parents in the same place is, for many, an extreme change. As best as possible, describe the new schedule and routine. Just as your wedding day vision of the future has changed, so too has your child's vision of the future. Be honest about the changes and the weight they carry.

When Jesus promised knowing the truth would set us free, we would not be free from dealing with sin, but its penalty. Likewise, spoken truth does not keep us from experiencing pain, but it does give us the freedom to feel it and seek help from our family and the Father through it.

Today, I will...write down the truths I need and want my child to know. I will be intentional to talk to them about these changes of life.

Help Your Children See Forgiveness

Today's Scripture: Matthew 19:13-15

Nestled between the Lord's response to the divorce and remarriage controversy of the Pharisees and the critical encounter Jesus had with the rich young ruler, we see one of the most tender moments in Jesus' ministry: parents bringing their children to Jesus. Matthew records they were brought to Jesus to be blessed (Matthew 19:13). Luke provides the reminder of Jesus how only the converted believer's heart to become as a child will gain entrance into heaven (Luke 18:17).

Sometimes divorce occurs out of necessity to preserve life and wellbeing. Sometimes it occurs regardless of the want and prayer for it to be avoided. Sometimes divorce occurs, and we recoil at the notion it ever did. Few, if any, want the negative consequences of divorce in their life, much less the lives of their children. Neither power nor predictability are in the hands of those enduring divorce, nor to know all the reasons they must now navigate this reality. The power we do possess as parents, grandparents and overseers of children is to continually bring them to see Jesus. Talmudic writings reveal how Jewish parents sought renown teachers for their blessing to be upon their children. No doubt this was the motive of the parents mentioned by Matthew and Luke. It, too, must be ours.

Children need to see Jesus and His forgiveness when divorce has occurred. Forgiveness is different from trust. Don't forget, the Lord's blessing of the little children comes in the wake of His teaching of forgiveness, "up to seventy times seven." Forgiveness means we are honest about the wound the offense has brought to our lives and the lives of those we love. Forgiveness also means we are honest about the strength God gives us to not be enslaved to bitterness.

Modeling a lifestyle of forgiveness for our children shows them the nature of our relationship with Jesus is not theoretical. His truth will set us free (John 8:32). If we are living out forgiveness, rest assured our children will be witnesses and be helped as a result of it.

Today, I will...led*live out the power of forgiveness before my children. I will speak words of forgiveness regarding those who have sinned against myself and seek forgiveness from those against whom I have sinned.*

THURSDAY

Garden Hoses & Fire Hydrants

Today's Scripture: Psalm 141:1-10

Today's world places strong emphasis on the emotions we feel as a result of any given circumstance or even concept thought. Significant effort is placed on trying to prevent negative emotions from being felt or taking negative emotions and attempting to make them only positive. Our thoughts cultivate our emotions. Our emotions help shape our behaviors. Attempting to avoid or dismiss negative emotions all together truly does not benefit anyone involved.

Kids and emotions are complex to navigate, to say the least. Adults and the art of navigating emotions are hardly simple. The most significant distinction between adults and children is the ability to regulate (if we choose to) our emotions. For kids, often they are feeling emotions with such intensity, it's a like a garden hose hooked to a fire hydrant...lots of pressure, little control. What results is misbehavior, outbursts, extreme mood swings, loss of interest in their activities, lying, or other uncharacteristic behaviors. If we're honest, adults respond this way too.

For kids, feeling anxious over existing conflicts, being the "deliverer" of messages or reminders, catching criticisms shaped from our hurts (i.e., "You're just like your father"), or calling for their agreement with your complaint leave children wrestling with their own feelings of fear and rejection. Kids feel a need to choose a side to reduce the uncomfortable feeling of the tension.

The Psalmist was so overwhelmed with emotion, he was compelled to "cry out" to God. Many reasons exist for this choice; chief among them, he knew he could. Help your child by gifting them with understanding how hard it is to make sense of confusing things we feel. They may blame you. Be strong enough to endure it, and hear it. Do not use them for your communication between you and your ex. Be interested in the child's time away from you with the other parent. You're ability to listen with gratitude for your child's well-being is no more affirming of another's actions you do not approve of, any more than your child's enjoyment of being with someone they love and miss.

Today, I will...pray for an understanding heart for how my child is trying to comprehend what even I have trouble explaining.

Boundaries in the Burden

Today's Scripture: Ephesians 6:1-4

Divorce delivers a lot of unwanted mail to the lives of families. There are chaos and confusion, rejection and resentment, and doubt and distance. Perhaps the most devastating delivery of divorce: its power to collide the worlds of "things we once believed would always be" and "what might have been." Within all this disruption comes the temptation to "lighten" and "ease"the standards and expectations on the children of divorce. The command to "honor your father and mother" does not come with a qualifier. Children are to regard the value of parenting, even if it is marked with less than desirable circumstances (Ephesians 6:1-2). Parents are not to provoke their children to wrath, but instruct them and guide them by God's word (Ephesians 6:4). In short, we need to set boundaries and keep them.

Accept criticism. Expect respect. Part of this new context of life will bring an understandable amount of blame and frustration toward the parents. Even under the best circumstances, it's not pleasant when your kids are upset with you as a parent. Give them permission to speak honestly, but respectfully. Giving them the space to share their frustration does not forfeit their honor owed to you.

Avoid taking sides. Kids will become upset with a parent. The other will potentially hear about it. Listen to the complaint. Resist the temptation (should there be) to "pile on" the other parent. Instead, reinforce reasonable discipline and corrections among both parents, in order to show growth, wellbeing, and character development are still shared interests of the parents.

Know when you are being manipulated (i.e., played). Guard yourself against seeking the role of "favored" among your kids. Monitor your motive for agreeing to or denying certain requests from your children. Remember too, kids are often living in the tension between two parents. The Lord can still train, even and especially in the midst of the burdens we carry (Ephesians 6:4). Seek God's will for you and your kids so that even in all the difficulty, "It may be well with you."

Today, I will...seek to honor my God, my kids, and my relationships, with the love of Christ teaching me to permit and prohibit where it honors Him.

WEEK 46

Encouraging Your Sons to Be Preachers

JON WARNES

The Motivation to Encourage Others

Today's Scripture: John 12:21

The Greeks who were on their way to Jerusalem had heard about the miracles of Jesus and that He was nearby. They sought to see Him, the One who had brought back to life a dead man…the unthinkable. What about those who come to your church today to "see Jesus?" Those who come are likely in pain and dead spiritually. Typically, we have a preacher who can show them Jesus. But what about the church of tomorrow? Who will be there to show them Jesus and preach the truth? Jesus departed two thousand years ago into glory and yet, like those who approached Philip (John 12:21) to see this amazing man named Jesus, there will continue to be an incredible amount of interest.

Why not encourage our sons to show future generations Jesus from God's word? The beauty of preaching is that preachers come from all walks of life, meeting the needs of millions with a million different personalities and needs. What's sad with our current American trend in the Lord's church is that pulpits are being vacated at a seriously quick rate. No, not every preacher is or must be preaching full-time. Sure, it would be nice, but why not before sending your son to college for a secular job, encourage him to go to future preacher camps in the summer and attend a free school of preaching for two years while he is still young? This will add to his existing foundation, so that he will be additionally equipped to lead, teach, and preach within congregations in his future. Of course, he can still hold down a secular job after the ministry training, but help him accomplish it before the opportunity to show Jesus to others slips away.

Today, I will…*talk to my son(s) about a ministry training plan to help those who "wish to see Jesus" for years to come.*

Give Your Son the Chance To Save Lives

Today's Scripture: 1 Corinthians 1:17-31

I remember well the first time I took CPR training in the Air Force. It was a requirement for all in military service to take a basic Life Saving course. It was a bit uncomfortable, especially in such a large group setting, but what was more uncomfortable was making sure I did it right. The "dummy" used was obviously not even close to real life, but for those serious about knowing the right techniques if ever faced with reality, that "dummy" was going to really give our training a test and see if we could "save" its life. It may sound contrary to the whole "free will" concept, but what if we made Bible preacher training a requirement for our sons in the Lord's church? I know, a bit too much, but maybe it really isn't too much. After all, isn't learning the Bible and being able to teach others the truth a basic Life Saving course?

Until the Lord comes for us, there will always be a need to help save souls for God's beautiful purpose. There is no better time than now to instill in your son the desire to be a saver of lives by using God's word and to be adequately equipped to preach His glorious and perfect word. In 1 Corinthians 1:17-31, there is much about wisdom, foolishness, and how preaching saved those who believed (v. 21). Now, I don't want to go as far as calling unsaved people "dummies", but I remember very well how ignorant (foolish) I was to God's word, and it took a man trained in biblical Life Saving skills to help save this foolish man through sound preaching. For that, I am so thankful to God! What a beautiful thought it is to think we can encourage our sons to be preachers trained in Life Saving, all for God's glory.

Today, I will...*consider taking my son(s) to meet or call several area preachers and talk about the importance of preaching.*

Run the Race with Beautiful Feet

Today's Scripture: Romans 10:14-15

"How then will they call on Him in whom they have not believed? And how are they to believe in Him of whom they have never heard? And how are they to hear without someone preaching? And how are they to preach unless they are sent? As it is written, 'How beautiful are the feet of those who preach the good news!'" (Romans 10:14-15).

You probably figured at some point I would use the ol' beautiful feet Bible illustration when it came to this topic of encouraging our sons to preach. It's awfully hard to resist and ignore because the word picture is truly a beautiful and inspiring one. Not only can you imagine it, but think about the possibilities for your son(s) to be the ones humbly delivering the word of God both to the lost and to the saved.

My wife and I did not set out to raise a bunch of preachers, but we did set out to raise Christian men (and women) who would take our feeble Christian training, make it their own, and excel even more than their parents did or even imagined. I thank God that the men of our family have decided to be preachers and to deliver the Bible to all who will listen…with their beautiful feet. What significantly contributed to this happening was placing the family in a "Think Souls" environment on a regular basis. What this means to me is putting yourself within a congregation that is evangelistic and sees not only the immediate need for delivering the word of God, but looks long-term at ensuring the Bible will continue to be taught for years beyond yours and my lifetime. And what's more important is to breathe this mindset in your home 24/7. This life is about "Thinking Souls" and our son(s) need to see it from our beautiful feet first.

Today, I will..._study Romans 10:14-15 with my son(s) and with much excitement encourage them to be spokesmen for God._

Teach Them Early to Be Eager To Be Ministers

Today's Scripture: Romans 1:15-17

"So, I am eager to preach the gospel to you also who are in Rome. For I am not ashamed of the gospel, for it is the power of God for salvation to everyone who believes, to the Jew first and also to the Greek. For in it the righteousness of God is revealed from faith for faith, as it is written, 'The righteous shall live by faith'" (Romans 1:15-17).

As a young parent and adult, I thought I could measure up a young boy/man pretty well and determine if he would be a good fit for ministry or not. Boy, was I wrong! After years of spending time in a school of preaching environment and being part of several congregations due to my time moving in the military and ministry, I have been amazed at how many different young men have taken an eagerness to preach. There are so many different personalities in the pulpit...and I am SO glad for it.

It shouldn't surprise me, though, knowing Jesus' disciples were not one-size-fits-all robots. The same goes for our own sons. I love seeing how God has developed each of my sons into various types of ministers for the Lord's sake. Each, by his own decision, has answered the call to be a minister by using his love for God, love for God's people, and using his own personality to be the best minister he can be for the Lord's church. All with an eagerness to see saints in the church be strengthened and souls who are lost become saved. One important factor we can instill in our boys at home is to show them we are eager for them to learn the Bible well enough so they can help a lost world and a needy church.

Today, I will...pray with my son(s) about learning even more about the powerful word of God so he will develop an eagerness to share it the rest of his life to God's glory.

What You Say at Home Will Be Said

Today's Scripture: Deuteronomy 6:6-9

"And these words that I command you today shall be on your heart. You shall teach them diligently to your children, and shall talk of them when you sit in your house, and when you walk by the way, and when you lie down, and when you rise. You shall bind them as a sign on your hand, and they shall be as frontlets between your eyes. You shall write them on the doorposts of your house and on your gates." (Deuteronomy 6:6-9).

"The Shema" (Deuteronomy 6:4-9) is a powerful text of Scripture that is not only beautiful to recite from memory, but it is chock-full of principles from God to parents. It's no secret, how we behave as parents around the house will usually equate to how our children will behave to their children. As parents, we can motivate like none other. That is God's incredible design of family. So, how will we motivate and encourage our young sons to strongly consider ministry? By placing God first in our own lives and in our home without compromise.

No, it's not about just having a Bible or many Bibles on the mantel or bookshelf, nor having decorative verses on the wall. It's also not just about making sure we are only in the pew on Sundays and Wednesdays. It's about distributing, breathing, and ingesting God's word at home first and allowing it to produce an abundance of fruit from every member of the family. If you wish to see your son(s) be preachers, I'm pretty sure your intentional and loving parenting towards that goal will also produce the fruit of ministry.

Today, I will...*be intentional in helping develop a spirit of ministry within my son(s) at home, no matter if he latches on to a full-time work or not. The hope is he will speak of God and live for Him daily...and forever.*

WEEK 47

Teaching Our Children to Be Spiritual Leaders

MIKE JOHNSON
(KENTUCKY)

Fathers Guard the Door

Today's Scripture: John 10:7, 9

Doors are a very important part of our houses and our cars. Doors keep things out that might want to get in but are not wanted. So, we lock our doors and even install alarm systems to ensure the safety of all behind those doors. Doors also allow access to those who are accepted. However, we need to unlock the door or turn off the alarm for them to enter.

Doors serve as a visible symbol that we will invite into our lives those whom we wish. We welcome people to our homes through our doors. We paint the doors and hang wreaths to give a welcoming appearance to our homes all the while monitoring the comings and goings of people.

Jesus said of Himself, "So Jesus again said to them, 'Truly, truly, I say to you, I am the door of the sheep...I am the door. If anyone enters by me, he will be saved and will go in and out and find pasture'" (John 10:7, 9). He fills the role of a physical door in a spiritual sense. He is the one who determines who and how someone may enter the sheep fold over which He has control.

Now, consider the spiritual role of fathers who guard their doors. In a physical sense, fathers take this obligation seriously. No father wants to expose his family to the dangers of the world without doing all he can to protect them.

But, what about the protection of his family spiritually? God calls fathers to be the spiritual leaders of their homes. How would things be different in our homes if fathers were as concerned about their family's spiritual safety as they are about their physical well-being? What steps would these fathers take to ensure that spiritual safety?

Today, I will...*tell my children that my greatest concern for them is their spiritual safety.*

278

Mothers Provide a Home

Today's Scripture: Acts 12:1-17

While fathers are guarding the home, mothers are making the home a place where everyone wants to be. She is the emotional hub of the home. When Paul instructed Timothy concerning the older women teaching the younger women, his instructions included, "...manage their households..." (1 Timothy 5:14). That includes so many things that relate not only to the physical side, but also to the spiritual side.

There is a woman who has been overlooked in her contribution to Christianity. She raised a man who became the author of the second gospel of Jesus Christ. He was a missionary with Paul and Barnabas (Acts 13). Even though he left them on the journey, he became a man whom Paul, 11 years later, asked Timothy, "Get Mark and bring him with you, for he is very useful to me for ministry" (2 Timothy 4:11).

This man was John Mark. His mother was Mary (Acts 12:12). His uncle was Barnabas (Colossians 4:10). He was Peter's son in the faith (1 Peter 5:13). He was the author of the Gospel of Mark. Mark's mother deserves much praise for his contributions to the Christian faith. She molded him by her actions and decisions.

We learn about this woman in the event described in Acts 12. Peter was in prison. The Church prayed constantly for him. In response to their prayers, God miraculously delivered Peter from prison. Peter went straight to the place where the Church was gathered together praying for him—the house of John Mark's mother (Acts 12:12).

Mary created a home where the Church was glad to gather. She gave her son the opportunity to meet the faithful people of his day—Peter, James, John, Barnabas. Mary helped to mold Mark into the Christian leader he became through using her home as the contact point for him to be exposed to the people and training he would need in his future ministry.

Today, I will...
open my home to Christian people who will influence and teach my children.

WEDNESDAY

Aspire that They Learn To Teach Themselves

Today's Scripture: Hebrews 5:12-14

"The sign of a good leader is this. When a job is complete, the people will say, 'We did this ourselves.'" I found this statement and have kept it on my desk for a number of years now. It has such a powerful message. We are thinking about how we train our children to be spiritual leaders. I want to give three key words to describe that training: aspiration, inspiration, and perspiration.

In this devotional, consider aspiration. The dictionary definition of aspiration is: "the hope or ambition of achieving something." Our aspiration for our children first must be that they learn to lead themselves before they can lead others.

Hebrews 5:12-14 is a text that may not have been properly understood through the years. I know I had missed the point. The text reads, "About this we have much to say, and it is hard to explain, since you have become dull of hearing. For though by this time you ought to be teachers, you need someone to teach you again the basic principles of the oracles of God. You need milk, not solid food, for everyone who lives on milk is unskilled in the word of righteousness, since he is a child. But solid food is for the mature, for those who have their powers of discernment trained by constant practice to distinguish good from evil."

I have thought for most of my preaching life that I could use this passage to encourage people to teach Bible classes. While that could be the natural outcome, that is not the primary point of the passage.

The Hebrews writer is telling his readers that they have a responsibility to learn to teach themselves. They should not choose to rely on what others say about a Bible topic or passage. Spiritual leadership begins with learning how to teach yourself. That is a key to spiritual maturity. Are you teaching your children how to learn and not just telling them all the answers?

Today, I will...begin to collect the resources my children will need to find the answers for themselves.

280

Give Them Inspirational Images

Today's Scripture: Philippians 1:12-14

What is it that inspires you? What gets your motor running, your heart racing, and your sight engaged? Maybe you have been inspired by the words of a coach or friend. Or, maybe you have been inspired by some great piece of music or art. Or, maybe there is an image in your head from something you have seen in the past that continues to inspire you whenever you remember it.

Who of us was not inspired by the brave actions of the first responders on 9/11 racing up the stairs of the twin towers into the danger the people scurrying down the stairs were trying to escape? Those images still stir something within all of us.

There was another great inspirational moment in the history of our country. It began with these words, "Four score and twenty years ago..." Abraham Lincoln's Gettysburg address was only 273 words. He was not even the main speaker of the day. That title went to a man whom you may never have heard of, Edward Everett, former Secretary of State. His speech lasted for 2 hours and it was delivered completely from memory. However, he would later say, "I wish that I could flatter myself that I had come as near to the central idea of the occasion in two hours as you did in two minutes."

The second word in training our children to be spiritual leaders is inspiration. Paul gave us some inspirational words from behind the walls of his imprisonment. "I want you to know, brothers, that what has happened to me has really served to advance the gospel...And most of the brothers, having become confident in the Lord by my imprisonment, are much more bold to speak the word without fear" (Philippians 1:12, 14).

We must inspire our children through our own lives. They must see us doing what we preach. They must hear us handle difficulties and difficult people well. These can be inspirational images for our children as they grow to spiritual maturity.

Today, I will...*pray for ability to inspire my children through my faithful life.*

Always Let Them See You Sweat

Today's Scripture: Matthew 7:13-14

In 1984, the Gillette Company launched a new series of TV commercials for its Dry Idea antiperspirants that introduced what eventually became one of the most famous ad slogans of all time. The TV commercials featured celebrities who each mentioned three "nevers" for their profession—ending with "never let them see you sweat."

That is good advice for any of us who are public speakers. No one wants to see the sweat marks in the armpit of your shirt! If you are a basketball fan, you may know of Buzz Williams. He is the coach at Texas. He is as famous for his obvious sweating as he is for his coaching!

While we don't desire others to see us sweat, there is another way in which we should want them to see us sweat. The third word in our series on teaching our children to be spiritual leaders is perspiration. My dad often said, in response to my complaining, that hard work never killed anyone.

Jesus clearly stated that the Christian life will not be easy. "Enter by the narrow gate. For the gate is wide and the way is easy that leads to destruction, and those who enter by it are many. For the gate is narrow and the way is hard that leads to life, and those who find it are few" (Matthew 7:13-14).

As we train our families toward spiritual leadership, the commercial slogan will not work. We should amend it to say, "Be sure to let them see you sweat!" Some parents do not allow their families to learn from sweating. They allow their children to take the easy way out, doing only just enough to get by. It is not easy to develop a life of discipline that includes Bible reading and prayer. It is not easy to face some things that the world will throw at us. But, these are necessary, and our children need to see us perspiring so that they will learn how to do it themselves.

Today, I will...*determine to nudge my family into something that stretches them and causes them to sweat.*

WEEK 48

Helping Our Children to Think Positively About the Church

MICHAEL BATES

Speak Positively About the Church

Today's Scripture: Philippians 4:8

Our thoughts are extremely important (Philippians 4:8). The thoughts of children are especially important. The story is told of two young brothers who were constantly getting into trouble. Their mother had become quite perplexed as to what to do to correct their delinquent behavior. Not knowing what else to do, she reached out to her preacher who had witnessed first-hand the poorly behaved boys, as they had often gotten into trouble at church. The preacher had the mother bring the oldest boy into his study first. After a long time of really getting nowhere with the boy he shouted, "Do you know who God is? Do you know where God is?" At that the young man jumped from his seat, ran from the preacher's study all the way down the street to his house. He then ran upstairs and locked himself in his closet. The interested younger brother came near to the closet door and asked, "What did the preacher say?" The younger brother replied, "God's missing and they think we had something to do with it." The young man had the wrong idea about what this was really all about.

Did you know our words about the church greatly influence our children's thoughts about the church? And we must not misguide their thinking about the church of our Lord. If we speak negatively in their presence about the church, they are most likely to think negatively about the church, too. But if we speak positively about the church, they are more likely to think positively about the church. As a preacher once said, "We have fried preacher and stewed elder for lunch on Sunday and wonder why our children grow up not loving the church." He's on to something. Imagine if we spoke positively about worship, Bible class teachers, the song leader, the preacher, the elders, deacons, and all other members!

Today, I will..._resist the urge to utter a single complaint against any person in the church, but instead speak complimentary of them before my children._

Love the Church Like Jesus Does

Today's Scripture: Ephesians 5:23

A young man, a Bible major at one of our fine Christian universities, delivered a devotional one night for his peers. He had an exceptional visual aid drawn on a large, white poster board. The picture was an hourglass drawn to cover nearly the entire surface. On the top of the hourglass was written, "Jesus died for . . ." and on the widest part of the hourglass was written underneath, "The World." Then about half-way down the upper portion of the hourglass these words were written, "The Church." And as the hourglass neared its narrowest point right in the middle, but still on the upper portion, this word was written, "Me." The young preacher explained how in the broadest sense Jesus died for the world (John 3:16). Then he demonstrated how Jesus died for the church (Acts 20:28). Then he made it even more personal, making the case that Jesus died for each person (Galatians 2:20).

The bottom half of the hour glass was a mirror-image of the top half. However, the bottom half had these words, "Therefore, I have a responsibility to… myself, the church, and the world." It was a tremendous lesson. Try to draw this on paper.

In helping children think positively about the church, pointing them to the things Jesus loves may help. If Jesus loves something we should, too. Jesus loved the church so much that He "gave Himself up for her" (Ephesians 5:23). The church is so important to Jesus that she is pictured as His bride. To show husbands how to love their wives, the Holy Spirit directed Paul to use how Jesus loves His bride as the model. If children have attended a wedding, remind them that the bride and groom vowed to love each other for the rest of their lives. The love Jesus has for His bride, the church, is even greater than this. And if Jesus loves the church so much then we should, too.

Today, I will…_show my children how Jesus loves the church._

Desire Deeply to Be with the Church

Today's Scripture: Matthew 6:33

Sporting events often draw very large crowds. People either love the sport being played or they love someone participating. Concerts can draw large crowds, too, and tickets can even be difficult to obtain due to the many people who desire to be there. They either love who is performing, the songs they sing, or the person who may attend the concert with them. Even hospitals can draw large numbers of people. When loved ones are ill or having tests and surgeries, we want to be near to support them. You see, we do what we love or do things with and for those we love. A former elder often said, "We do what we really want to do." That is, we take the necessary efforts to do what we really desire.

That's even true regarding our relationship with Christ and His church. When we really love Jesus and His church, every effort is made to make Christ and His church the top priority (Matthew 6:33). Is that what our children see in us? Are we showing them, by the choices we make in life, that Jesus and His church come first? If children learn best by example, what are we teaching them? Hearing parents complain about assembling with the church of our Lord at any time is quite discouraging. When children hear parents and grandparents offer one excuse after another as to why the family doesn't engage in the work of the church, they often deem it as unimportant.

However, there is a better way. We love the Lord so much we want to be there to worship, fellowship, and engage in His work. We love His church to the point that we want to be together with those of like, precious faith. Those times where we can get away from the world and find the oasis of God's people should be our greatest desire.

Today, I will...be determined to show greater joy about putting Christ and His church first in the life of my family.

Be An Active Part of God's Family

Today's Scripture: 1 Timothy 3:15; Luke 8:19-21

The word "family" is a special word for many people. It has such distinct meaning and application in our lives. Even those who do not have the warm, loving family they desire still dream and even pray for that reality. For many years people have described other relationships as "family" even though there may be no blood relation. One might refer to people at work as my "work family." Athletic teams often refer to themselves as "family" and even have it printed on their practice attire as a reminder. Some may refer to dear friends as "family" because of the closeness of their relationship. It is a most endearing term, "family."

One of the ways the church is described is by that same idea. Paul wrote to Timothy, "If I delay, you may know how one ought to behave in the household of God, which is the church of the living God, a pillar and buttress of the truth" (1 Timothy 3:15). What is a household? It's a family, isn't it? We could relate other passages which use familial type terms such as God being our Father and we being His children, Jesus as our older brother, etc. For instance, Jesus referred to His disciples as being His mother and brothers (Luke 8:19-21).

What if we instilled within the hearts of our children the same truth? The church is my spiritual family. We are blood-related through Christ. This is God's will that I have a special

"family" with which to grow closer. This family shares joys and sorrows, trials and victories. This family helps us grow in the faith to be more pleasing to God. This family helps me when I am weak and sinful (Galatians 6:1, 2; James 5:16), and I am happy to help any of them. Church just isn't a place to go; it's a place of love and belonging.

Today, I will...look for ways I can be a better family member in His church.

God's Provides Through the Church

Today's Scripture: Genesis 6-8

Among some of the most well-known Bible characters and events among children would have to be Noah and the ark. The minds of children are enthralled at the thought of all those animals, such a huge boat, and so much water! In more recent history there has been a lot of effort by teachers in Sunday school and VBS to make the account of Noah, the ark, and the flood come alive. Think of the many tourists who have been to the Ark Encounter in Kentucky and imagine the wonder in the eyes of children as they behold such a massive vessel.

One of the things to stress in that passage (Genesis 6-8) would be that God provided a place of safety for those who were faithful to God. Sure, the storm and the flood were scary, but inside the ark there was peace and security. Our children desire the same peace and security to feel safe. That's one of the roles for parents: to help our children feel safe and secure, especially at home.

What if we helped our children to look at the church as Noah's ark, a place of safety? This is where God can give us the best care and protect us from our enemy, Satan. It's a place of support and encouragement in a world that only seeks to tear us down. It's a place where we are renewed and regenerated to face the harsh world again. The church can help us be fed and clothed so we are adequately prepared to live as sojourners and pilgrims on this earth until we reach our heavenly home. We don't have to worry if God will provide for our every need because He has, He does, and He will (Matthew 6:25-34; Philippians 4:19). He has provided a place of safety, peace, and security. He knew we would need it.

Today, I will..._explore ways to show the children in my care that God provides care to our family and within the church._

WEEK 49

Dealing with Conflict in the Family

DALE JENKINS

Dealing With Conflict Within The Family

Today's Scripture: Matthew 5:9

The first book I remember seeing about the family was *Vestibules of Heaven* by Mid McKnight. It focused on the idea that there are no thrills in life like a family united in Christ who love each other...BUT the reality is many families do not enjoy the idea and few experience the perfect. Many reading this tend to believe that all confrontation is bad. That is simply not so. And, it becomes a challenge to a functional and healthy family. All confrontation is not bad:

God contends with satan over Job (Job 1:8; 2:3). Jesus contends with the money changers in the temple (Matt. 21). Paul contends with the Judiazers in the church (Just read Galatians). Barnabas contends with Paul over John Mark (Acts 15:39).

Often born from the labor of Christ-like contentions is the fruit of better understanding, better communications, better relations, and better directions for the lives of those involved. While we are NOT advocating for mean-spiritedness, nor aggressively seeking out conflict, the notion that all conflict is bad and should always be avoided can lead to damaging results. It can cause one to lie about a situation rather than telling a painful truth. It can cause one to hide an uncomfortable situation rather than deal with it. It can cause one to embrace a sinful action rather than face it with fact. While Jesus said: "Blessed are the peacemakers" (Matt. 5:9), we know that even He faced conflict and did not shy away from it when conflict could be productive (Mark 11:15-18; Matt. 23).

We've seen people who sweep conflict under the rug, thinking avoiding it will make it go away. This rarely works. What most of us need to learn is how to use conflict to the Glory of God and how to defuse conflict that pushes people away from God. We need to learn to take our selfishness out of the conflict and think of the other person and what is healthiest for them. This week we will focus on some specific conflicts that seem very relevant in families today and face these dragons. Because if satan can get us cross with our families, since they are dearest to us, he might break our spirits.

Today, I will...*pray for that the spirit of those in my family will deal with conflict in a healthy manner. In Jesus Name, AMEN.*

If They'd Only Stay Little

Today's Scripture: Matthew 19:4-6

For many parents the most challenging conflict comes when their child begins to grow up and thinks for himself. This is natural.

It is only natural that it is hard for a parent to let go. We prayed for our children even before they were born. We nurtured and protected them from the moment they came into the world. We tried to train and teach them, to mold them, to shape them into godly men or women. And, now, now they are grown. Now they have taken what we have taught them and have learned to think on their own and to make decisions. They will make decisions differently than we would.

It is only natural, even biblical, that a child becomes an adult. That child will "leave his father and mother." That child will form his own family and raise his or her own children. But what do we do in that awkward time as they turn from children to adults?

So, what should a parent do as his child grows?

We should increasingly give them opportunity and responsibility. We should help them think through questions, doubts, and challenges to their faith. We should pray. We should strive to be who we say we are. Nothing destroys connections like hypocrisy. We should be honest about our own mistakes as a child. We should challenge them to live lives of faith and to grow their faith. We should question them on actions that are not true to God's Word and encourage them to do right for right's sake but not badger them.

But first, we must value the time we have now. Numerous studies from varied groups reveal that most parents spend an average of between one and two hours per day in direct interaction with their children. Make the most of this time, and if we do, we will increase the likelihood of the time in the future being richer.

Today, I will...*take time with children encouraging them in every good thing.*

When My Child Chooses Differently

Today's Scripture: Isaiah 49:15-17

I don't suppose there is anything more challenging and conflicting for a Christian parent than when his child choses a different lifestyle than one directed in and by Jesus. It is crushing and hard to move forward when this happens. You dwell on it. You pray about it. You might even want to shake your child back to reality and say "How? What? Why?" You know that the life he is choosing is not the one you taught them. And, you are tormented by a feeling of failure. That verse in Proverbs haunts you (Train up a child in the way he should go; even when he is old he will not depart from it - 22:6). You tend to forget that this verse is a proverb. You also tend to twist it into somehow removing the free will that God gives to every person, even your child whom you trained to live right. And you forget that if every time a child goes astray it means a parent has failed, it would make God the greatest parental failure of all. Yet, even with those reminders, the hurt in you heart is real.

Your reactions are typically anticipated. You want to talk some sense into your children's heads; you want to warn them, to plead with them, to help them see clearly that this is not acceptable, not biblical, not right. And, you are tempted to bring it up over and over and over. This chapter is on dealing with conflict, and of course, this is a major source of conflict. Here's a suggestion that you might try.

Call a meeting. Make it as formal as possible. Explain, in as unemotional a way as you can what you believe (Yes, they already know) and how that will not change because the Word of God does not change. Then, taking your time, assure them of your love for them. Tell them that just because they have made these decisions does not mean you do not love them (Does God stop loving those who rebel against Him? See Jeremiah 31:3; Romans 8:35-39) and that your love for them will not change regardless of their decisions (Isaiah 49:15-17). Tell them that you will treat them with love at all times. Then tell them that this is never to be confused with your acceptance of their life choices, but that it is based on your love. In this way you make it clear where you stand, but you also make it clear that you still love them, because you do.

Today, I will...*pray for all of those who have gone astray from the Heavenly Father.*

292

THURSDAY
"My" Father and Mother?

Today's Scripture: Mark 3:31-35

I didn't realize at the time but she was speaking for a lot of young people: "Do I have to honor my mom and dad when they don't love the Lord?" Talk about conflict in the heart of a young person who wants to be pleasing to God but lives in a house where He is not honored. The Bible is clear: "Honor your father and your mother" (Exodus 20:12; Matthew 19:19; Ephesians 6:2). This verse shares with only a handful of others a unique fact. It is a command stated by every member of the godhead; God in Exodus, Christ in Matthew, and the Holy Spirit in Ephesians. Ephesians 6 reminds us "which is the first commandment with promise; That it may be well with thee, and thou mayest live long on the earth." With that as a backdrop what is the believing child of an unbelieving parent to do?

She is to honor her mother and father. That does not mean to approve of them; it does not mean to follow their morals, nor does it mean to adopt their beliefs. And it certainly doesn't mean she has to obey their instructions IF those instructions would cause her to sin. But she is to honor the fact that they are her parents, that they brought her into the world, and surely that she caught some good things from them. Honor them. Honor them in the same way she prays for and honors a president who does not espouse Christian morals. Even though He obviously did not agree with him and his morals, Jesus paid tribute to Caesar (Matthew 17:24-27 KJV). And, while Jesus certainly honored his mom to the very end of his physical life (John 19:25-27), He did not let her keep Him from obeying God (Mark 3:31-35).

Honor my parents? Yes. Bottom line - because God said so.

Today, I will...*make contact with my parents (if possible) and let them know I love them. I will honor them regardless.*

FRIDAY

The Better Bargain

Today's Scripture: Mark 10:7-9

Marriage can be a factory for conflict: Take two people raised in separate homes with differing understanding of work division and responsibility and varying levels of expectations and put them together forever. Take two people who each have their own baggage from their raising, from life, and from experience and put them together. It can certainly be an opportunity for what Paul Faulkner called "unscheduled discussions"—i.e., fights!.

While this is not to be a primer on how to keep from fighting, I do want to plant a seed in your mind. Do you remember when you first saw/asked out/ had interest in your spouse? Remember how special you felt when they accepted that invite or when that invite was extended? Remember how amazed you were that THIS person was interested in YOU? Remember how the relationship progressed and how honored and in love you were when they asked or accepted the proposal for marriage?

For some of you, it's been a long time. For some of you where acid words are the norm or icy actions are the standard, it may be hard to go back in your mind. So let me help you a little. You felt like you were getting the better end of this deal. As men like to say, that you "out kicked your coverage."

So, try to go back to that emotion. I have found that as long as we keep believing we got the better deal than our spouse, things go much better. But if we ever begin to believe we could have done better or worse, our relationship can be in serious deep water. But if both parties can keep that feeling of "I got the better end of the deal," then marriage, with all its obstacles, should go better.

Remember it is and has always been God's intention that people marry for life (Mark 10:7-9). It is His plan that only death separate the two He united (1 Corinthians 7:29). He never promised it would be easy, but it is worth the effort. Nobody celebrates a 50th anniversary of a divorce!

Today, I will...*if possible, let my spouse know that I believe I got the better end of the deal.*

294

WEEK 50

Having Fun in The Family

DAVID SALISBURY

God Likes Fun

Today's Scripture: Psalm 126:1-2

When I was in college, there was a small Bible bookstore close to campus that I enjoyed visiting. One day I saw a cheaply made 8x10 framed picture of Jesus, and I knew I had to have it. My college kid budget wouldn't allow me to buy much "art," and I certainly didn't have a place to put this picture, but I had never seen a picture of Jesus like this before. It was Jesus with a goofy grin on His face. You can tell He's either just about to laugh or just had a good belly laugh. If you asked 1,000 Christians what expression they imagined being on the face of God or Jesus, I bet almost no one would say they picture God laughing.

We tend to think of religion as serious and God as someone who deals with serious things. We may talk about joy and could even imagine a smile on God's face but outright laughter? To some people, that almost seems blasphemous.

But consider this: We are made in the image of God, so laughter and our enjoyment of fun come from Him. In Job 8:21, Bildad talks about God's blessings and says, "He will yet fill your mouth with laughter." In Psalm 126:1-2a, the writer says, "When the Lord restored the fortunes of Zion, we were like those who dream. Then our mouth was filled with laughter, and our tongue with shouts of joy." The ability to laugh and enjoy life is a gift of God. Modern medicine is still discovering the benefits of laughter and having a sense of humor, but it was Solomon in Proverbs 17:22a who said, "A joyful heart is good medicine." Ecclesiastes 3:4 reminds us there is a time to laugh, and Isaiah 62:5 tells us that God "rejoice[s] over us." Indeed, God enjoys laughing along with us at the things in this life that are funny!

Today, I will..._enjoy a good laugh and thank God for the ability to have fun._

TUESDAY

Families that Laugh Together

Today's Scripture: 2 Corinthians 6:9

"Hey, dad! Did you know 10+10 and 11+11 are the same? Yup, 10+10 is 20, and 11+11 is 22!"

"Mom, I saw the funniest meme today..."

"Hey kids, I remember one time in church when the funniest thing happened, and we couldn't even laugh because it was in the middle of a prayer!"

Something special happens when families laugh together. Taking time for laughter that doesn't embarrass anyone unites us as a family. When we share something we find funny, we give others a glimpse of how we see the world and what things are important to us.

We get a sense of belonging when we laugh together at the same things. When our family has "inside jokes" only we get, it makes us feel special. We are clued in to something those outside our family know nothing about. That special knowledge is also a key that we can give to special friends and allow them to share in that sense of belonging. Family jokes can also serve to remind us of the unique blessings of being part of this family.

Sharing funny moments is also a great way to make memories. A lot of family stories have a humorous element to them. As children grow and leave home, the funny stories we remember bring us back together and remind us of who we are as a family.

The health benefits of laughter have been well documented, but the relational benefits are even more remarkable. When we share laughter, we share joy. 2 Corinthians 6:9 reminds us that "God loves a cheerful giver." While we often think about that in terms of the money we give at church, what better way to be a cheerful giver than to share something with your family that makes you laugh?

Today, I will...*share something funny with my family and laugh together.*

Plan Some Unplanned Time

Today's Scripture: Galatians 6:8

Spiritual discipline can conjure up stern images. It's easy to picture a finger-wagging, guilt-inducing, nagging church lady who reeks of too much perfume. Or maybe it's a self-righteous hellfire and brimstone preacher who speaks in King James English even at home. They say things like, "You should read your Bible every day and pray for at least 30 minutes. Be at church every time the doors are open. Give at least ten percent." Spiritual discipline sounds like about as much fun as doing a Bible reading plan that features Leviticus, Numbers, Ezekiel, and all the speeches in Job. But at its heart, spiritual discipline is just intentionally doing the things we know we ought to be doing because they are good for our souls. It is choosing what God says is good for us over what we want to do at the moment. And there's sound logic behind that! Paul says in Galatians 6:8, "For the one who sows to his own flesh will from the flesh reap corruption, but the one who sows to the Spirit will from the Spirit reap eternal life." Sowing to the flesh means just doing what comes naturally to us. For many of us, doing what comes naturally often involves a lot of work. There's work, but there's also housework and errands to run, meetings to attend, and to-do lists to be made and followed. If we're doing well, we might include being at worship and Bible class and spending time in daily devotion. But playtime seems like a waste of the time we have. Discipline teaches us to invest our time in the things that really matter.

So does playtime really matter? Fun time, by definition, has no agenda to it. It is non-utilitarian and includes imagination, creativity, and spontaneity. Part of free time together is intentionally including moments for rest and recreation. It connects us to the idea of Sabbath time. If we believe in discipline, we should deliberately include time for all phases of our family's spiritual life, including fun time.

Today, I will..._plan a family fun time—whether at home or out—and commit to keeping that time free for family fun._

THURSDAY

Crafting as Creation

Today's Scripture: Psalm 139:13-14

God is a creator, and He has shared with us the ability to create things. Spending time creating something is a great way to have fun in our families. Families with younger children can enjoy Play-Doh, Legos, and building blocks. Older children can begin to learn creative hobbies like woodworking, knitting, drawing and painting, gardening, building models, and quilting (just to name a few). Don't be afraid to try new things and learn together! It's not about producing a masterpiece (though you may discover previously unknown talents); it's about the process of imaging something and bringing it into existence.

When we create something, we gain insight into God as our Creator. Before we can create something, we must first have it in our minds. We learn what God meant when He told Jeremiah, "Before I formed you in the womb I knew you" (1:5). As we create and see the level of detail it takes to make all the pieces of a project come together, we learn about God's wisdom and power. We appreciate what David said in Psalm 139:13-14, "For you formed my inward parts; you knitted me together in my mother's womb. I praise you, for I am fearfully and wonderfully made. Wonderful are your works; my soul knows it very well." And when a project is done and meets with our approval, we learn something of God's approval of us, too. Genesis 1:31 reminds us, "God saw everything that He had made, and behold, it was very good."

Take time as a family to specifically learn a creative hobby. When you create something together, you will have many opportunities to discuss faith and family values. You can study the artisans of the Bible from Bezalel (Exodus 31) to Huram-abi (2 Chronicles 2) to Jesus Himself (Mark 6:3). You can talk about the value of work and doing a job well and how to support your family while doing something you enjoy.

Today, I will...*make something and share it with my family as we talk about God as a Creator.*

Devotional Fun

Today's Scripture: John 6:63

Family devos are a great way to share your faith with your children. But getting children interested in them can be a problem. If your devotionals resemble a church service, you may get pushback from your kids. But there's no rule that prevents us from making devotionals fun! So as you lead your family in devotional time, take a few extra moments to think about how you can make it fun.

Can you teach David and Goliath (1 Samuel 17) and research the size of the rock David would have used (It's bigger than you think!) or the type of sling he would have used? Then, when you read the story, can you take a moment to imagine how the people involved might have felt?

When you read a story involving multiple Bible characters, such as the account of Gideon in Judges 6-8, can you each take one person and read their part of the story? Perhaps you can use different voices for different people in the story.

As you study the account of Peter walking on water (Matthew 14:22-33), can you act out what happened? Have some fun and imagine what the disciples might have said to Peter LATER after it was all over, and they were back on land. I wonder how long it was after Peter got out of the boat before he remembered that Jesus had given him a new name that meant "rock."

Can you take the Beatitudes in Matthew 5:2-11 and rewrite them to rhyme? Since they were initially designed to be hymns, can you take one of the Psalms and sing it?

What can you do to make the Bible come alive in your family devotionals? Jesus says in John 6:63, "The words that I have spoken to you are spirit and life." And Hebrews 4:12 tells us, "The word of God is living and active." So in our devotional times, we can help our family see the relevance of God's word when we make it alive for them.

Today, I will...*plan a family devotional that is fun as well as educational.*

WEEK 51

Encouraging Your Daughters to Marry Faithful Men

KIRK SAMS

Guarding Our Daughters

Today's Scripture: 1 Peter 3:1-7

As I write this, my daughter has just turned thirty. It seems my daughter's birthdays, more than my own, have a way of making me feel my age. How is it possible that she is in her thirties with 2 wonderful girls and a relatively new baby boy? But these fleeting thoughts on aging give way to reflections on the past and how much simpler it felt to raise a daughter and a son decades ago (Funny thing is, I remember my mom saying the same thing to me when my kids were little.). I sought to raise my daughter to withstand the tidal wave of feminism that threatened her femininity. My daughter is, to this day, a skilled and dedicated mother. But the world seems a scarier place than it was then and parenting a more daunting task. How will my granddaughters, so happy and carefree in their girlhood, resist the lies and insults the world is sure to hurl at them?

"We can't assume that a Christian home or a good church will inoculate our daughters against toxic feminist messages."

With all the cultural confusion over gender-related issues, we may be tempted to panic and throw out the biblical playbook. But we must not flinch as we follow the gospel plan for raising our daughters. Neither can we be apathetic, assuming that a Christian home or a good church will inoculate our daughters against toxic feminist messages. We need to be alert and shrewd—preparing our daughters to discern and reject the false teaching about womanhood from our culture (1 Peter 3:1-7, Matthew 10:16).

We should stick close to Scripture as we walk the same path of faithfulness as the godly parents before us did.

This week we will look at the passages and principles that will prepare us to guard and to guide our daughters in their search for the right spouse for life.

Today, I will..._continue to pray for the courage for parents to remain Biblically strong in raising their children, especially our daughters._

TUESDAY

Training Our Daughters

Today's Scripture: Titus 2:3-5

Faithful parenting, now as always, requires faithful sowing. When we plant a garden, we don't throw seeds haphazardly into the ground and expect neat rows of our favorite vegetables. Instead, we select our seeds and plant straight rows in order to reap a good harvest. In the same way, we must be intentional to sow seeds of biblical womanhood into our daughters' lives.

Put simply, biblical womanhood is God's delightful design for women as revealed in the Bible. In fact, when Paul tells Titus how to build a church that lights up a dark and evil age with the gospel, he tells him to make sure the older women pass along the heart and habits of godly womanhood to the younger women (Titus 2:3–5).

As Christian parents, we must not neglect to include the fundamentals of biblical womanhood in our daughters' education. Consider: Am I preparing my daughter to be the kind of woman who is strong enough to submit to her husband? Is she determined enough to complete the difficult task of raising children? Is she creative enough to build a home that is both a greenhouse and a lighthouse, cultivating the gospel message and beaming it out into a dark world? Is she intelligent enough to see how studying history, bible study, and horticulture can be used in her gospel mission?

Most importantly, faithful parenting requires faith. We put the seeds in the ground, but at first, we don't see how or even if they are growing. We simply watch, water, and repeat. The seeds won't sprout if we don't plant. They won't survive if we don't pull the weeds. They won't thrive if we don't water. But ultimately, we have to trust God to bring the increase (1 Corinthians 3:6). He promises that we will reap a harvest if we do not give up (Galatians 6:9).

How do we keep from giving up? We remind ourselves that no matter how our culture heaves and shifts, Scripture's truth, relevance, and power will remain. God is still in charge. From age to age He sits enthroned. He rules over seasons, stars, and tidal waves of feminism (Psalm 29:10). Let us train our daughters to love their husbands and children and be models of good works; that is power modeling (Titus 2:3-5).

Today, I will..._continue to teach my daughter that biblical womanhood is more powerful and transforming than worldly womanhood._

Guiding Our Daughters

Today's Scripture: Deuteronomy 7:2-5

The Bible does not oppose inter racial marriages, but it does warn strongly against inter religious marriages. Make sure you hear me clearly here; it is not wrong to marry a person who has different religious beliefs than you, but it is very dangerous. God throughout His word reminds His children that this choice impacts so many other choices in our lives. The major reason for the warning is the potential of the relationship to draw us away from God and to be drawn to something else as our primary interest. Notice the multiple warnings.

Joshua 23:11-13 "So be very diligent to love the Lord your God, because if you ever turn back and cling to those who remain of these nations by intermarrying with them and associating one with another..."

Judges 3:5-8 The Israelis continued to live among the Canaanites, the Hittites, the Amorites, the Perizzites, the Hivites, and the Jebusites, taking their daughters as wives for themselves, giving their own daughters to their sons, and serving their gods. The Israelis kept on practicing evil in full view of the Lord.

1 Kings 11:1-5 King Solomon loved many women who were not from Israel. He loved the daughter of the king of Egypt, as well as women of the Moabites, Ammonites, Edomites, Sidonians, and Hittites. The Lord had told the Israelites, "You must not marry people of other nations. If you do, they will cause you to follow their gods."

Ezra 9:12 "Therefore do not give your daughters to their sons, neither take their daughters for your sons, and never seek their peace or prosperity, that you may be strong and eat the good of the land and leave it for an inheritance to your children forever."

Nehemiah 13:24-27 "I made them swear in the name of God that they would not let their children intermarry with the pagan people of the land. Wasn't this exactly what led King Solomon of Israel into sin?"

God's warnings are timeless.

Today, I will...continue to study and make sure I have both *mentored and mirrored a biblical relationship before my children as husband/wife so that they see the benefit of godly choices.*

Praying for my Daughter's Future Husband

Today's Scripture: James 1:17

I am pretty sure that I at some point said to both of my children that I wish that our culture was such that the parents chose the future spouse of their children. After that they rolled their eyes and made fun of me, thinking I was not serious. I remember sharing how important that selection is considering life and eternity.

Abraham intentionally sent someone with instructions about choosing a spouse for his son Isaac. This woman was not from people who would influence her to not follow Jehovah God. As parents, we want the best for our daughters and that includes a perfect mate. Many of us pray that our daughters will marry a man who is a dedicated believer, who is equipped to lead and teach her and his family. We also pray that he will be motivated by a sincere desire to glorify God through his life and the life of his family, We hope that he will be faithful in his church attendance and service in the church.

While it may initially seem presumptuous, praying for a perfect husband for your daughter is not. In fact, it is biblical. James 1:17 tells us, "Every good and perfect gift is from above, coming down from the Father of the heavenly lights." The truth is, if you are seeking God's ways and following His principles, the husband God brings into your daughter's life will be a perfect gift from Him.

As Christian parents, we pray for our children each day. God has entrusted our daughter to us. We know the Lord knows better than we do what she goes through on a daily basis. We know that God can get closer to her, take care of her, free her, protect her and heal her. Our daughter deserves a husband who is after God's own heart, who is completely in love with Jesus. If you entrust your daughter to God, then trust the direction He will lead her and her future husband.

Today, I will...continue to pray for God's guidance and grace as my children hopefully make a choice that will not only impact their eternity but also, if God provides, their children's as well.

Helping Our Daughter Choose God's Man

Today's Scripture: 1 Samuel 25

There are many different things that women look for in men. Some seek wealth and security, others seek physical appearance, still others seek men with social standing. However, many women look deeper than that and value men of character who will be faithful and lead them spiritually. For many ladies, finding a Godly man is tops on their list. How do you marry a Godly man? Furthermore, where are they and how do you meet one?

Because of the move away from church attendance and the desire to have a spiritual experience, I believe our young people are not allowing themselves to be in an environment that will allow them to meet, date and eventually marry the right person. Part of that is absolutely that they must be the right person as well. However with the limits of interaction in the best environments, the search for a spouse can be done in an environment that is not always conducive to finding a biblical spouse (1 Samuel 25).

You will need to trust what God says more than what your natural mind or those around you tell you. Many women miss their opportunity to marry their king David because they meet him when he is still running around in the wilderness avoiding Saul. However, take a lesson from Abigail and recognize and marry your man of God when the opportunity presents itself, even if it is unexpected.

It's important that your daughter's future husband is equipped to lead in the ways of Jesus so that he can disciple and be a great example to your daughter and her children. It's important that he is reminded of God's unconditional love for him and that he reflects that love every day.

I must allow the word of God to give my daughter the proper desire to marry someone who will assist her in becoming what God wants her to be, not what the world wants her to be.

Today, I will... *continue to pattern my life after God' s word in hopes that our daughters will choose a spouse that will assist them in being a husband or a wife that submits to each other and to the Lord.*

WEEK 52

Teaching Our Children to Respect Authority

BROCK JOHNSON

I Think Peter Said It Best

Today's Scripture: Ephesians 6:4

My phone rang one Tuesday afternoon. I answered, and a female voice spoke, "Is this the preacher?" The woman's son was disruptive in school, had gotten in trouble with the police, was disrespectful at home, and she had no idea how to "fix him." A mutual friend told this struggling mother I would be able to give her some Bible verses to help her. There was a problem. I met with the woman and her husband three times and learned that God, the Bible, and faith had no place in their lives. How would Bible verses have influence in the son's disrespect for authority if he was never taught to respect God and His authority?

"Fathers, do not provoke your children to anger, but bring them up in the discipline and instruction of the Lord" (Ephesians 6:4). This Scripture is foundational in teaching our children to honor authority. When parents fail to bring children up according to God's design, both children and parents become exasperated trying to establish who is in control. Parents provoke children and children provoke parents (and other authority figures). As fathers and mothers we must raise our children to understand the authority of God, because all other authority branches off that trunk. I think Peter said it best, "To Him belong glory and dominion forever and ever"(1 Peter 4:11b). Authority as a parent is God designed and God given, and with that great power comes great responsibility (shout out to Spider-Man's Uncle Ben). As Christian parents our first responsibility is to teach children to honor God's authority, that all authority belongs to Him, and that authority figures serve important roles in our lives. If you want your children to respect authority, begin by instilling a love for God's authority.

Today, I will..._assess myself and evaluate whether I am bringing my children up in the discipline and instruction of the Lord. I will pray for God's guidance in leading my children according to His will._

The Sincerest Form

Today's Scripture: 1 Corinthians 11:1

Children are natural imitators. Parents use that fact to display children's brilliance. You have done it. "Sweety, what does a cow say?" and your child replies, "Moo." You proclaim, "He knows twelve other animals." How did your child know what a cow said? Well, he listened to you say, over and over, "A cow says moo." Your child is imitating the example you set. It is said, "Imitation is the sincerest form of flattery," and I say that leading by example is the sincerest form of teaching.

Parents are the first authority figure in children's lives. Thus, it is parents' responsibility to teach children to respect authority. If you treat authority figures with respect, your child will honor that authority also. If you ridicule their teacher, coach, a police officer, or undermine your spouse's authority, how will they interact with those authority figures? Jesus led by example. He never asked His disciples to do something He would not do first. Jesus told His disciples, after washing their feet, "For I have given you an example, that you also should do just as I have done to you" (John 13:15). Leading by example is the sincerest form of teaching.

I have said to my children, "Do as I say, not as I do," and "Actions speak louder than words." These sayings represent a mindset. In our context one sends a message of hypocrisy, "I can disrespect authority, but you cannot," and the other a message of leadership, "Follow my actions." The Apostle Paul understood Jesus' ability to lead by example, which Paul clearly stated in 1 Corinthians 11:1, "Be imitators of me, as I am of Christ." Do you want your children to respect authority? Lead them with sincerity, show them how to respect authority, then they will flatter you by following your lead.

Today, I will..._pray to God for wisdom to lead by example, in all things. I will assess how I speak about and interact with authority figures, so my children have a Godly example to follow._

It Is God's Will

Today's Scripture: Ephesians 6:1-9

I like the movie, *Matilda*. It is about a kind, brilliant little girl being raised by parents who demand respect from their daughter, though they have not earned it. In one scene Matilda's dad asserts his authority saying, "I'm smart; you're dumb, I'm big; you're little, I'm right; you're wrong," because Matilda questioned his business practices. Matilda bruised her father's ego; she exasperated him, so he put her in her place. After all, she was supposed to respect him because he was her father. Your children are supposed to respect you because you are their parent, right? Actually, children are supposed to honor their parents because it is God's will. We are supposed to honor authority because it is God's will.

Ego gets in the way of relationships sometimes. Often, parents provoke children into "respecting" them because the children challenge the parents. This holds true for other authority figures also. Policemen might assert authority intimidatingly, as might teachers, or political figures. (You challenge my authority and I will put you in your place.) This writer's (non-expert) opinion is that this happens because people are taught the "what" but not the "why" of respecting authority.

Ephesians 6:1-9 states many "whats:" children obey parents, fathers do not provoke children; servants, obey masters; masters, stop threatening servants. It is easy to get lost in those things and miss the "whys:" children, obey in the Lord, it is a commandment; Fathers, do not provoke your children, but bring them up in the Lord; servants, serve your masters as if serving Christ; masters, stop threatening your servants, because He (the Lord) is your Master also. The last part of Ephesians 6:6 sums it all up into, "...doing the will of God from the heart." Applying authority in a Christ-like way, and respecting authority in a Christ-like way is not about us receiving the respect we deserve. It is about glorifying God because it is His will.

Today, I will...*guide my children in respecting authority because it glorifies God. I will strive to keep His will above mine.*

THURSDAY

Appointed by God

Today's Scripture: Romans 13:1-2

"He is not my president." It is on bumper stickers; it is on t-shirts; you may have said it. He is your president, though, and you should pray for him, and you should respect the office he fills. In 1 Timothy 2:1-3 Paul tells Timothy, "First of all, then, I urge that supplications, prayers, intercessions, and thanksgivings be made for all people, for kings and all who are in high positions, that we may lead a peaceful and quiet life, godly and dignified in every way. This is good, and it is pleasing in the sight of God our Savior." When Paul wrote this, the emperor Nero was in rule. Nero is known for terrorizing Christians, yet Paul said to pray for all rulers. How could Paul say that?

Paul knew every authority that exists is from God. He even wrote it, "Let every person be subject to the governing authorities. For there is no authority except from God, and those that exist have been instituted by God" (Romans 13:1). All authority comes by and through God. Your authority as a parent, the president's authority, a teacher's authority in the classroom are all God designed. Not only should we respect the authorities who govern our lives, and teach our children to do the same, we are expected to do it. Paul continues, "Therefore whoever resists the authorities resists what God has appointed, and those who resist will incur judgment" (Romans 13:2).

Paul is not telling Christians in Rome or Timothy to support the actions of ungodly rulers. He is, however, calling all Christians to respect authority figures and pray for them. Also, we need to understand it is pleasing to God when we honor authority and teach our children to do the same, and it displeases God when we do not.

Today, I will...remember that God established authorities and governing bodies to fill a role in mankind glorifying Him, and He expects His people to honor authority. I will pray for God's guidance in leading my children to understand the same.

What a Beautiful Blessing

Today's Scripture: Romans 13:7

My oldest daughter was a baby and my in-laws were keeping her so my wife and I could get away. We were in a bookstore, in Gatlinburg, TN, and I was reading a version of the Bible called the "MANual." An older woman asked, "Are you a father?" I replied, with my chest out, "Yes ma'am, I am a daddy." I thought I understood what it means to be a daddy. The woman said, "What a beautiful blessing. You get to teach your child to love God, to be loved by God, to respect and honor God, and to live in a relationship with God." With each statement, my chest sank slightly. I had underestimated what it means to be a daddy. "I am sure you will do fine," she said; the conversation ended, and I left with new perspective on my job as a daddy.

Teaching our children is a beautiful blessing. One important thing we teach them is that in relationships there are roles. When we teach our children to honor God and His authority, how to love Him and receive His love, and to understand the roles in that relationship, we prepare them to do the same with authority figures. Paul said, in Romans 13:7, "Pay to all what is owed to them: taxes to whom taxes are owed, revenue to whom revenue is owed, respect to whom respect is owed, honor to whom honor is owed." Teach them their teachers love them and have purpose in their lives, and they deserve respect. Teach them that law enforcement protects them and fills a purpose in their lives and deserves respect. Teach them that we love them and express to them the purposes we fill in their lives, and when they respect and honor us, it pleases God. Do we want our children to respect authority? We get to teach them. What a beautiful blessing!

Today, I will...talk to my children about relationships with authority figures and pray for guidance in teaching them to fulfill their roles in those relationships.

312

WEEK 53

Encouraging Your Minister's Family

CRAIG EVANS

Letters to a Preacher in Need Of Encouragement

Today's Scripture: 1 & 2 Timothy

As I was pursuing my Bible degree at FHU, I remember being told it would be wise for us to read 1 and 2 Timothy. But why? While most of the epistles are written to churches, these letters are written from an older, experienced preacher to two younger preachers. They are filled with life lessons and wisdom needed for ministers to serve in a way that pleases God and blesses the church.

Should only ministers read these books? No, everyone should. If someone wants to try to get a glimpse of the demands and challenges of church work, they should read these books often. Look at Paul's list of challenges in ministry:

- Be an example of Jesus in speech, in conduct, in love, in faith, in purity (1 Timothy 4:12).
- Devote yourself to reading scripture (1 Timothy 4:13).
- Grow spiritually (1 Timothy 4:15).
- Watch your life and doctrine because your salvation and others depend on it (1 Timothy 4:16).
- Withdraw from evil and greediness (1 Timothy 6:3-10).
- Pursue righteousness, godliness, faith, love, patience, and gentleness (1 Timothy 6:11).
- Fight the good fight and take hold of eternal Life (1 Timothy 6:12).
- Fan the flame of the gift which is in you (2 Timothy 1:6).
- Share in suffering (2 Timothy 1:8).
- Dig into and handle correctly God's Word (2 Timothy 2:14-15).
- Remember there will be times of difficulty (2 Timothy 3:1).
- Preach the Word, reprove, rebuke, and exhort with complete patience and teaching (2 Timothy 4:2).
- Do the work of an evangelist and fulfill your ministry (2 Timothy 4:5).
- Remember there is a crown laid up for the faithful (2 Timothy 4:8).

Paul ends 2 Timothy by saying, "The Lord be with your spirit." He ends by encouraging Timothy. If you want to better understand the challenges of ministry and the need for encouragement, read 1 and 2 Timothy.

Today, I will...read 1 and 2 Timothy to gain a better understanding and appreciation for those who devote their lives to ministry and to see a need for encouragement.

Organ Donors & Heart Transplants

Today's Scripture: Ephesians 4:29

One of the biggest days in many of our lives is the day when we get our driver's license. It is a day of anticipation and excitement for the teenager and a day of anxiety and added car insurance expense for the parents. I remember the details of this exciting day from driving with my mom to the DMV in a silver Chevy Cavalier station wagon (try not to be too jealous), to Rufus, the man who gave me my road test. I remember hearing those life changing words, "You passed," from Rufus. I remember driving home, and then driving to a friend's house to celebrate. While I remember the joy and excitement of that day, I also remember a sobering part of that day. When filling out the paperwork there was a question: "Do you want to be an organ donor?" I found myself having to contemplate life or death on this exciting day. What does being an organ donor have to do with encouragement?

To have courage means to have heart, and to encourage someone means to "give heart." There is not a person on earth who doesn't need encouragement. Having read yesterday's devotional and 1 and 2 Timothy, I hope you see the need for encouragement in the life of a minister and his family. I don't know if your preacher is your favorite preacher or one of your least favorite preachers, but I do know you can make him a better preacher this Sunday by encouraging him today.

Paul challenges the church in Ephesus, "Let no corrupting talk come out of your mouths, but only such as is good for building up, as fits the occasion, that it may give grace to those who hear" (Eph. 4:29).

You may never know when a preacher's heart or his family's heart is broken. They may be struggling spiritually, emotionally, mentally, physically, or financially. There may be a family issue, or they may possibly be on the verge of giving up on God, church, ministry, their family, or even continuing to live. What I do know is your encouragement can give heart to the heartbroken when they need it, and that encouragement can make a difference.

Today, I will...*encourage my minister's wife.*

The Power of the Prayer Lists

Today's Scripture: James 4:16

I have yet to be a part of a church family that doesn't have a prayer list, and I have yet to be a part of a church family where people do not covet their name or a loved one's name being included on that list. One of the blessings of being a preacher is the mentioning of your name in public prayer, and usually that prayer is for me to have a "ready recollection" of the things I have prepared. I am thankful each time I hear my name mentioned in prayer. Charles Spurgeon said, "No man can do me a truer kindness in this world than to pray for me". I want to add to Spurgeon's quote, "No man can do me a truer kindness in this world than to pray for me, unless it is to pray for my family as well."

If you want to encourage your minister's family, begin to include your minister's wife and their children on your prayer list, both public and private. If it is your private prayer list, let the minister's wife and children know you are praying for them. Pray for their physical, emotional, mental, and spiritual health; pray for their spirit; pray for their peace; pray for their friendships; pray for their faith; pray for their extended families; pray they hold up under pressure; pray they withstand temptation; and pray for them to have true joy

If you pray for your minister's family in private, let the family know you are praying for them. You could also ask them for specific needs to pray for them.

Today, I will...*pray specifically for each member of my minister's family and will let them know they were prayed for.*

THURSDAY

Important Jobs

Today's Scripture: 1 Thessalonians 5:11

It seems many important jobs in corporations have initials associated with them. The prestige of being a CEO-Chief Executive Officer, CIO-Chief Information Officer, CFO-Chief Financial Officer, or CTO-Chief Technology Officer is one for which many strive. Those acronyms carry with them the meaning of a job and job description. Are there acronyms for jobs at your congregation? I have heard some referred to as the CCC, those are the Chief Church Complainers and the Chief Church Critics. There are some who seem to believe their calling and spiritual gift is to complain and criticize which leads them to also become the CCD-Chief Church Discourager. The problem with CCCs and CCDs is there can be more than one holding that position at a time. Many times, the criticism and discouraging words fall on the shoulders of the minister and his family.

There is another job that is available and is needed: the CCE-Chief Church Encourager. What if you were determined to be an encourager to your minister's family?

Paul tells the church in Thessalonica to "encourage one another and build one another up, just as you are doing" (1 Thessalonians 5:11).

What are some ways to encourage your minister and his family?
Pray for them.
Send a note of appreciation.
Offer childcare or pay for a babysitter so they can have a night out.
Don't have unfair expectations of the preacher's wife and children.
Offer a place for the family to take a trip and stay.
Take a meal.
Send a gift card to them.
Talk positively about them to elders.
Give him a vacation (as one person has said, "Give your preacher a vacation. If he is good, he deserves it, and if he is not…well the church could use the break.")

CCEs find ways to make sure the minister and his family know they are truly loved and valued. If you are wondering how to do this, just ask your minister's family what would bless them the most. Praying we choose to be a CCE!

Today, I will... *intentionally encourage my minister's children.*

FRIDAY
Making a Difference

Today's Scripture: Hebrews 3:13-14

Amy Glass was a friend at Freed Hardeman University who made a great impact on my life and many others. Amy passed away in a car wreck shortly after graduation. She was an amazing encourager and had an incredible smile. A scholarship was established in her name and a triathlon was started to raise money for the scholarship. I chose to participate in this triathlon one year. The triathlon consisted of a ¼-mile swim, a 12-mile bike ride, and a 5k run. You could complete it yourself or put a 3-person team together to complete each part. Since they do not make floaties for adults and I had rather not ever be seen in bicycle shorts, I chose to put a team together where I would run the 5k. I trained from January to May for this event and equipped myself with the best running shoes I could find. I was ready.

The swimmer and cyclist completed their parts, and it was up to me to finish. I started strong but quickly developed a blister on my heel. My good shoes were diminished by mediocre socks. I stopped to adjust my socks often and walked slowly. I was frustrated and dejected knowing it was going to take a while to finish. As I stopped to adjust my socks, a lady whom I had never met ran up beside me and said, "Let's go," so I started running with her. She engaged me in conversation, and I continued to run with her for over a mile, not stopping or thinking once about my blister. Because of her encouragement, my pace, my attitude, and my energy all increased, and when I crossed the finish line, I was met with cheers and the feeling of joy from finishing strong.

The Hebrew writer tells us in Hebrews 3:13-14, "But exhort one another every day, as long as it is called "today," that none of you may be hardened by the deceitfulness of sin. For we have come to share in Christ, if indeed we hold our original confidence firm to the end." Remember as you encourage your minister and his family, you are not only encouraging them to stay in ministry but even more importantly, to stay faithful to God for the rest of their lives.

Today, I will... *write a note, send a text, or call my minister and his family and let them know I appreciate them, knowing my encouragement can make an eternal difference.*

318

Titles Available from TJI

Keys to Effective Ministry (Jeff & Dale Jenkins)
Weekly Joy for Senior Saints

The Living Word: Sermons of Jerry A. Jenkins
Before I Go: Notes from Older Preachers

Thoughts from the Mound (Jeff Jenkins)
More Thoughts from the Mound (Jeff Jenkins)

Beyond the Valley of Death (Jeff Jenkins)

All I Ever Wanted to Do Was Preach (Dale Jenkins)
I Hope You Have to Pinch Yourself (Dale Jenkins)

The Preacher as Counselor (Dale Jenkins and others)

Don't Quit on a Monday (Jeff & Dale Jenkins)
Don't Quit on a Tuesday (Jeff & Dale Jenkins)
Don't Quit on a Wednesday (Jeff & Dale Jenkins)
Don't Quit on a Thursday (Jeff & Dale Jenkins)
Don't Quit on a Friday (Jeff & Dale Jenkins)
Don't Quit on a Saturday (Jeff & Dale Jenkins)

Five Secrets and a Decision (Dale Jenkins)
Centered: Marking Your Map in a Muddled World
(Dale Jenkins)
*On Moving Well: The Scoop-Meister's Thoughts on Ministry
Transitions* (Dale Jenkins)
Praying Always: Prayers for Preachers (gift book)
(Jeff & Dale Jenkins)
You're Fired! Now What? (Dale Jenkins)

A Minister's Heart (Jeff & Dale Jenkins)
A Youth Minister's Heart (Jeff & Dale Jenkins)
A Mother's Heart (Jeff & Dale Jenkins)
A Father's Heart (Jeff & Dale Jenkins)

Immerse: A Simple Look at Baptism (Dale Jenkins)
We Think You'll Love It Here (personalized for guests)

His Word (Daily devos from the New Testament)
His Life (Daily devotionals from Jesus' life & ministry)
My Life (Daily devotionals covering the Christian life)
His Family (Daily devotionals studying the church)
My Family (Daily devotionals studying the home)

The Glory of Preaching (Jay Lockhart &
Clarence DeLoach)
Profiles of Faith & Courage: Interviews with Gospel Preachers
(Dennis Gulledge)
Me, You, and the People in the Pews (Tracy Moore)
From Mother's Day to Father's Day (Paul Shero)
Little Fish, Big Splash (Mark Neaves &
Shawn Weaver)
The Three Little Ministers (Philip Jenkins)
Choice Over Circumstance (Drake Jenkins)
Pocket Guide for Preachers: 1 Timothy
(Joey Sparks & Cole Wade)

Free Evangelism Resources by Jerry Jenkins:
God Speaks Today
Lovingly Leading Men to the Savior

To order, visit ***thejenkinsinstitute.com/shop***

Made in the USA
Middletown, DE
05 January 2023

19680126R00201